▶ ENDORSEMENTS

"Lee Ellis continues to honor the ethos of service, first in his own leadership and then in his passion to teach others. His military experience—and his years of captivity in the Hanoi Hilton—gave him a deep foundation of strength, resilience, and wisdom. His dedication to writing is yet another act of service, from which we can all learn."

— *Jim Collins, author* Good to Great, *co-author* Built to Last

"…There are few that have made significant strides on making 'knowing yourself' operational and real as Lee and Hugh have in this marvelous book. Reading this book is a compelling adventure. If you follow the path, you will change for the better!"

— *Richard Boyatzis, Distinguished University Professor, Case Western Reserve University, co-author of the international best seller,* Primal Leadership *and the new* Helping People Change

"This is the book that I have longed for during my decades in managing talent, and Lee and Hugh have brought the two together with a clear and action-focused model. Having seen the positive impact of DNA Behavior on my teams, this is a must-read for leaders who desire to build strong teams by accelerating natural talents in an authentic and lasting way."

— *Belva White, CPA, MBA, Vice President for Finance & Treasury, Emory University*

"Hugh and Lee's book is an insightful and inspirational read for everyone who has a passion for leading and developing people, and guiding change is the ultimate leadership test. I highly recommend this book as a practical guide for leaders who are trying to build a high-performance business."

— *James A Combs, President and CEO, National Advisors Trust Company*

"Lee Ellis and Hugh Massie have crafted a powerful how-to manual for leaders and those who aspire to lead. Their science-based insights will help readers maximize natural talents, overcome struggles and discover their most rewarding career fit."

— *Stuart Parker, CEO, USAA*

"*Leadership Behavior DNA* has been such a valuable discovery process for me and my team's personal awareness and cohesiveness. If you apply the principles and insights in this book, you will gain a competitive edge in the marketplace that will yield long-term dividends for you and the people that you serve."

> — *Nancy Richardson, CEO, SAS Shoes*

"*Leadership Behavior DNA* provides a great framework for helping leaders develop themselves and their teams by identifying their strengths and struggles. The ten minutes it takes to complete the assessment will be best 10 minutes anyone has spent to improve their leadership skills and enable teams to reach their full potential."

> — *Ralph de la Vega, Chairman of the De La Vega Group, former Vice-Chairman of AT&T, Inc., and author of* Obstacles Welcome

"[Reading *Leadership Behavior DNA*] exceeded all of my expectations! If you want to leverage your natural leadership strengths in order to build strong trusting teams, as well as create a dynamic culture around you, this book is a must-read!"

> — *Gerald V. Goodfellow, Brigadier General, USAF (Ret.), Executive Director, Louisiana Tech Research Institute*

"The book moves the needle on the need for personal behavioral self-awareness to how you deal with different styles. Until now it has been hard to adapt that knowledge for disrupting how we lead, perform, and relate with each other."

> — *Raghu Misra, CEO and Founder of Wired2Perform, Jacksonville, FL*

"Building a healthy team and company culture has been the heartbeat of my work over the last 33 years, and *Leadership Behavior DNA* is a must-read primer on the validated, scientific process to help all leaders learn the soft skills of managing diverse talents and differences."

> — *Dee Ann Turner, Former Vice President, Talent and Vice President, Sustainability (Retired), Chick-Fil-A; Communicator, Consultant, Coach, Dee Ann Turner LLC*

"The insights in this book are like drinking at a well. You can return regularly to draw fresh insights…This book is a must if you are interested in understanding your own talents, behaviors and leadership style or how to bring the best out in any individual or team."

> — *Malcolm LeLievre, CEO and Founder of Brilliant Fit, Melbourne Australia*

"In *Leadership Behavior DNA*, Lee [and Hugh] give us the tools to understand others so that we can intentionally and empathetically impact both culture and performance. Putting them into practice has made me a better leader and better human being."

— *Kathy Schwaig, Ph.D., Provost and Senior Vice President for Academic Affairs, Kennesaw State University*

"I highly recommend this book to every leader that realizes that they can always become better. It's the perfect resource to gain a deeper understanding and be able to lead your people to greater results. This will absolutely change how you lead and change your organization."

— *Debbie Gordon, CEO of Cloud Range Cyber, Nashville, TN*

"Leadership Behavior DNA is a must-read for today's leaders who need to attract and motivate future teams."

— *Mary C. Kelly, PhD, Commander USN (Ret), Author of* Who Comes Next? Leadership Succession Planning Made Easy

"This book draws out that focusing on your strengths alone is not enough. The reader will learn about the relevance of managing struggles, as they are strengths overplayed that can quickly derail performance. You will receive Lee and Hugh's coaching tips on how to capitalize on your strengths and manage your struggles. I highly recommend this book."

— *Tobias Maag, CEO of Sencopar, São Paulo, Brazil*

"I've used DNA Behavior® in my counsel to CEOs and boards. The approach and principles Lee and Hugh speak to in this book are on point and highly relevant in understanding and optimizing relational and results-based leadership. You will refer back again and again."

— *Tony Mitchell, national speaker, Board Director, CEO advisor*

"[Hugh and Lee] help bring more science to leadership, which begins with understanding one's self. It provides leadership tools and learnings that will help you lead better on all fronts of your life; business, personal and family."

— *John Bly, Principal of LBA Haynes Strand and Board Member of Entrepreneurs Organization 2016-2019, Charlotte, NC*

"*Leadership Behavior DNA* is a road map to aid in the growth and development of a high functioning leadership team. Having personally seen the impact that Lee and Hugh can make in an organization really excites me to get my hands on this dynamic leadership tool."

> — *Billy Sims, Sr. Vice President, Policy Administration, Southern Farm Bureau Life Insurance Company*

"The world of business needs authentic leaders at all levels. This book defines the characteristics of great leaders, and you'll be inspired and surprised. But above all, you will be grateful you read it. I highly recommend this book."

> — *Steve Mintz, CEO of PG Wireless, Atlanta, GA*

"Fantastic read! This is the culmination of years of work on human behavior curated in a fascinating and inspirational manner. Hugh and Lee unlock the code to understanding your own leadership style and then how to lead others in the most efficient and effective way for top results."

> — *Dana Bradley, Principal of Performance Holdings, Board Member of Entrepreneurs Organization 2017-2020, Charlotte NC*

"Once again, Lee [and Hugh] have created a framework that will help us as leaders to challenge ourselves to improve no matter how experienced we are. These real-world insights will help leaders continue to strive to be better tomorrow than they are today."

> — *Carol Burrell, President and CEO, Northeast Georgia Health System*

"Thank you, Hugh and Lee, for an actionable and inspirational guide to understanding and leveraging hardwired leadership behaviors. We all face a vast amount of change and complexities, and this book is an important guidebook to help thrive and lead while life happens."

> — *Susan Bradley, CEO and Founder of The Sudden Money Institute, West Palm Beach, FL*

"In leadership development classes, I tell participants that 'if you cannot lead yourself, how can you lead people?' Lee and Hugh have mapped the DNA to understanding your leadership traits, and every leader must read their book."

> — *Dr. James T. Ward, Facilitator and Manager for Leader Development Programs, Naval Air Systems Command (NavAir)*

"If you want to understand how successful teams work, how your leadership impacts them, this is the book for you. Insightful and practical it spells out the importance of understanding different behaviors and how to self-manage. Highly recommend this book."

> — *Rick Kent, CEO and Founder of Mentoro, Atlanta GA*

"If your approach to leadership includes making others better because of your presence, then you really need to understand WHO you're leading. The practical models in this book are powerful in understanding your people. These models are essential to success whether leading in your home, your business life or yourself. I highly recommend this book."

> — *Brian Brault, Global Chair of the Board of Directors, Entrepreneurs Organization 2017-18*

"Your team deserves a leader who understands team dynamics and has the tools and ability to bridge individual differences to build sustainable unity and trust. Lee and Hugh have combined their experience with research and delivered a guide that is realistic, practical, easy to understand and implement."

> — *Dan Olson, Vice President, Armament Systems, Northrop Grumman Corporation*

"*Leadership Behavior DNA* is a compelling read and is essential to developing higher levels of leadership performance; within oneself and throughout an organization. This manuscript serves as a model for affecting leadership, and it's a must read for those interested in taking leadership to the next level."

> — *Steven D. Allen, JD/MBA, Head of Aviation, QBE North America*

"Hugh and Lee's book is a mustread for those with a passion for leading and developing people. The practical approaches will change the way you work, the way you lead, and the impact you have on the world."

> — *Clayton J. Delaney, CEO, Black River Wealth Ltd.*

"This book reminds all leaders of the critical importance of continuous learning. Between the lines of this well-written text and practical approaches are insights to the value of attentive listening, thinking before acting and the demand to maintain your awareness of the situation and yourself. A great addition to any leader seeking to make greater impact!"

> — *Craig Pfeiffer, President & CEO, Money Management Institute*

"An eye-opening read for unlocking the mystery to fulfilling your God-given potential by discovering the keys to maximizing human performance for achieving personal, team, and organizational success."

> — *Michael Beduze, CEO of Davinci Global Consulting*

"Leading and operating from an understanding of natural, hard-wired behavior is the hidden competitive advantage in developing a dynamic people culture—the kind of culture that attracts and develops great talent for the benefit of the organization and the individual."

— Warren Rustand, Summit Consulting Group, Dean of Entrepreneurs Organization Leadership Academy, Former YPO Chair, Tuscon, AZ

"An excellent book addressing the need for leaders to first identify and address their strengths and struggles in order to best motivate others within their organization. I plan to share this book with all our employees as a tool for growing our future leaders in our company. This has the makings of a best seller!"

— Mike Santiago, President/CEO, Polaris Aviation Solutions

"[*Leadership Behavior DNA*] is a brilliant framework for exploring the harmonious balance needed between the key orientations of results vs. relationships. Lee and Hugh's combined and diversified understandings and experiences have brought an urgently needed synergy for leadership wisdom and success in developing talent and managing differences."

— Archie B. Carroll, PhD, Scherer Professor Emeritus of Management, Terry College of Business, University of Georgia

"Having seen LBDNA in action across several organizations, I truly believe it is a phenomenal framework for organizations to learn how to successfully grow together. And the benefits were immediately apparent in every team that I witnessed. Another great addition to my organizational behavior toolkit!"

— Dr. Robert H. Lass, Colonel, USAF (Retired), Director of Education, Louisiana Tech Research Institute

"This book draws out that focusing on your strengths alone is not enough—struggles must also be managed. By reading this book, you will receive Lee and Hugh's [valuable] coaching tips."

— Kent Gregoire, CEO of Symphony Advantage and Master Key Executive, Boston, MA

"The book offers a very well-balanced narrative which presents concepts, fundamentals, scientific studies and the authors' extensive experience in a very straightforward way. And, it equips us to manage both sides of the behavioral coin, enabling us to achieve outstanding performance. It is a true masterpiece for leaders and people who aspire to lead in any type of organization."

— Adriana Prates, CEO and Founder, Dasein Executive Search, Brazil

LEADERSHIP BEHAVIOR
DNA

DISCOVERING NATURAL TALENTS AND MANAGING DIFFERENCES

LEE ELLIS | HUGH MASSIE

FreedomStar
Media·

Readers should be aware that Internet Web sites mentioned as references or sources for further information may have changed or no longer be available since this book was published.

Published by FreedomStar Media®

ISBN (Softcover Trade Edition) 978-0-9838793-9-8

Cover design: Michael Sean Allen
Interior Art and Layout Design: James Armstrong and Michael Sean Allen
Copy Editor: Georgina Chong-You
Select iconography from Vecteezy.com

Trade distribution is provided by the Greenleaf Book Group. To purchase this book for trade distribution, go to www.GreenleafBookGroup.com.

For media requests and interviews, go to FreedomStarMedia.com

Publisher's Cataloging-in-Publication Data
Title: Leadership behavior DNA : discovering natural talents and managing differences / Lee Ellis ; Hugh Massie.
Description: Includes bibliographical references and index. | Dawsonville, GA: FreedomStar Media, 2020.
Identifiers: LCCN 2019913978 | ISBN 978-0-9838793-9-8 (pbk.) | 978-1-7336322-1-8 (ebook)
Subjects: LCSH Leadership. | Success in business. | Personnel management. | BISAC BUSINESS & ECONOMICS / Leadership | BUSINESS & ECONOMICS / Management
Classification: LCC HD57.7 .E4173 2020 | DDC 658.4--dc23

Special Sales
FreedomStar Media resources are available at special discounts for bulk purchases for sale promotions or premiums. Special editions, including personalized covers or bookplate inscriptions, excerpts of existing books, and corporate imprints, can be created in large quantities for special needs. For more information, please contact us at Contact@FreedomStarMedia.com or 678-455-9514.

Printed in the USA

20 21 22 23 24 – 10 9 8 7 6 5 4 3 2 1
1st Printing

▶ Contents

Section 3 – *Managing Team Differences*

▶ FOREWORD

The science behind studying and assessing human differences and behaviors has advanced considerably over recent years. Today, behavioral and cognitive scientists can better account for individual differences and how those differences contribute to observable behaviors.

In over 30 years of my work in the fields of psychology, human development, and learning, I've witnessed the tremendous growth and insight we have today in understanding the unique ways that humans are wired and develop. The insights, arising from the unification of research in brain science and behavioral and cognitive psychology, are helping to transform leadership development. My work directly benefits from the application of these behavioral discoveries for helping leaders to develop and improve reflective practices as well as effectively leading in an increasingly complex world with cognitive and moral reasoning. I've seen the benefits in a variety of contexts working with leaders in business, education, and government, wanting to develop throughout the entire course of their professional life.

In this book, Lee Ellis and Hugh Massie delve deeper into the application of the unified research discoveries to better assess leadership and account for individual behavioral differences. Drawing from statistical research, they lay out a simple and easy to understand system that one can readily apply to self and others. Using real-life examples, they describe how *strengths* and *struggles* are networked together in each person, clarifying what others observe as the unique package of each human being.

Further, the examples and stories provide refreshing and timely teaching for practical leadership development. As Ellis and Massie highlight, a "strengths only" approach is not enough to develop as a leader. Yes, they focus on the strengths of natural talents as critical for career success. But for leader growth they clearly illustrate the need to adapt our behaviors to compensate for missing talents. Additionally, they share many examples of the negative impact, even damage that comes when leaders overuse or inappropriately respond with their key strengths.

You'll see a well-organized and systematic presentation of strengths and struggles that is foundational to understanding self and others. But knowledge is not sufficient. We must adapt, and they provide specific coaching for learning how to shift our behaviors in the moment to become more balanced in our approach to achieving results and connecting with people.

In an era where pressure for results and the rate of change are dramatically increasing, there has been an unintended negative consequence: employee engagement is reportedly the biggest challenge in organizations. The lessons here will equip even the most results/task focused leaders to adapt and connect with the hearts and dreams of their people, show value, and lift their energy—increasing both productivity and retention.

The promise of growth through adaptation offered by Ellis and Massie is not meant to be fulfilled from an armchair embrace of a good read. Yes, this book is a good read. No, actually it's a great read. The words easily lift off the page and flow into the mind with sincerity and conviviality rarely encountered outside of conversing with family and friends. And, as can readily happen when talking with family and friends, such conversations can go beyond exchange of words among minds to touch the heart of each wherein feelings and the will to understand, share, and respond reside. In fact, as I was writing this foreword, I shared the concepts in this book to a group of colleagues, which led to a spontaneous two-hour conversation about their own personal journey to become better leaders!

Very few books written on leadership offer these fundamental insights with a call to respond. There is an expression widely used in the corporate and military arena that "leaders are readers." I believe that readers of this book will respond to become better leaders—with the opportunity to be known as "great leaders."

Andrew G. Stricker, PhD
Sr. Advisor, Human Development and Learning
United States Air Force

▶ PREFACE

Tools that Connect the Dots

Have you ever scratched your head, wondering why it took so long to get wheels on luggage? After all, the wheel has been used as a mechanical tool to bear weight for more than 5,000 years. Wheels moved catapults to lay siege to castles, supplied Roman armies, and rolled covered wagons across the frontier. But why not *luggage*? For centuries, no one connected the dots…

It was not until 1987 when the very practical and creative Robert Plath, a Northwest Airlines pilot and avid home workshop tinkerer connected wheels and a handle with luggage, identifying what was hidden in our collective blind spot.[i] His Rollaboard® took the lug out of luggage and quickly disrupted airline travel, for the better. Aircraft interiors were reworked for carry-on luggage, leaving travel (and our backs) better ever since.

So, it isn't unheard of for something that has been plainly obvious to everyone for millennia to be completely ignored as a

1938 - 1987 ------- 1987 - CURRENT

practical tool for everyday use. Just as humans struggled with their luggage, most of us still struggle with managing *individual differences* in our day-to-day lives.

Individual Differences Lead to Conflict

The challenge of relating to these individual differences in human behavior has been evident in every family and workplace since the beginning of time. However, being able to clarify and manage differences consistently has never really been done effectively in society, especially in the workplace. Here's an example: the reserved/introverted executive who can't comprehend why her outgoing/ex-

troverted manager can't just go in his office, shut the door, and work for a few days to crank out the report that will be due in two weeks.

Similarly, this lack of understanding and appreciation of differences between outgoing salespeople and task-focused operations people, for example, is legendary for causing conflict. Yet even to the casual observer, the root cause is obvious: people are not just performing different functions; they *themselves* are different.

These conflicts arising out of differences are natural; they're inborn behavioral responses (our DNA) that create disconnects, impose barriers, and block performance for all involved. However, if the people involved could have a clear and objective view of themselves and realistic expectations of others, it would lighten the load on all relationships. These revelations about natural, hard-wired behaviors would enable us to better manage our own **strengths** and **struggles** while adapting our expectations and communication style to better relate to others. *With those powerful insights validated, systemized, and available online*, we can put the wheels on individual differences, opening the door for the dialogue essential to good leadership, collaborative teamwork, and ultimately: mission success.

Re-envisioning Leadership

This book provides a framework for re-envisioning leadership, showing you how to achieve a higher level of leadership perfor-

mance. When you objectively see and understand *yourself*—your own natural **DNA-driven Behaviors**—you have the knowledge and insight to grow to your full potential. As Cindi Filer, a successful leadership consultant in Atlanta, said recently in a presentation to a CEO group, "Self-awareness is the essential component of the mature behaviors needed by everyone—especially leaders."

As you grow more aware of your own natural behaviors, you'll also become more aware of how to achieve a healthy balance between results (mission) and relationships (people)—or what we call *leadership tilt*. Good leaders have to live in this tension of mission and people and it's all about having behavioral skills for both—which is not normal to our DNA and therefore often feels unnatural. With the insights about yourself, you'll gain clarity about others' Traits and see how to manage the differences among those you lead. You'll see how their ***strengths and struggles go together and are really two sides of the same coin***.

The good news is that much of the fog and friction you encounter at work and with your family will begin to clear, making relationships easier.

We know this sounds both familiar and challenging. You know it's real and present in every situation, but you may be thinking—can I really do this? Based on many years of work with leaders across the globe, we can assure you that you can, and also, that you and those around you will be very happy with the outcome. So why not engage in this challenge and gain mastery? We'll provide a scientific and practical framework and lots of examples and stories to help you connect the dots. Additionally, you will see how we have put it all into an on-demand system and language that you can access and use.

Though your authors come from different backgrounds and continents, we share a perspective that is undergirded by years of data and ongoing research. Perhaps more importantly for you, the reader, we have decades of successful practical experience employing these online tools to help thousands of people in both their professional and personal lives.

In this book we'll go deep into unpacking the *natural behavioral Traits*—the ***strengths***, ***struggles*** and communication styles that inherently come with our DNA. In fact, we have trademarked the label ***DNA Behavior*®** and will use it often in the chapters ahead. It's a scientific framework through which we see how we can use our inherent differences to achieve higher performance as individuals and as teams.

From our experience, gaining an objective view of ourselves is the foundation of self-awareness, which is a prerequisite for growth. Other than character, understanding and managing our unique ***DNA Behavior*** is the most important determinant of success. This understanding will also equip each of us to see others more objectively, leading to relating and managing people more effectively—to their joy and everyone's success.

We've tried to put both wheels and handles on these concepts of human behavior to make them easy to apply in every interaction. If properly used, we know from experience that the knowledge and stories presented here will change your life for the better and, in the process, equip you to bring greater freedom and energy to those you lead and with whom you interact.

▶ INTRODUCTION

As the title portrays, this is a book about leadership behavior DNA—two ideas intentionally married together. Most of the book is focused on clarifying and explaining **DNA Behavior**, our natural talents. However, you will see that it's presented with a focus on the powerful role it plays in helping leaders develop themselves, develop others, and manage the differences that are inherent on any team.

What Are the Best Traits Required to Be a Great Leader?

It's an honest question, one we've heard many times in our work, but we believe that what's underneath this is another question: *"Do I have what it takes to be a great leader?"* The answer is a resounding yes, but there's a catch, so here's how we respond: "Your Traits—yes, the ones you already possess—are the very best for you. If you understand and develop your **strengths** and manage your **struggles**, you can be a great leader."

Do you Celebrate the Unique and Different of the Human Domain?

Regardless of our diversity (culture, gender, ethnicity), we're different as a result of the coding in our DNA—our deoxyribonucleic acid—the double helix, which bears the print of how our unique human characteristics will be expressed. In the pages ahead, we will focus on one area of our *default* DNA—the natural talents that give each of us our unique "go to" behaviors.

A keen understanding of **DNA Behavior** is one of the most useful and powerful tools a person can have. This book is your gift, and like gold, the concepts here are both valuable and enduring. Moreover, they are accepted currency in every culture and country in the world. But additionally, these tools work for our personal relationships as well. So regardless of where you are in your professional life, these tools apply across the spectrum.

Understand and manage self; understand others and learn to manage differences, apply the Platinum Rule, and you'll have a people culture: a workplace that attracts and retains the best talents and gets the best results.

Our first goal is to help you gain objective insights into who you are and understand your natural **DNA Behavior.** In the pages ahead, we're going to dissect eight Factors with sixteen Traits of behavior that will help you understand and develop more of the positive aspects of what makes you tick. As you'll see, there are many great leaders with Traits like yours. You'll realize that you're capable of being a highly successful leader—someone who gets results, who attracts and inspires others to follow your lead.

As you honestly assess both your natural **strengths** and **struggles**, (we provide an equal number of each for every Trait), you'll be able to see others' **strengths** and especially their **struggles** from a more objective and compassionate perspective. Others are unique and talented, just as you are. There is no hierarchy of talents. They are all valuable and worth celebrating. We each possess many talents—our own unique array—but they're occasionally hidden from view and must be coaxed out.

We hope that you'll see that as a leader, part of your job is to recognize talents in others and call them out, affirming their value and increasing the inner confidence of people around you.

Once you understand yourself and others, you're equipped to manage differences: learning to connect with people in ways that work for them, setting realistic expectations, while remembering that what you effortlessly do well may challenge others, and vice versa.

The Platinum Rule

At the heart of our work is the wisdom of **the Platinum Rule—** **_Do unto others as they would like to be done unto._** We use it to bring success at every level of leadership and teamwork. It's a simple and powerful tool for successful relationships across the board, but sometimes hard to grasp and requires intentionality.

The idea is to recognize how the other person likes to be connected with and related to, and then respond based on their preferences. For example, if they are big on logic, give them the logic in bullets and avoid unnecessary fluff. If they are big on feelings and relationships, include more about the people and your feelings about the issue. This is a simplified explanation, but operate with this concept in place and you'll overcome the barriers of differences and reap the benefits of a culture that truly gets the best out of everyone. Moreover, the respect given in this approach to managing differences motivates people to do and be their best, which benefits everyone at every level of an organization.

Let's Dive into Some Details and Define a Few Terms:

Creating a People Culture

We know that to some readers, the expression "people culture" may sound like the latest "Kumbaya" fad. Don't be deceived by these soft-sounding words. People do the work and this book will illustrate how to understand, lead and manage the behavior of different people in a way that inspires them to their best performance. This kind of leadership enables a positive, high-energy culture—a culture that collaborates to execute strategy and achieve superlative outcomes. Not accidentally, this is the kind of culture that also attracts and retains the best talent, which is the driving force and the secret sauce behind successful organizations.

There is never just one culture that fits all organizations or one strategy that directs every business. But there is a common denominator: human behavior. Using these behavioral insights, you will be able to pinpoint misalignments between an existing culture and strategy. These tools will enable users to focus on managing the *people* part of aligning culture and strategy to deliver outstanding people performance and business results.

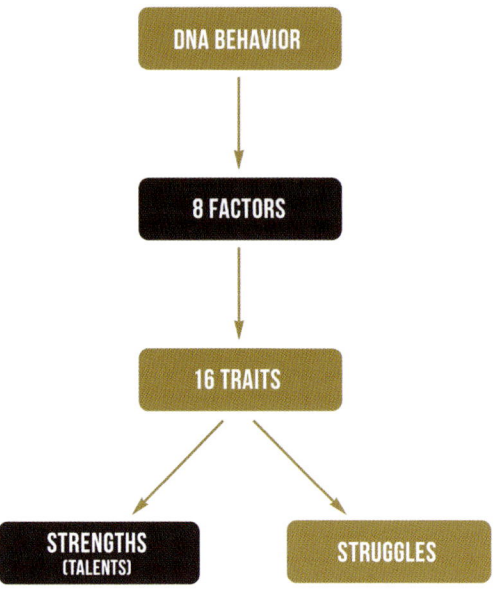

DNA Behavior

Here, we're talking about behaviors which are our natural talents—behaviors that can be quantified with eight Factors and sixteen Traits that we're born with and the ones that dominate our style, personality, and even the way we view and respond to others and situations. Most importantly: our **DNA Behavior** predicts our **strengths** and our **struggles**, which are the important critical insights for leadership and teamwork.

Strengths (Talents)

These are behaviors that come naturally and where we typically excel. It's critical to understand that our talents are mainly by default—they come with our DNA; they're different for each person and that's key to understanding our uniqueness. We will use these two terms interchangeably throughout the book.

Struggles

Not only does our natural DNA predict our talents, or natural **strengths**, it also foreshadows our **struggles**, which are typically the absence of talents—**strengths** that are missing from a person's natural **DNA Behavior**. For example, listening—one of the most important leadership and relational skills—is a **struggle** for many people. Listening takes patience, which is often in short supply. And if it isn't addressed in an individual, it can quickly be perceived as a weakness.

Struggles can also result from the overuse of our **strengths**. How? Being decisive is an important behavior (a strength) in many situations, but when overused, it becomes micro-management and control. No one on the receiving end likes the way that feels. It's also debilitating to the development of others who need to grow confidence by making decisions themselves. So, in many ways, overuse of this **strength** is a leadership downer.

Here we must highlight a crucial point. Many of the assessment and self-discovery processes in use take a **strengths**-**only** approach. We agree that focusing on your **strengths** is crucial for your own best performance. However, for working with other people (or leading and managing others to their best performance) we must deal with our own **struggles**; they're the obstacles to good relationships. We'll make the case for addressing **struggles** as the primary key to personal and leadership growth. As you read through the list of **struggles** associated with some of your own key Traits, you'll see those **struggles** are the areas where you must be most intentional to adapt your behaviors, because extra effort is required. When a leader falters, it's often due to a failure to adapt in an area of **struggle**. That's when they get in their own way.

> *"I have had more trouble with myself than with any other man I have ever met."*
> —*Dwight Lyman Moody*

Personal Growth Is the Key to Becoming a Great Leader, No Matter What Kind of Work You're Engaged in

While your natural style may be different from others, we'll show you that presidents, CEOs, military heroes and leaders across vocations possess many of your specific Traits. Importantly, these examples will illustrate how leaders with any combination of Traits can be successful. Our research has shown that there is no single leadership Trait that differentiates great leaders from average leaders. The payoff comes from knowing these Traits in ourselves and seeing them in others and mastering them in every interaction. So, know yourself, be yourself and continue to grow. Your talents will be sufficient to achieve your goal of becoming a better and likely, a great leader. And please pay it forward: use the knowledge you've gained about **DNA Behavior** to help others develop and grow. It pays off across the board, yielding great dividends for your organization.

SECTION 1

THE FUNDAMENTALS OF DNA BEHAVIOR AND LEADERSHIP

CHAPTER 1 ▶ THE UNIQUE BIRTH OF DNA BEHAVIOR

The things you are passionate about are not random—they are your calling.

—Fabienne Frederickson[1]

Separately and before we ever met, we were struck by the powerful idea of capitalizing on natural bent—our individual uniqueness—to maximize talents and manage differences.

The authors of this book, Lee Ellis and Hugh Massie, are both similar and different in our talents. We tend to see the same big picture vision quickly, yet we may respond differently because some of our Traits are different. Of course, we also come from different experiences, and our passion and calling for work is slightly different too.

Discovering Our Calling: Freeing People to be Themselves, Which Solves Problems and Promotes Success

If you judged us only by our early professions, you'd never expect that we would be teammates. There was nothing in our backgrounds to indicate that our passion and calling would be collectively focused in the field of human behavior.

In his first career, Lee was a US Air Force officer, fighter pilot, and flight instructor, holding leadership positions at every level along the way in his twenty-five-year military career before retiring as a colonel.

Hugh grew up in Australia and became a recognized CPA in Sydney, Singapore, and Bangkok, working in a leadership role with one of the world's most acclaimed accountancy firms before founding his own wealth management company in Sydney. In the past few years, Hugh has also become a global leader in *Entrepreneur's Organization* helping bring together over 13,000 successful business owners from diverse cultures and various stages of life and personal evolution.

What unites us is our shared interest and experience with individual uniqueness, used to maximize talents and manage differences among people. When we saw peer-reviewed scientific research that supported our shared instinct, we were hooked. Though we didn't know one another and lived on opposite sides of the earth, we had seen how the idea of *natural talents—DNA—*the ones each person brings, could revolutionize how people work and interact.

> *"You cannot teach talents. You must select them."*
>
> **—Gallup**

It's been nearly two decades since we began to discuss our common interest in natural behavior and how capitalizing on natural talents could address several objectives like the ones listed below.

What is the Value of Relationships?

Hugh's early vision for using behavioral assessments was toward helping financial planners better understand themselves and their clients in order to build more durable relationships, empowering them to make more confident decisions. Think about it like this: markets and values go up and down, but relationships and trusted emotional connections can keep clients engaged through cycles of the economy and transitions of life. In recent years, Hugh has been using his expertise in understanding how **DNA Behavior** and money intersect to help leaders globally make organizational decisions, enhancing their people culture and addressing different employee motivations in the workplace.

How Do We Make Career Choices and Manage the People We Have?

Lee began working with talent measurement in 1990 when he led a team that developed a four-part assessment package to help people understand themselves objectively and make good career choices. By understanding their natural talents, passions, skills, and values, people can understand their shape—a square peg belongs in a square hole—so they can look for job templates that are a match. In 1996, he began using them to coach leaders on hiring and managing their people and in 1998 went full time into leadership coaching and team development using behavioral assessments as the foundation for his business. Over the years, Lee has personally assessed and worked with thousands of leaders and his assessments have been used worldwide by millions.

How do We Move Toward a Business and Organizational Focus?

Because of this basic understanding of natural behavior gained early on, friends and colleagues began to ask us for help in various ways related to business—particularly areas that related to the human domain: hiring, managing, motivating, developing and retaining people. After gaining insights using other assessment tools, some of which we had created, owned and used, it was clear that we needed to develop and refine a new assessment that incorporated both the latest research and our deep experience gained from years of coaching and training work with clients. To develop this new tool, we worked with Industrial/Organizational Psychology experts for academic validation.

This effort brought us the "best in class" **DNA Behavior** assessment, employing eight Factors of behavior that represent sixteen powerful Traits. The scientific core of this book focuses on sharing these performance Traits, which we believe are the solution to successfully working with people and succeeding in relationships of all kinds.

"The man who is born with a talent which he is meant to use finds his greatest happiness in using it."
—Johann Wolfgang von Goethe

Here are Some of the Key Applications of Our Research and Experience:

In Hiring

We see how crucial it is for a person's *natural talents* to be matched to their task—to achieve work productivity needed for the company and job satisfaction and success for the employee. There is no better predictor of job fit than natural talents. Even with the information and technology of the twenty-first century, we see that many organizations are not applying the concept of *talent fit* to the hiring and team development process. Across corporate hiring, we see several obsolete and inefficient mind-sets that ignore the talent model. (See Checklist "Due Diligence for Hiring" at Appendix A.)

The industrial model treats people like machines: hire them, plug them in and expect them to operate effectively. The problem here is that the individual's shape (square, round, or other) is not considered, and talents and passions are wasted. Then there's the **car-salesman model**, which finds those who fit by trial and error. You just keep hiring and firing until you find those who can do it.

Next, we see the **non-human transactional model**, in which I pay you and you work. And to some degree, this is the extended use of the **military boot-camp model**, which believed a trained and motivated person should be able to do anything. Just give the orders and it will happen. (It's great for military bootcamp and orientation, but not for the day-to-day workplace.) None of these approaches is able to maximize productivity or job satisfaction. So, whether it's at home or at work, conventional wisdom is not commonly applied to talent management. What is needed is a process that is based on natural, default talents, which you now recognize as *DNA Behavior*.

If others are truly different from me in this or that way, then I will have to manage them differently to help them succeed and to be more successful myself.

Leadership and Management

Leaders must see the vision and accomplish the mission, but to do that they must operate effectively in the human domain. Leadership is about influencing others and that requires two critical components: *knowing* oneself and *understanding* others.

Leader development only comes through personal growth, and this requires self-awareness. Think of this as management information—the insights required to make decisions and act. To develop self and others, you need to know what you are managing, with an understanding of what to do more of and what to do less of—what's working and what isn't. That knowledge is best and most efficiently gained by understanding talents: your *natural **strengths*** and ***struggles***—your natural ***DNA Behavior***.

We learned that as a person gained self-awareness, another light bulb came on: they could take this new insight, using our scientifically validated assessment and apply it to better understanding others. Users saw clearly in a scientific, mathematical and graphical way specifically *how* people are both similar and very different. Accessing the data of these differences works to quantify what was perceived as previously unquantifiable. How are we different? How do these differences manifest? For many people, articulating this information is a monumental challenge. We removed the challenge with quantifiable information.

Sure, everyone knows that people are different—that's obvious, but now a curtain was pulled back and there was so much more. Using this new tool and lens for understanding ***behavior*** and ***talents***, we could show very specifically how people were different. This is insight and understanding that could have previously taken years to fully understand, so we sped up the clock. In a one-day workshop, we regularly accelerate trust and managing difference within teams to a level that would normally take six months to a year or more.

We began to understand that individuals could not be trained or "rewired" to operate like and in effect be someone else. And very importantly, we personally learned that they could never be like us in areas where they had different ***DNA Behaviors***. They could learn to adapt if they wanted to, but it was fruitless and frustrating (to both parties) to try to change them. Think about it: changing ourselves is a difficult challenge, but changing other people is impossible, either at work or at home. Trying is a fool's errand.

"You must be the change you wish to see in the world."

—Gandhi

Then the next light bulb came on—the game-changer for leaders: If others are truly different from me in this or that, then I will have to manage them differently to help them succeed. This also helps me to be more successful in my role as a leader. This is about bringing *freedom* to people and it's what good leaders do: free people to be all they can be. And knowing the unique talents of an individual equips the leader to encourage, develop, and apply those talents to the success and well-being of everyone.

Team Development

Teams are collections of individuals. Humans are unique and that means there will be some differences. Differences naturally divide, yet teams need cohesion, trust, and unity. When people know themselves and understand that others are different, they can learn to accept and respect differences. This is also where the **Platinum Rule** mentioned earlier comes into play. We can adapt our behaviors to fit their needs to bridge the gap of differences.

With this understanding and the essential qualities of acceptance, and respect, people learn to value the unique talents of others, making it much easier to set aside judgment and skepticism, allowing others to be themselves. And many of us learned that most of what we see in others' behaviors are not about how they experience or react to us; it's just them being themselves—we don't need to take it personally.

So much of what gets in the way of relationships is that we focus first on the *struggles* of others, which can impact how we relate to them. The bottom line is that the behaviors of others who are quite different from us can irritate us. We judge them because

8

they don't respond the way we might, in any given situation. It's so easy to take their conduct personally or judge it as a character problem, when in fact, it's just their **struggles**—part of their unique DNA. And it's likely that they are not seeing our **struggles** clearly either.

These insights, often gained in face-to-face team workshop experiences accelerate trust, allowing transparency and vulnerability, which lead to even more trust. The foundation for this more accepting perspective is anchored in people gaining self-awareness and self-confidence that come from accepting themselves as okay while not being perfect.

DNA Behavior Frees People to Soar Higher

This **DNA Behavior** process will be much easier and natural if you can answer yes to these crucial, foundational questions: Do you have a positive worldview about people? Do you value people? Do you enjoy inspiring others to achieve goals and grow as a team?

Regardless of your worldview, or what kind of work you do, or whether or not you're a member of a large team, we know that this knowledge of what makes you—and those around you—tick, can transform how you think about yourself and others. Such revealing information is not always easy to face head-on, but the benefits are tremendous.

We put it this way because those among us who are able to see ourselves objectively and then buckle down and deal honestly with the issues of our own personal growth always find ourselves celebrating on the other side of this journey. Honestly, it's about becoming more mature, and the *self*-awareness and *situational* awareness that come from directly facing our own **DNA Behavior** pay dividends every day. Think of it like being released from the shackles of an old mindset, like being freed from carrying your luggage in your hands: though we know it's possible to do it the old way, it can be so much easier. You can quickly go from struggling to carry something to rolling smoothly, and we'll show you how.

Quick Coach Notes

Key Point

Natural behavior provides the needed insights for self-awareness and understanding differences, and it becomes the foundation for leadership development, managing others, and all relationships.

Questions

1. How self-aware do you think you are? What do you think others would say?
2. What has been your experience in growing in self-awareness? Recall key moments along the way when you gained a more objective view of your own natural behaviors; what was that like, and how has it impacted your personal and leadership growth?
3. As a leader, how have you helped others gain more self-awareness? What has been the response and outcome of that awareness?
4. Can you think of a time when a relationship with another person has improved because of your understanding and acceptance of that person as being different from you? Reflect on what you learned or could learn from that experience.

PREFACE ENDNOTE

i   (See page xv.) Bernard Sadow patented wheels on regular suitcases with a tow strap in 1972, but it did not catch on. https://www.nytimes.com/2010/10/05/business/05road.html)

CHAPTER 1 ENDNOTE

1   Fabienne Fredrickson is the founder of Boldheart® and Boldheart.com (formerly The Client Attraction Business School and ClientAttraction.com). Fabienne's company has repeatedly been ranked by *Inc.* magazine as one of America's Fastest Growing Private Companies. She is the author of *Embrace Your Magnificence: Get Out of Your Own Way and Live a Richer, Fuller, More Abundant Life.*

CHAPTER 2 ▶ UNDERSTANDING STRENGTHS— MANAGING PEOPLE

I'd rather have a lot of talent and a little experience than a lot of experience and a little talent.

—John Wooden, Legendary UCLA Basketball Coach

Former Secretary of State General Colin Powell (also former Chairman of the Joint Chiefs of Staff) highlighted the importance of people to organizational success when he said, "Organization doesn't really accomplish anything. Plans don't accomplish anything either. Theories of management don't much matter. Endeavors succeed or fail because of the people involved. Only by attracting the best people will you accomplish great deeds."[1]

"Endeavors succeed or fail because of the people involved."
—Gen. Colin Powell

Regarding the ***strengths*** side of the behavior coin, do you have an abiding sense of the importance of people and can you see the strengths in those around you? Have you bought into the idea that humans are innately special and every one of us has the potential to be an extraordinary contributor—if we use our best natural talents and work hard to de- velop them? We believe that leaders have a responsibility to provide encouragement, a healthy environment, and the opportunity to develop talents through practice and hard work. We see this clearly in athletes, but it's just as true in every other field.

Learning to appreciate and value people and our different talents is crucial to developing a good mindset for leadership. It's easy to admire the famous ones, but it's important to value those who do the behind-the-scenes work that is so crucial to success. One example that is close to home for us is intercontinental air travel.

Hugh regularly returns to Australia to check on family and business interests. Lee has made trips to Asia for speaking engagements. These journeys require fifteen to sixteen-hour non-stop flights over water or the frozen Arctic. Our lives depend on the reliability of the aircraft and crew.

On these flights, both of us like to pause and give thanks for those amazing people who conceptualized, designed, built, and now maintain the airframes and especially the engines that reliably keep turning for hours on end, taking us safely to our destinations. This may seem like a mundane example, but when you know there are no emergency airfields within hundreds, perhaps thousands of miles, this criticality becomes very clear, making the point: humans and our curiosity and ingenuity are remarkable with almost unlimited potential. At work, it takes talented people to make things happen and get the results needed to accomplish the mission. They deserve good leadership and a workplace where they are valued and appreciated.

This point also illustrates that most work is done in concert with others—in which we pool our *strengths* to reach a shared goal. Though the technology of modern life allows us to work in more isolated ways, it hasn't made most of us more independent. It seems that the need to communicate and collaborate with others increases every day. Without the talents of others working in a team effort, we'd still be living in caves, hunting and fishing to survive. The bottom line is that we need each other, and we need different talents, regardless of our different behaviors.

People are essential for success, but leading and managing them requires a positive mindset, the courage of a tiger, the empathy of a saint, and the skills of an engineer.

Sure, everyone knows people are critical to success, but like wheels and luggage, too often our insights about ourselves and others are disconnected. There is no framework or online system for practically using what is intuitively obvious. The result is that too often, we don't develop ourselves and others, and we don't apply the insights of human behavior to leading and managing others. People are not mechanical and too many leaders are still viewing the work of their people as just a transaction or a mechanical step in the process. Right up front, we want to challenge you to evaluate your perspective on the importance of people.

We offer this challenge because we know how hard it is to understand, lead, and manage people. If you are going to maximize talents and manage differences for success, you will need a positive mindset about people—those around you and those you don't know. It is people who make everything happen and we're more productive when they're using their talents and feel valued and important. With these considerations in place, the environment is set for people to experience meaning in their work.

We know that people and relationships are an important part of life and success. But there is a tension that comes with it. People are not always predictable; they have feelings, emotions, sensitivities, and baggage from past experiences. Case in point: in a casual conversation at the end of a recent workshop, an IT systems specialist commented, "I'm so glad I don't have to manage people. I'm just not cut out for it. I love my job without that responsibility." His comment demonstrated good self-awareness and his recognition of the tension introduced when people come together. Helping leaders gain this kind of self-awareness is exciting and at times a challenging and risky business.

Have you ever met a talented, confident, self-aware leader who is perfect in almost every way, yet missing one thing that's obviously holding them back? Whether it's a missing element in their naturally wired behaviors or an unresolved issue from a childhood experience, everyone notices there's a problem—except them. **Self-awareness** is key in leadership and managing relational dynamics.

Let's use as an example a particular leader coached by Lee, who had an impressive track record that leaned heavily on his *strengths*. He graduated from West Point and served in an elite military unit.

After completion of his military commitments, he became a management consultant for one of the top national firms, eventually becoming a leader in a Fortune 500 communications/technology company. When Lee met him, he was president of one of their most important divisions. For the story, we'll call him Tom.

Tom is bright, a great problem solver and very mission-focused, or as we often say, results-oriented. It was obvious that he was a good person with strong character and integrity. He seemed to be an ideal fit for his role. But in working with his team, it became clear that there was a missing element in his leadership.

One day, Lee asked Tom how his team was doing. He replied that they were doing a great job. Lee looked him in the eye and replied, "But you never tell them that…and some of them are starving for feedback. Most of what they hear from you relates to the next problem to solve."

"I don't give that kind of feedback because I don't need it and hadn't considered them to either," responded Tom, to which Lee replied, "But Tom, you were an officer who led soldiers, I know that the military teaches you about taking care of your people." Shifting with a bit of discomfort, he responded, "It's not part of my life experience and it seems kind of 'hokey' to me."

What Tom had not become aware of was the reality of his natural **strengths** and **struggles**. In what we call **Leadership Balance**, every Factor (and fiber) in his **DNA Behavior** was strongly tilted toward **Results**—mission and almost none towards **Relationships**—people.[2] He was woefully out of balance in these two critical components of leadership. He had good values, but he was just being true to his results-focused DNA and it was just not in him to affirm others. It would have to come from learned behaviors, and that's always a challenge.

Lee knew they had to start somewhere with a specific action to shift Tom's mindset and behaviors, so, he asked him what he thought about the work done by a team member who had organized and managed an off-site retreat two weeks earlier. Tom replied, "She did a great job." Lee responded, "Have you told her?" It won't surprise you to hear his answer: "No—not really."

This was the perfect opportunity to begin his development, so Lee asked Tom to come up with a simple script of affirmation for him to execute. To Tom's credit, he accepted the task seriously and practiced his script, even though it was uncomfortable—too "soft and fluffy" for a results-oriented guy like him. Lee coached him that if he delivered the message believing it was genuine and deserved, it would be well received. But he would need to put so much positive energy and enthusiasm into it that it would feel very unnatural and awkward to him.

This was new and scary territory for Tom, a former Army Ranger, but drawing from his strong character and commitment to grow as a leader, he executed his plan. The results were predictable. His team member had known that the event went well, but to hear it from her boss was very special; it lifted her spirits and brought a warm smile to her face. And of course, she proceeded to pass it down. You see, **emotions and energy are contagious**, and the morale of her team was lifted as well. They knew they had brought value and now it was confirmed and affirmed by their leader, giving a surge to their confidence and equipping them for their next challenge.

Tom sensed that he had done a good thing, and this emboldened him to become more intentional about giving appropriate, simple, positive, and specific feedback to his team. In this way, he overcame a *struggle*. His adapted behavior clearly impacted his entire team. The positive energy was obvious, and they went on to exceed their annual goals while enjoying their work and camaraderie even more. After a few months, Lee was closing out with their last coaching meeting. As they sat down in his office, Tom asked if Lee could stay a few minutes after the meeting; he had someone he wanted him to meet. Of course, Lee agreed. At the end he excused himself, returning with a lovely lady wearing a big smile— his wife.

She explained that she wanted to meet Lee to share what had happened at home. They had a 13-year-old son, and Tom's growth as a leader paid off at home, changing their relationship. Tom was listening to him, showing more patience with him, and they were really connecting in a way they had not done before. Lee looked at Tom with a big smile and would have hugged him right on the spot for the great work he had done…but he was not sure they were ready for that. Lee doesn't recall what he said, but ever since, Tom's been one of his heroes and an example of courage for his own growth. Though initially he had been uncomfortable, Tom had leaned into the pain of his doubts and fears and done what he knew was right. In doing so, he had gained a new and powerful balance in his approach to leadership, greater success at work, and a stronger connection with his son.

The Bottom Line

We use Tom's story not because it's unusual, but because it's so typical of the leaders we work with. You can't grow until you know, and the revelations of **DNA Behavior**—self-awareness—can be life-changing.

To grow as a leader, knowledge is not enough; you must change your behavior. And to change your behavior, you need objective insights and honesty about how it impacts others. When you change your behavior, you grow as a person. **When you grow as a person you have more influence, better relationships, and you help others reach their full potential.** Tom's personal growth in this one area positively affected the entire culture of the organization. And as a footnote, the last time Lee saw Tom, he shared that he and his now adult son were headed out on Saturday to run a half-marathon—together.

This is a good place to qualify the context of our experience and stories used in the book. We work mostly with good leaders and rarely see bad ones. Bad leaders are usually very insecure and terrified that someone might hold up a mirror; they can't face the reality of their imperfections. Their fears preclude true vulnerability and they lack the kind of courage that comes with being secure with themselves. Without that kind of inner confidence, people will not have the courage to see themselves objectively and accept ownership of the problems they're causing.

> *When people are fearful of vulnerability and lack humility, they won't pursue objective self-awareness, the essential for maturity and the foundation for all growth.*

Absent self-awareness and courage, it's unlikely they will ever change, short of a derailing train wreck that forces them to change willingly with remorse and humility, or unwillingly and probably with resentment.

Fortunately, this was not the case in the story above. Tom had strong character, he was a person who truly wanted to do the right thing and he had courage, the kind of courage that enables a person to make hard choices and operate outside of his comfort zone to do what is right. Winston Churchill understood this and expressed it best.

> *"Courage is rightly esteemed the first of human qualities… because it is the quality which guarantees all others."*
>
> **—Winston Churchill**

Are Talents (Strengths) Behaviors? Are You Talent-Smart? Let's Find Out

Dictionaries typically define talent as a *"natural aptitude or skill"* with synonyms: *strength*, gift, knack, bent, aptitude, and flair. Notice the word "natural"—that's key to understanding **DNA Behavior**. Here we define **strengths** as the talents that flow out of us by default. Children sharing the same biological parents and home environment may share the same values, but more often than not, their talents and behaviors are different. If you have siblings or children, you've seen how **nature** determines those differences and typically overrides **nurture**.

17

Hiring, Developing and Managing Others—Talents Point the Way

Like the use of wheels to haul cargo, the wisdom of using individual talents as the key criteria for making career and life choices is not a new idea. Some 2,400 years ago, Greek playwright Aristophanes pointed the way when he said, "Let each man [or woman] exercise the art he knows."[3] In the first century AD, when writing to the Romans, Saint Paul took a similar line: "Since we have gifts that differ according to the grace given to us, let each exercise them accordingly."[4]

More recently, some unknown sage has offered perhaps the best advice for parents who are guiding their children: "Our job as parents is not to mold them; it's to unfold them. God has already given them their shape."

The Gallup Organization, well known for conducting public opinion polls, is also one of the leading management consulting firms in the world. For decades, they have collected data on workers, managers and the workplace by surveying millions of people and hundreds of thousands of managers in more than four hundred companies.

Gallup's research conclusions (1984-1998) were presented in a landmark book entitled *First Break All the Rules: What the World's Greatest Managers Do Differently*, first published in 1999. The authors, former Gallup consultants Marcus Buckingham and Curt Coffman used Gallup's extensive research to document the value of understanding and using talents as the focus for matching people to positions. They concluded that great managers "select for talent . . . not simply experience, intelligence, or determination."[5]

A major conclusion from Gallup's research is captured in the authors' definition of talents: ***"Any recurring patterns of behavior that can be productively applied are talents."*** (emphasis added) They go on to say, "The key to excellent performance, of course, is finding the match between your talents and your role."[6]

Gallup's research validated our own long-held view and the often-ignored conventional wisdom about matching people to jobs. Furthermore, their conclusion that talents are *behaviors* provided solid confirmation from a reputable outside source to the concepts that we felt so passionately about and upon which we had built our work and companies.

You will recall that in the Introduction, we used the words talents and *strengths* interchangeably. That's a good way to think about it here—if you keep in mind that with our talents, we get not only the *strengths*, but also the other side of that coin—the *struggles*, and those will be covered in Chapter Three. Of course, both sides of this behavioral coin are going to be unpacked in almost every chapter in this book. But here we are focusing on the crucial importance of using *strengths* as the key to success in our work professions.

Recognize Diverse Talents and Strengths to Build a Winning Culture

The evidence is clear that the most successful companies are those that know the individual natural behaviors of their people and help develop their *talents/strengths* accordingly. When you mix in a focus on attracting good people, treating them with respect and dignity to make it clear they're valued, and developing them based on their *strengths* and their dreams to achieve their potential, you have the ingredients for a "high performing" *people culture*. With this knowledge, you can treat them as people—not "talent," which is like another species. Into that splendid mix, you only need to add one more thing: it's important to have some fun, in spite of the fact that it may seem antithetical to the mission of work itself. Fun builds camaraderie and trust, relieves stress, and opens up communications—and it releases positive energy.

Southwest Airlines, known for its unorthodox "fun" environment and the only major airline that showed a profit for forty-five straight years, makes clear its priority for dealing with employees: "Give people the freedom to be themselves."[7] The implication is clear: don't try to remold them. Create the parameters and allow people to be themselves, which enriches the culture and an organization's success. Even hard work feels like fun if we are using our *strengths* doing something we feel is valued and important and it's taking us toward our dreams.

In his best-selling book, *Job Shift*, Ken Bridges wrote, ". . . We are finding that the most successful organizations are made up of people doing what they like to do and believe in doing, rather than of people doing what they are 'supposed to' do."[8] In a similar vein, Peter Cappelli, writing for the *Harvard Business Review*, concluded his article on the challenges of retaining talent with the following words: "One thing is for sure: as the early years of the new century unfolded, executives will be challenged to abandon their old ways of thinking and adopt more creative ways of managing, retaining, and, yes, releasing their talent. Those who begin this difficult process now will be one step ahead of the game."[9]

Talent Mismatches Cause Problems for Everyone

Jim Collins emphasizes the need for recognizing and managing talents in his book *Good to Great*, where he writes about not only getting the right people on the bus but also getting them in the right seats. Thanks to Jim's simple but brilliant word picture, hardly a week goes by without one of us hearing that expression. This book is intended to help you do just that—match people's talents to the right roles and then manage them differently based on their uniqueness.

Ask yourself if you would be attracted to a work environment where your talents are likely to be mismatched and then remolded or, instead, one where they're matched and unleashed.

The logic seems basic, doesn't it? But just because conventional wisdom seems so obvious doesn't mean that it's commonly applied in today's work world.

When we place people in jobs in which their primary work does not exploit the **strengths** of their natural talents, we condemn them to a future somewhere between failure and mediocrity. This sets up a lose-lose situation in which the individuals and the organizations suffer, and no one is happy or as productive as they want to be and the role requires.

Another way to illustrate the value of matching talents to tasks is to think of swimming upstream versus downstream. When people are using their talents, it's like swimming downstream. Going with the current (your natural bent) is efficient and fun. After a long day of work, you may be tired, but you feel great because you've been going with the flow and you've traveled quite a distance. You know you've been highly productive and just as importantly, those who are watching are cheering your progress.

On the other hand, when people are mismatched, it's as if they are swimming upstream. Can they do it? Of course, they can, but it requires much more energy, it's stressful and exhausting, and the progress is slow. And when the sun rises the next day, there's little excitement about getting back in the water.

Regardless of whether we use Gallup's research or simple illustrations like square and round pegs, seats on the bus, or swimming, the message is the same. People generally achieve their highest productivity and work satisfaction when they identify and use their unique **strengths**.

> *"The secret of joy in work is contained in one word—excellence. To know how to do something well is to enjoy it."*
>
> **—Pearl Buck**

Yes, joy, satisfaction, confidence, and excellence in the workplace are the natural outcomes when you identify, unfold, and exploit talents—your **strengths** and those of others. The principle to remember is that by matching the individual **strengths** to the tasks, everyone benefits. But as in almost every other area of life, the "other shoe" has to fall, or more appropriately here, there is another side to this coin.

An understanding of talents is essential for career planning, but it's not sufficient for individual and leader development. Reflect back to the story of Tom shared earlier. His natural blind spot was in his **struggles**; it was his non-talents and his overuse of his **strengths** that were undermining his leadership. So now we must turn the coin over and address this crucial issue that so often gets avoided—our **struggles**.

Quick Coach Notes

Key Point

Leaders must learn to recognize talents because they are the best predictors of work success. Getting people in the right slots where their talents are aligned to their roles is a critical responsibility for leaders.

Questions

1. What has been your experience in the past regarding understanding and using or misusing your own talents?
2. To what degree have you considered talents in assigning work to your people? What worked, what didn't, and what have you learned?
3. Given the insights in this chapter, are there any adjustments in the roles and assignments of your people that you might want to consider? If so, how will you approach those adjustments?

ENDNOTES

1   *A Primer on Leadership*, Lesson 15, General Colin Powell, Retired Chairman of the Joint Chiefs of Staff.

2   In Chapter 4 we share more about the challenge of leadership balance. You will see that the neuroscientists call it the "neural seesaw."

3   https://www.ccswv.org/johann-von-goethe/

4   Romans 12:6 (NASB)

5   Marcus Buckingham and Curt Coffman, *First, Break All the Rules: What the World's Greatest Leaders Do Different* (NY: Simon & Schuster, 1999), 67.

6   Ibid 71

7   As quoted in National Religious Broadcasters magazine, "The People Department," May 1998.

8   William Bridges, *Job Shift, How to Prosper in a Workplace Without Jobs* (Boston: Addison-Wesley, 1995).

9   Peter Capelli, "A Market-Driven Approach to Retaining Talent," *Harvard Business Review* (January–February 2000).

CHAPTER 3 ▶ STRUGGLES: THE OTHER SIDE OF THE COIN

Sometimes, struggles are exactly what we need in our life. If we were to go through our life without any obstacles, we would be crippled. We would not be as strong as what we could have been. Give every opportunity a chance, leave no room for regrets.

—Friedrich Nietzsche

You already know that the ***strengths*** of our talents are the keys to success at work. Here, we'll examine the concept of ***struggles*** and see how they affect work—especially leadership, teamwork, and all relationships. As you'll see here and in the chapters ahead, ***struggles*** are directly tied to the ***strengths*** of our natural ***DNA Behaviors*** as well. As mentioned earlier, we like to think of them as the other side of the coin. The better you understand this connection, the more objective you'll be about your own ***struggles*** and the better you'll be able to understand yourself and others. The principle that comes out of this is so crucial we'll make it a bold statement:

You cannot grow as a leader without self-awareness and that includes awareness of struggles and how they can hold you back.

The tendency of individuals and much of the leadership literature is to ignore the dark side. After all, why not focus on a person's ***strengths***? The problem is that for every ***strength*** there is usually a corresponding ***struggle***, and a ***struggle not managed will*** *be experienced by others as a weakness.* To illustrate this, let's look at the example of a person with a talent for working accurately with details for extended periods. This talent might be essential for someone who is a diamond cutter, a copy editor, a design engineer, or an accountant.

Typical Strengths

1. Accurate and exact with detail
2. Good with process and procedure
3. Thorough and prepared
4. Determined to "get it right"

Typical Struggles

1. Tend to be inflexible or too fixed
2. May be too reliant on procedures/rules
3. Have difficulty with improvising
4. Perfectionistic to avoid mistakes

We know that this talent for accuracy and detail encompasses *strengths*, such as those listed above. But look at the *struggles* that usually go with these *strengths*. Note that we call them *"struggles"* and not weaknesses. Generally, if we make some effort to adapt our behaviors a bit in our *struggles*, they will not be seen by others as weaknesses. This is where we need to apply adaptive or learned behaviors, modifying our natural behaviors in some situations to be more effective. The best leaders learn to be very intentional about adapting their behaviors so as not to get in their own way.

Struggles will typically not be seen as "weaknesses" if we actually struggle with them and adapt our behaviors.

Overcoming Struggles that Result from Non-Talents and the Miracle of Adaptability

When we talk about *struggles*, we think first of areas of non-talents. Reflecting on the previous example—a talent for detail-oriented work—it's possible for this person to use the learned behavior of becoming less picky, more spontaneous, and more flexible. However, it will require intentionality and extra energy, and certainly, you would not want to put that person in a job in which his or her success depended primarily on overcoming those *struggles* on a regular basis. That would result in swimming upstream. **Still, the good news is that we humans have an amazing ability to adapt and overcome *struggles* or adversities in the moment to be more effective in nearly any given situation.**

We use the word "overcome" in relation to *struggles* because it fits so well. In fact, on several occasions, people have actually used the word overcome to describe the process it took for them to achieve those skills and truly integrate them into their behavior. Most people we work with are amazed by the accuracy of their *DNA Behavior* results; we rarely receive pushback, but when we do, it's most likely related to the talents of organization and detail. Over the years, we've worked with three individuals, all of whom had earned PhDs, who challenged their assessment results in this area. In each case, they believed that they should have scored in the *Planned* (accurate, detailed, organized) range, rather than the *Spontaneous* (generalist, not detailed, rely on instinct, "wing it") range. As we discussed their assessment results with them, all three asserted: "I have struggled with being disorganized, not detailed, and too spontaneous, but I overcame those problems."

Elaborating on the misalignment of these three individuals' self-perception, each was saying that the drive required to complete their doctorate degree was so strong that they temporarily did what was needed to reach their goals. There is no doubt that many years of dedication and commitment were required by each of these people. We asked them if they were still 'overcoming' in these areas and they replied that they were. This validated their true Trait as being *Spontaneous* because they have to intentionally *struggle* to be planned, methodical, and organized.

Adapting Behaviors to Overcome Struggles at Work

Even small changes that may not initially seem impactful can create a lot of leverage. This example helps us see clearly the difference between **strengths** and **struggles** and our ability to *adapt behaviors* to deal with our **struggles**. If being **Planned** had been their real talent, they would not have had to "overcome" their **Spontaneous** Traits in order to achieve their goals. So, the principle to emphasize is that to perform a function to achieve a goal (or to work with someone with opposite strengths), it may be necessary to adapt your behavior to the situation.

Initially, adapting may be a challenge, but usually, a small change in behavior yields big results. Human survival is the story of adaptation and if we've been doing it since leaving the caves, we can certainly do it now in our modern world. And don't forget you're not trying to reinvent yourself; you are adapting to be more effective in a specific situation. You are not abandoning your core DNA.

If you reflect back to an assignment that was stressful for you, a time when you felt like you were a round peg in a square hole, most likely you were working in an area where the talents needed were missing in your natural skill set. From the previous discussion, you now have a clearer view of that issue. But even when our work is a good match for our talents, we still have to operate in some areas that are not our natural behaviors—we have to stretch and adapt. The good news is that we humans can do that.

Our Struggles Also Come from Strengths Overdone

If you've read objective reporting about high-profile leaders, you'll see that they all had **struggles** that accompanied their talents. For example, one of Winston Churchill's biographies had the following to say about his **strengths** and **struggles** when he took over as First Lord of the Admiralty at age thirty-seven.

"Churchill rose to this challenge with incomparable vigor and self-confidence. These characteristics were precisely the ones to which he owed both his failures and his successes as First Lord. For as Admiral Bacon said, 'Churchill's vices were simply his virtues in an exaggerated form. Dash became rashness. Assurance became cocksureness. Churchill's overflowing energy was difficult to harness. His overwhelming faith in himself closed his mind to the opinions of others.'"[1]

Churchill is not the exception where this concept is concerned. A cursory review of history indicates that many famous leaders have fallen, not because of their non-talent *struggles* but because of the misuse of their *strengths*. Because our *strengths* are responsible for so many of our successes, it's easy to over-rely on them to our detriment.

In 1966, psychologist Abraham Maslow captured this tendency with a word picture that is so simple and yet so powerful that it's become famous.

> *"To a man who only has a hammer, everything he encounters begins to look like a nail."*

It seems straightforward enough, but how do you apply this abstract simile in the context of our discussion? We think it perfectly illustrates how we overuse our own tendencies, falling back on our *strengths* over and over again—assuming they will always work. Most of us have experienced this "blindness of excess" from a confident, quick-minded, decisive person who has been "right" so often that he or she quit listening to anyone else's ideas. Or maybe you know a kind, supportive, helpful soul, who helps everyone and can't say no to anyone, until one day he or she physically and emotionally wears out. We are all susceptible because the consequences from overdoing our *strengths* can be very subtle at first because they're our *strengths* and they work for us, for a while, until we begin using them in situations where they're not appropriate.

Struggles Undermine Relationships and Teamwork

Once, during a session with a group of senior managers, Lee was explaining that most people identify with their *strengths* but sometimes push back on some of their *struggles*, especially if they are from *strengths* overdone. This led to a very profound comment about *struggles* from a fellow in his mid-50s who remarked, "I know where you got this list of *struggles* in my report. You called my first wife. I heard about them every Saturday for years."

His response was certainly funny, yet also sad and insightful about the problem of *strengths overdone* and the power of *struggles* to undermine relationships. Understanding this connection enables us to see talents more objectively and more predictably. Most important for leader development, it helps us gain the self-awareness needed to adapt and grow.

> *Strengths are critical for individual performance, but Struggles are the fertile ground for leader and team development and all relationships.*

In the same way that an understanding of talents and *strengths* can point the way to better success in our work, an understanding of *struggles*—ours and others—can guide us to better relationships and ultimately a healthier culture. Here's a common example: Consider two very different people whom we encounter on almost every team—we'll call them Jason and Sophia.

Jason is a highly engaging extrovert who enjoys having fun so much that at times he's the office "entertainer." He tends to talk too much, can be overly optimistic, often doesn't finish what he starts and thrives on being the center of attention. Despite these natural *struggles*, his talents are a good match for his work, and he is very productive. Jason's *struggles* irritate the reserved Sophia because when he's around, it's difficult for her to get any work done. His struggles can exasperate her, and she doesn't see how they link to his talents.

Of course, Sophia also turns off engaging Jason at times. She can be cold and distant and when she does speak up, her words can be curt or negative. Her approach comes across as secretive and even quietly self-righteous. She never shares much about her life and really seems distrustful of everyone. Despite her natural behaviors, her talents are also a good match for her work, and she is very productive in her role.

Employing the Platinum Rule Rescues Relationships and Builds Trust

Clearly, these two are like night and day—oil and water—and they definitely don't appear to go together. The irony is that they need each other and can make a great team if they work together toward a **Platinum Rule** relationship. We use this term a lot in our **DNA Behavior** training because it's simple—and compliments the **Golden Rule**. The **Platinum Rule** says, "Do unto others as they would like to be done unto." It turns out that this is one of the most powerful ways to actually carry out the Golden Rule.

In our example of Sophia and Jason, the **Platinum Rule** means that each must adapt some of their natural "go to" behaviors when they are together to relate to the other person the way *they (the other person)* likes it—not demand they adapt to them. If the reserved Sophia acts friendlier to Jason and he limits his effusive expression around her, their dynamics change dramatically. This goes back to the leverage we mentioned earlier; a little change can make a big difference.

The stealth benefit of the **Platinum Rule** is that each person is showing respect and gaining respect from the other, increasing *trust*. Adapting like this brings out the best in both and facilitates alignment so they can work better together. As you might suspect, adapting to align our behaviors with others can be a very challenging undertaking and requires a great deal of self-awareness. But you can see that a **strengths**-only approach can be a big turnoff that undermines all the relationship pieces needed for good collaboration. With this minor adjustment, these two individuals can be more productive, and less stressed, each day.

> *Struggles not managed will be seen as weaknesses. To grow as a leader, you must confront your Struggles. It's how you avoid getting in your own way and achieve greatness.*

During Lee's time as a Vietnam Prisoner of War, the living situation varied from isolation to cells of four to six people, but eventually he spent almost two years locked up in one large room with 52 strong-willed, competitive aircrew cellmates. There were no inside walls in this cell of roughly 1800 sq. ft.; it was packed with bodies and the only place you might be able to get alone was the "two-ho-ler"—basically a squat trench over the sewer in a small room at one end. The POWs slept elbow to elbow on a raised concrete slab. There were some hard times, but it was the perfect laboratory to learn about human nature and practice the Platinum Rule—long before it was so named. Here is how he describes it:

> "In this enlarged 'sardine can', you could not hide nor pretend. Your best and worst behaviors were on display 24/7 day after day, month after month, year after year. Packed together so closely with our struggles so open and obvious, we could see how they were problematic. First, we saw it in others who irritated us. But over time, in ways that were sometimes subtle and often blatant, we learned of our own gaps and shortcomings. It was there that we came to accept that we were all unique and that we could not change others. In effect, there was a mirror there to show us what we had not seen before. In this suspension of time in the camps, we were motivated to go to work and so we did.
>
> "With little to do, most of us decided it was a good opportunity to grow and develop. We soon organized an educational **program** with formal academic classes six days a week. It was optional, but most guys engaged in some of the classes. The teamwork in that cell became remarkable.
>
> "We organized everything, assigned and rotated duties, and most importantly learned the power of respecting and caring for others—even those who irritated us the most. Only twice in those 20 months did someone raise their voice at another, and in both cases, they apologized before bedtime. Besides a greater awareness of the unique *strengths* and *struggles* of each person, we also learned to live the ***Platinum Rule*** and it paid off in ways that continue to bind us together. Our cell's turnout for reunions is the highest of any of the seven large cells in that camp."

This powerful concept of relating to others the way they like it is universal and one you can begin practicing immediately at home and in every relationship. In the chapters that follow, you will see specific ways to connect with each Trait—*the way they like it*. Try it and you will see this miracle of adaptability firsthand.

Keep in mind that some whose **strengths** are more social and relational might rationalize the need to be kind when in fact they are being too soft in managing relationships and weak in driving towards results—not holding people accountable. Again, the key is to leverage your **strengths** but manage the **struggles** sufficiently through awareness and adaptation, so they do not derail performance and demoralize teams.

Remember, great leaders are more concerned about being effective than they are about being "right." They read the situation and adapt appropriately to avoid derailing behaviors that undermine their credibility and team success.

We hope you can see that a *strengths*-only approach will leave you potentially making a series of destructive decisions or continuously damaging key relationships and justifying it as acceptable because "that's just who I am."

Quick Coach Notes

Key Point

Talents are the key to work success, and ***struggles*** provide the insights needed for our personal and leadership growth and, especially, for building teamwork and relationships.

Questions

1. Consider three situations where you have not been fully successful. What ***struggles*** contributed to the problems?
2. Think of some of your best leaders and try to recall how they managed their ***struggles***?
3. Have you used the ***Platinum Rule***? What was that like and how did it work? Have you asked your people to communicate with you based on your preferred way? If not, the Trait chapters will provide you some good insights.

ENDNOTE

1   *Winston Churchill: A Biography*, Piers Brendon pg 62-63, 1984, Harper & Row, Pub. Inc.

CHAPTER 4 ▶ LEADERSHIP FUNDAMENTALS

There is no decision that we can make that doesn't come
with some sort of balance or sacrifice.
—Simon Sinek

Before we launch into the science of defining and measuring ***DNA Behaviors***, we want to address five points that are crucial to good leadership development. The first will help you put leadership and behavior in a clear context regarding mission and people. The second will help you confront the doubts and fears that all leaders face. The third will clarify your responsibility to be accountable and help others be accountable. The fourth highlights the challenge of living in the tension of paradox. And finally, courage—the quality that frees you up to meet the personal and professional challenges you will face as a leader.

1. **Understand Leadership Balance and the Leadership Attributes Model™**

Many years ago, we developed the ***Leadership Attributes Model*** shown below. It has stood the test of time as a simple graphic that encompasses every element of leadership. All the levels shown are important, but for this book, we mainly focus on the Natural ***DNA Behaviors*** layer that shows Mission/Results and People/Relationships. Other than the Character layer at the bottom, this is the most critical area for your leadership development and success.[1]

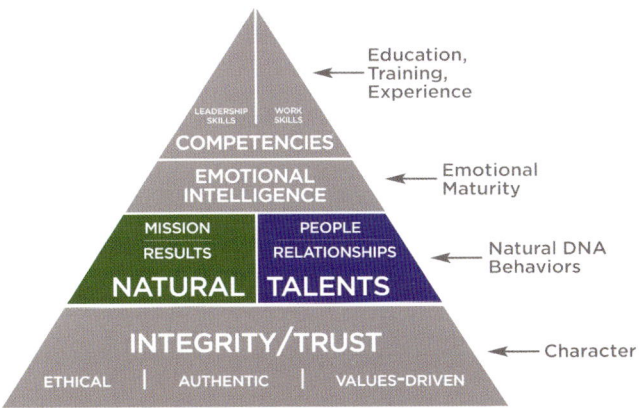

Almost the entire contents of this book relate directly to these two areas of Mission/Results and People/Relationships. Doing both may sound easy, but it isn't—most of us don't enter this world with talents for both. Eighty percent of us are born with talents more suited for one than the other. Early on we called this your "bent," but we now have termed this your leadership tilt. You can see below how that works.

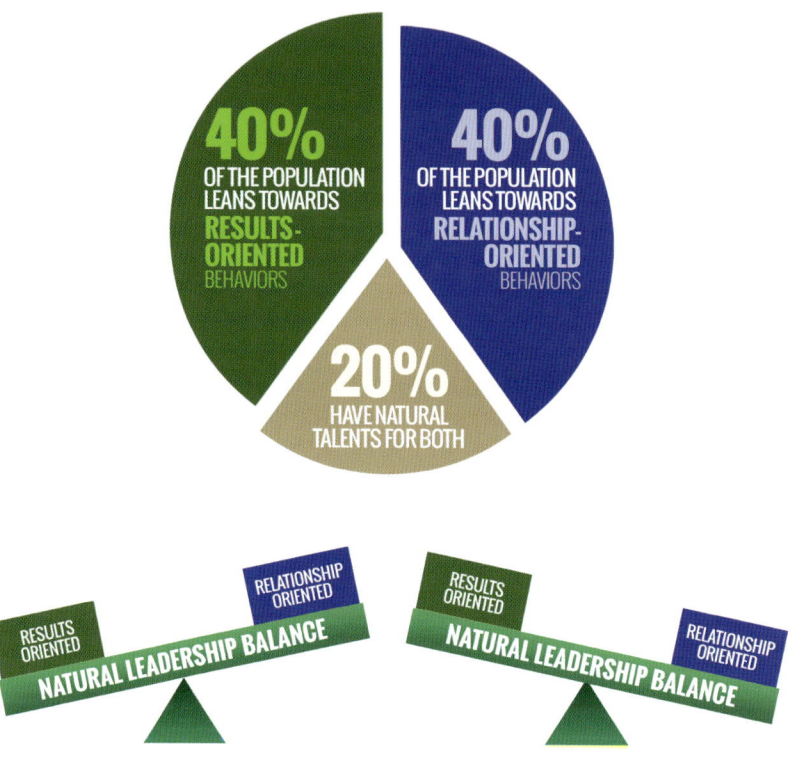

No doubt we can all agree in principle that both mission and people are important for success—but here is the problem. Research shows that forty percent of the people in any general population are born with natural talents *(DNA Behaviors)* for Mission/Results and forty percent are born with natural talents for People/Relationships. And the twenty-percent that are born with some of both will default to Mission/Results when there is the slightest pressure to "get 'er done."

What this means is that to be a truly effective leader 80% of you reading this book will have some good natural talents for one (that is your tilt) but also have to adapt your behaviors to develop a few good skills in the other to develop your **Leadership Balance**. Doing some of both well is a requirement and thus becomes the starting point for of all leadership development.

Check yourself on this list of leadership attributes (behaviors) associated with Results/Mission and Relationships/People:

Results-Oriented	Relationship-Oriented
• Big picture, visionary, strategic • Strong focus on tasks, good problem solver, analytical • Results focused, goal oriented • Decisive, give direction, firm • Set standards, expectations & boundaries • Hold people accountable	• Good listener, open to consider others' ideas • Care, connect to show concern for others • Trust people to do the job • Supportive, lend a helping hand • Take time to develop people • Give encouragement & positive feedback

Learning to employ attributes from your lightweight or scarce side will require commitment and intentionality because you are fighting against your natural behaviors, which are hard-wired. Modern brain scans (FMRI) show that there are two networks in the brain. Neuroscientists tend to call these: the task network and the social network.[2] These two networks closely parallel the concept explained above and depicted in the leadership balance and tilt graphics. They use the term neural seesaw which may be an even better way to describes the issues of balance and tilt shown above.

Dr. Richard Boyatzis, famous for his research and writing in *Primal Leadership* and *Resonant Leadership*, talks about these two competing neural networks frequently in his teachings. We encourage you to check out his books and YouTube videos.[3]

The research shows that the brain is not good at simultaneously doing both of what we call Results and Relationships. That's why it takes commitment and intentionality. Later in the book, we'll share more specifics on our personal experience of what it takes to gain a better balance—but the bottom line is it requires self-awareness, internal motivation, and a willingness to struggle with your *struggles*. Yes, like many of the good things in life, it takes effort, **but the rewards are great when you are able to operate successfully in both Results and Relationships to accomplish the mission and take care of your people.**

This is the challenge you must engage if you want to be a "great leader." Research of more than 60,000 employees showed…[4]

- If a leader had primarily a very strong focus on results, only 14% had the chance of being seen as a great leader.
- If they had mainly a very strong social skills focus, only a paltry 12% had the chance of being seen as a great leader.
- However, an astonishing 72% had the chance of being seen as a great leader if they were strong in both results focus and in social (relationship) skills. Social skills are a great multiplier. This seems obvious and like good common sense.

But not so fast—remember the problem of balance—the leadership tilt and the neural seesaw. And remember that 40/40/20 distribution of natural talents. It's going to take self-awareness and effort. Our goal is to equip you to do both (results and relationship) and be one of those great leaders.

Launching you on that trajectory is one of the main goals of this book. As you read ahead, you'll see that five of the eight Factors in the *Leadership Behavior DNA* model predict your natural talents toward either Results/Mission or Relationships/People. The DNA Behavior Traits associated with each are highlighted at the end of the next chapter and then in each chapter where they play a role in a specific Trait.

2. Get Rid of the Baggage: Gain Inner Confidence to Overcome Insecurity

Doubts and fears are a major problem for all leaders. These insecurities undermine behaviors and prevent us from the courageous actions to affirm, encourage, and support, as well as clarify expectations and boundaries, correct, confront, and hold people accountable. The most obvious evidence of being human is emotion and the most undermining of all emotions are doubts and fear. Yes, in a true fight or flight situation, they can save our lives, but those times are rare. Yet those emotions are always lurking just beneath the surface in every one of us.

From many years of working with and coaching leaders, we know that everyone has insecurities, doubts, and fears. A little doubt is helpful to keep us humble, but beyond that, those insecurities can cause us to withdraw, hold back or procrastinate, or in some personalities, attack and try to dominate or bully others. Both extremes are unhealthy and cause us to do dumb things that undermine success—ours and others. So, what can we do to increase healthy inner confidence? How do we move from Insecure to more Secure?

We should qualify that this is not a **DNA Behavior** issue, though the direction of our response (inward or outward) may be tied to our DNA. It's really a baggage issue from our nurturing—or lack thereof—and mostly not a nature issue.

The problem is that we all have insecurities. Deep down most of us *struggle* to accept ourselves as being valuable, worthy, or "enough" and those doubts come rolling in when certain situations arise. To be who we want to be and can be, we must find a way to believe in ourselves. Sometimes that can come from experience and achievement, but it's best when we learn to push aside those old "lies" that we picked up along the way and accept the encouragement, affirmation, and words of truth that come from others. Often, we will need the support of others who can help us set aside the fear and our "protective strategies" in order to see the source of the lie and discover the truth of who we really are.

Let's use Lee's friend Greg as an example. Greg was a top five percenter at West Point, graduated Summa Cum Laude from Harvard (MBA) and became very successful in everything he worked at. Yet he was miserable—until he met with a therapist. In one session, his therapist took him back to his childhood, when he overheard an argument in which his mom said to his dad, "Well, you know we did not plan to have him."

It was accurate, but a casual remark uttered in a moment of emotion. His parents always loved him as much as all their other children. He had a great childhood, but that one sentence drove him to achieve more and more, while always feeling unworthy and unwanted. Greg's case may be a bit extreme, but it makes the point that even the most successful achievers struggle with self-doubt.

The reality is that we all have doubts about our self-worth at times. For many of us like Greg, our insecurities drive us and though we are rewarded on the outside, internally we are paying a price that often negatively impacts our family and our closest relationships. Like termites, insecurities eat out pockets of doubt and fear that can eventually weaken even the strongest leaders."[5]

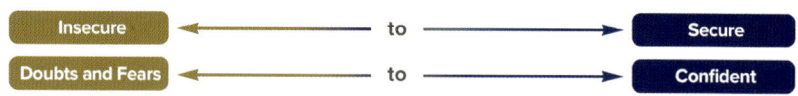

This leads to an important starting point and question: How do we get comfortable in our own skin?

When Lee was working on his 2012 book *Leading with Honor: Leadership Lessons from the Hanoi Hilton,*[6] many years after the Vietnam War, he asked his closest POW teammate, his cellmate and leader for more than three years of his five-plus years in the POW camps, "What was I like as a POW?" Ken replied, "When you were captured, you were not yet comfortable in your own skin. When you came home you were." The sacrifice, suffering, and periods of solitude and introspection, along with the trust, confidence, and compassion extended to him by his leader Ken, took Lee to a new level of inner confidence that anchors his self-image and informs his work today.

Few among us are going to be POWs, so how does the typical person grow in confidence? Honestly, much of it must come from accepting and believing the encouragement and affirmation of others. If you stop and reflect on your life and career, you will likely recall specific people—coaches, teachers, mentors, friends, leaders, and even family—who spoke confidently about your value and future potential. They treated you as important and spoke words into your life that launched your career or changed your trajectory to be more confident in yourself. In other words, often our greatest opportunity to grow more self-confident and capable is when we hear and believe the truth about ourselves from those who care about us and whom we trust.

As you read ahead, remember that you have what it takes to lead effectively, but it must be confidently expressed in your own unique way. Self-awareness, self-belief, and humility are the foundations for having the necessary confidence to become a great leader, and we want to help you get there. With these and a good understanding of human behavior, you'll be able to grow, develop others and manage each person uniquely based on their individual differences. Some of you may be thinking, "I got this." For others, this may sound a bit challenging at first, but with courage and intentionality, it's quite doable. We've helped thousands of people to use these skills, grow in confidence and humility, and we will do the same for you in this book.

It's Time to Pay Back the Bank

We hope that as a leader you see it as part of your calling, your stewardship, and your duty to pay back the bank. Even to pay it back with interest. Remember the times your leaders showed compassion and caring for you. Recall how they pointed out your talents, believed in your potential, and connected with your dreams, and how that has positively shaped your life and work. Reflect on the impact their words and attitudes had on your growth and consider your responsibility to share that kind of gift with those you lead.

In his new book, *Helping People Change: Coaching with Compassion for Lifelong Learning and Growth*, Dr. Richard Boyatzis and his co-authors bring together decades of research and experience to drive home the point that a caring leader (or coach, mentor, friend) relates to people in a way that facilitates their growth, helping them to be all they can be. They say, "Great coaches inspire, encourage, and support others in the pursuit of their dreams and the achievement of their full potential."[7] They call this coaching with compassion. This is what Capt. Ken Fisher did for Lee in the POW camps, and it's what we call the leader's responsibility to "Connect with the Heart" as a critical action in the *Courageous Accountability Model*™.[8]

Keep that thought, because in the upcoming chapters on Traits we will show you how to affirm others' talents and potential very specifically.

3. Accept and Embrace Accountability and Expectations

As leaders we have a responsibility to hold people accountable and we can only do that effectively when we set the example and provide clarity about our expectations. Often, we see leaders struggle to articulate what they expect and require of those they lead, leading to damaged relationships and failed missions. Lacking clarity on outcomes and standards, expectations are left to each person to interpret according to their own mindset. What is needed is confident leadership that can guide people forward and help them succeed.

Leaders are required to accept and embrace **ownership of their authority**, **responsibility for outcomes**, and at the same time **care for and develop their people**. Without clarity on all three of those, teams will typically lack cohesion and cannot rely on one another to execute their roles.

Many have found the Courageous Accountability Model™ that Lee has developed (see Appendix C) to be a helpful coach to guide them through the challenges of setting the right example and helping others succeed. Of course *character, courage,* and *commitment* are the core of any leadership success, but it also takes the *clarity* mentioned above and then being able to *connect* based on individual differences (the focus of this book), connecting with the heart mentioned above, and then ongoing *collaboration* that ultimately leads to celebration or occasionally major *confrontation*. (For more on these italicized C words, refer to Appendix C.)

When you understand your natural **DNA Behavior** and deepen your confidence, expressing your expectations and holding people accountable becomes more natural, and for those you're leading—expected. Without confidence, leaders often struggle to assert their expectations, and they don't hold people accountable. Under those conditions, success happens almost by accident, when in fact, it can be so much more intentional, enabling teams to reach greater heights.

Undergirded by true self-confidence and humility, the practice of understanding and managing differences provides leaders with a clear pathway to achieve greater success. The knowledge and experience in this book will help you get there, but it's up to you to use it.

4. Recognize and Accept the Challenge of Living in Tension

One reason that life and especially leadership are so difficult is that many of the important choices and actions needed are not simple "Either/Or" choices. Quite often they are seemingly paradoxical—we have to do both—deciding on when to do which. Moreover, depending on our nature *(DNA Behavior)* and our nurture/upbringing, one of the choices is likely to be easier than the other—more comfortable, and more in line with our default behaviors. This goes straight to the issue of leadership balance and the paradox that leaders face in the neural seesaw. Like good parents, leaders need to be both caring and tough, and that is a crucial tension that leaders must deal with. Facing that up front can be helpful for working through the many other seemingly paradoxical situations, like this short list below, that leaders encounter.

The Paradox of Leadership Balance

Independent	*and*	a Team Player
Persistent	*and*	Knows When to Quit
Reality-Based	*and*	a Dreamer
Spontaneous	*and*	Planned
Serious	*and*	Fun
Results-focused	*and*	Relationship-focused
Leader	*and*	Servant
Strong	*and*	Vulnerable
In Control	*and*	Willing to Delegate
Competitive	*and*	Supporting
Visionary	*and*	Practical
Generalist	*and*	Specialist
Strategic	*and*	Tactical
Confident	*and*	Humble
Detached	*and*	Sensitive
Tough	*and*	Compassionate
Decisive	*and*	Gets Counsel
Opinionated	*and*	a Good Listener
Bold	*and*	Cautious
Quick	*and*	Patient

"Treating a paradox like a problem to be solved—and picking any one side of the paradox—only creates complication and frustration and other negative consequences."
—**Kevin Kruse**[9]

As you can see it can be quite intimidating to even think about the magnitude of these seemingly opposite requirements of good leadership. How could anyone get it right consistently? You probably can't if you are plagued by doubt. That's why genuine inner confidence is so critical—and why you need to continually grow in being comfortable in your own skin.

We think the best leaders are those who can live in paradox and seemingly "walk both sides of the street" at the same time. (Or as Laurie Beth Jones[10] calls it—a "Picture in Picture" mindset.) Operating successfully in the tension of these states that seem so opposite and paradoxical is not possible without a lot of situational and personal awareness that is grounded in a solid foundation of values, standards, and a clear leadership philosophy.

Leading in paradox usually demands more than knowledge; it requires wisdom. There will be times when you will need the wise counsel of someone who can see situations and people more objectively and help you exercise good judgment.

5. Grow in Courage

Whether it's gaining a leadership balance, growing in self-confidence and true security, holding yourself and others accountable, or living in the tension of seemingly opposite choices and behaviors, everything seems to circle back to courage.

The POW camps were a crucible that served as a testing ground for Lee to learn about himself and courage. He puts it this way. "The challenge was to reconcile my legitimate fears with my values, responsibilities, and commitments. Our captors offered us two choices—cooperate and make antiwar propaganda or suffer punishment and torture. It was there that I learned what we now have on our coaching card that we use in speaking and training: Lean into the pain of your doubts and fears to do what you know is right, even when it doesn't feel safe or natural. In the end, we learned that our suffering was a blessing. It prepared us for the hard decisions of life and leadership."

This truth has been recognized throughout history by great leaders and scholars of leadership. Author and leadership coach Gus Lee put it this way:

"Courage is the backbone of leadership. It remains the key force and the pivot point around which our other strengths are leveraged, high core values are preserved, and personal and institutional integrity are maintained."[11]

With those wonderful words of wisdom in mind, it's now time to introduce the science and framework of ***DNA Behavior***.

Quick Coach Notes

Key Point

Your view of yourself is foundational to your success as a leader. When you are comfortable with yourself, grounded in solid principles, and operating with a positive mindset about others, your backbone of courage will be strong; you will be able to handle the many paradoxes of leadership.

Questions

1. Recall a leader you've had who was naturally tilted toward results and one who was naturally tilted toward relationships. In reflection, can you see how they adapted (or could have) to gain a better balance?
2. Who spoke words of encouragement into your life giving you hope and a vision of who you are and who you could be? Who affirmed your dreams? Are you connecting with others in this way? How could you be more intentional about doing that?
3. Do others see you hold yourself accountable and live in vulnerability when you fall short? Do you clarify and connect in order to collaborate and help others succeed?
4. Can you think of an example of how courage took you through your doubts and fears to achieve success? What can you learn from that experience?

ENDNOTES

1   To clarify your Character values, be sure to check out the Honor Code at Appendix B.

2   Using brains scans (F-MRI) Neuroscientist observe brain activity that supports what we call the leadership tilt. They call it the "neural seesaw." It's the switching back and forth of two brain networks: the Task Positive Network (tasks, analysis, problem solving, results) and the Social Brain Network (relationships, connections, openness to new ideas and moral reasoning). Note: this Social Brain Network appears to be part of or an overlapping with the Default Mode Network.

3   https://weatherhead.case.edu/media/videos/list/ldd-boyatzis/play/boyatzis-brain-science-leadership

4   Based on research by James Zenger 2009 as related in HBR: Should Leaders Focus on Results, or on People? https://hbr.org/search?term=matthew%20lieberman, Matthew Lieberman, December 27, 2013.

5   You can read Greg Hiebert's story in his recent book, *You Can't Give What you Don't Have.*

6   In addition to this award-winning book, see *Engage with Honor: Building a Culture of Courageous Accountability.* Go to www.EngageWithHonor.com.

7   Highlighted as a "Key Learning Point" in their new book, *Helping People Change: Coaching with Compassion for Lifelong Learning and Growth* by Richard Boyatzis, Melvin L Smith, Ellen Van Oosten, August 2019, Harvard Business Review Press.

8   This model provides the framework for Lee's book *Engage With Honor: Building a Culture of Courageous Accountability.* See Appendix C for a graphic of the Courageous Accountability Model.

9   https://www.forbes.com/sites/kevinkruse/2013/09/09/how-leaders-use-the-paradox-secret-to-solve-tough-problems/#204cc26d3eb3

10 Laurie Beth Jones is the internationally known best-selling author of multiple books on spirituality and leadership, including *Jesus, CEO, The Path*, and *The Four Elements of Success.* She has consulted with leading health organizations as well as cutting-edge non-profits, and has been named one of the Top 30 Master Leaders in the United States by George Barna of the Barna Research Group.

11 *Courage: The Backbone of Leadership* by Gus Lee published by Jossey Bass, page 159.

SECTION 2

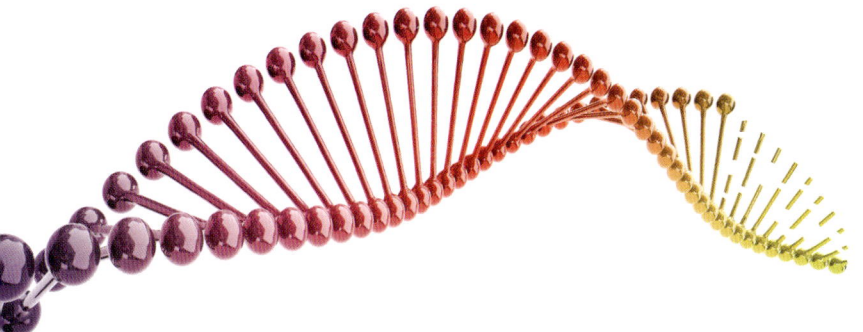

DNA BEHAVIOR FACTORS AND TRAITS

CHAPTER 5 ▶ MEASURING TALENTS

The heart of science is measurement.
—Erik Brynjolfsson[1]

Understanding DNA Behavior Scoring: A Quick Review

At this point, you can see how most of our talents and *strengths* are tied to our natural behaviors, which we call **DNA Behaviors**. The evidence is clear that our natural behaviors are part of our natural wiring with some possible further shaping in infancy. By age three, the die is cast, and like an ancient river, rerouting the direction of its flow is not easy.

Also, by now, you should have a good picture of why an understanding of talents is so important for leadership development, team building, hiring, managing for success and career planning. It's a powerful concept for both the individual and the employer, and regardless of where we are in our careers, this knowledge paves the way for better relationships and increased trust.

Matching talents to tasks not only increase performance and productivity, but it also reduces stress, improves health, and increases job satisfaction, which is directly related to employee engagement. Moreover, as you will see in the chapters ahead, understanding different talents is essential for effective communications and the collaboration needed in today's workplace. Ultimately, it's foundational for building a strong people culture.

Though we want to focus our work on our *strengths* as much as possible, it's critical to realize that our *struggles* emerge as some of the key behaviors that undermine leadership and relationships. Put another way, we limit our performance and we get in our own way if there is no adapting our *struggles* at the right time. That's why we can't ignore them: they surface anyway, so we may as well address them honestly, courageously and with compassion for ourselves. And here's another important reason to address our *struggles*: when leaders are vulnerable like this and others see them working on their area of *struggle*, they're seen as more genuine, humble, trustworthy and approachable. This confers credibility and promotes a desire to trust and follow.

Finally—A Rational Tool to Manage the Soft and Fluffy

No doubt, about 40% of you reading this book (and you're very likely to be among those who are naturally results-oriented) are starting to feel a bit queasy—after all, this material seems kind of soft and fluffy, and that's not your natural inclination. But you can relax. Our approach is about logic and facts—given that both of us are wired this way in our *DNA Behavior* style—and our next step is to explore the *rational* and *technical* aspects of measuring talents.

The underlying science that supports our work is important for several reasons, not the least of which is that many people still think of this subject as being 'soft' and subjective. Granted, human nature can be "soft" and subjective but it's also very rational and technical.

As you will soon see, with *DNA Behavior*, we are approaching it in a very rational, objective, and measurable way. This is why Hugh often describes himself as a "reformed CPA" saying, "I've come to learn how important measured behavioral insights are for trusting what we see, and ultimately achieving enhanced results."

Strict Rationality Kills Culture and Relationships

Most business leaders manage people and solve problems by numbers but do not appreciate that the source of the solution, in most cases, is human behavior. Ultimately, this is why both of us are heavily invested in the principle that valuing people and fostering enhanced relationships achieves better results. Or, viewed from the other side, *strict rationality (ignoring human qualities like individual differences and emotions) kills culture and damages relationships.* Nevertheless, having a scientifically verified model to diagnose the issues and blockages people are causing means the solution is more pinpointed, and those involved will buy in more quickly to what needs to be changed.

A study of talents can be very much like math or science: mathematical, statistical, realistic, predictable and quite objective. It's this scientific approach that makes knowledge of *DNA Behavior* so useful for individuals, teams, and organizations because it can be assessed, measured, and understood. It's also why often, those who dread one of our workshops leave as champions of this work and our way of understanding ourselves and one another, advocating for further use.

Once people see themselves objectively (celebrating their *strengths* and owning their *struggles*), it's much easier for them to see the people issues—in particular, miscommunication and misunderstanding of others' viewpoints. At this point they can operate with confidence, knowing they are equipped to both celebrate and manage differences. Remember the Rollaboard—a simple solution and improvement from which we all benefit, every day.

Stretching to Adapt—Imagine a Physics Problem

When the situation requires a person to adapt to a different behavior in order to be effective, we call that a "stretch." Consider this example of stretching to adapt:

As shown in the following graphic, a person whose score or default behavior is clearly on the right on Factor 1 is going to exhibit behaviors associated with the Take Charge Trait.

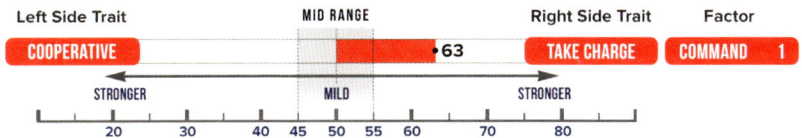

Their *strength* is to set the agenda and be in control. But what happens when they are restricted to very little authority and must follow someone else's agenda? (For example, what happens when they are working on a cross-functional team or go to their in-laws' home or some other setting where they are not in charge?) They have to adapt. We can do that, but it's not easy and requires extra energy. This intentional focus typically feels unnatural—maybe even stressful (remember Tom in Chapter 3). Also, like a rubber band that is stretched, when the pressure of the situation is removed (back in their office or home) they snap back to operate at their default natural behaviors, which require much less energy.

Lee once did a workshop for 110 managers and leaders from

a division of a Fortune 500 engineering company. He had no idea how the introverted, no-nonsense, and highly rational senior executive was receiving the information until he completed the session. At that point, the executive approached the microphone, unemotionally thanked Lee and then said to the group, "I think we can see this is really good stuff that will help us in many ways. I'd like for you all to take your teams through this training." Clearly, it was the logical and practical application of this information that impressed this highly results-oriented executive. He saw the value and wanted to exploit it further.

Similarly, one of the trainers on Hugh's team recently had the same experience with the skeptical leader of a highly fractured finance team at a prominent university. He had an "Aha" moment when team members objectively reviewed a written and graphical presentation of their scores. It was obvious to all that their natural behavioral differences were causing challenges and friction.

This new awareness opened the door for increased vulnerability that led to increased trust and a genuine, productive discussion. People began to see how they were each causing the issues and conflicts and, at the same time, began to take ownership of the solutions. A major breakthrough occurred, which has now transformed how this team operates. Once everyone took down their walls and started talking during and after the session, they began stretching and adapting—success came quickly.

Since this concept of stretching takes more energy, you can imagine what happens to a person who is challenged to consistently operate in a work situation that is not reasonably matched to their talents. Low productivity, stress, burnout, and absenteeism are likely. And some will just quit and move on to find a better work situation. Maybe you've already done that. Trial and error can always be an option as we refine our careers, but it's usually not the best starting point.

But even though a talent mismatch is very problematic, it's not as large a problem as the collateral damage caused by a culture dominated by those who rely solely on a rational, task-focused approach. Research indicates that most people who leave a company do so because they don't feel valued or cared about, so it's a relational/social issue. Addressing that issue is one of the major goals of this book.

Data and Research Are Revealing

As mentioned earlier, it was seeing the practical application of these human behavior Traits that attracted us to this field. Logical insights with such obvious use pulled us right in. But we wanted to take it to the next level and present these concepts more scientifically as clearly being natural *DNA Behaviors* that dictate so much of how we behave and interact.

Working with the academic experts on our team, the previously unquantifiable became measurable science through the statistical validation of the constructs we saw operating across the human domain. Essentially, through research and experience, we were able to confirm that the concepts of *DNA Behavior* are really the underlying science of human behavior so essential to personal and leadership development and good relationships.

Regardless of your bent, we think it would be helpful for your understanding to see the basics of how *DNA Behavior* measurement works. These measurement concepts will be used to unpack the explanations of the *DNA Behavior* Factors and Traits—insights that can make a powerful difference in your life, professionally, and personally.

As we laid out earlier, talents are the key to organizational success and keeping people fulfilled at work. Correspondingly, relationships are also essential for team performance—the kind of collaboration needed for higher quality, greater efficiency and better performance, which all lead to better execution, regardless of what business or industry they're applied to. Among the outcomes we see regularly is an increase in positive energy in the workplace, greater employee and customer engagement and better personal relationships, all of which move us toward one of our highest goals: improving our sense of meaning and purpose.

Everyone Has a Place on the Normal Curve

We'll be using our *DNA Behavior* assessment scoring scales as the basis for these explanations of natural talent measurement.

This assessment is used throughout the world and we believe it's the best available. We've included more information about it and how you can obtain the *Leadership Behavior DNA* Assessment on page 318. For the very best experience with this book, we recommend you pause and take it now. It's where the abstract becomes visible and practical, you could see it best in your own assessment of your **DNA Behavior.**

Let's take a closer look at the constructs that we'll be using. The array of commonly occurring behavioral talents can be plotted on graphs in the same ways as physical characteristics are. To illustrate how graphical information can be helpful, let's use size as an example and analyze how it might affect a person's career choice. The graph below represents weight increments on the horizontal axis and numbers of people on the vertical axis. To keep it simple, we've narrowed our focus to males and used sports occupations with weights typical for the average participant. This example is for illustration only and is not based on actual data, but you can see that it's close enough.

If we plotted the weights of all males globally, we would see a normal distribution curve that resembles the spread below. Most men weigh between 100 and 350 pounds.

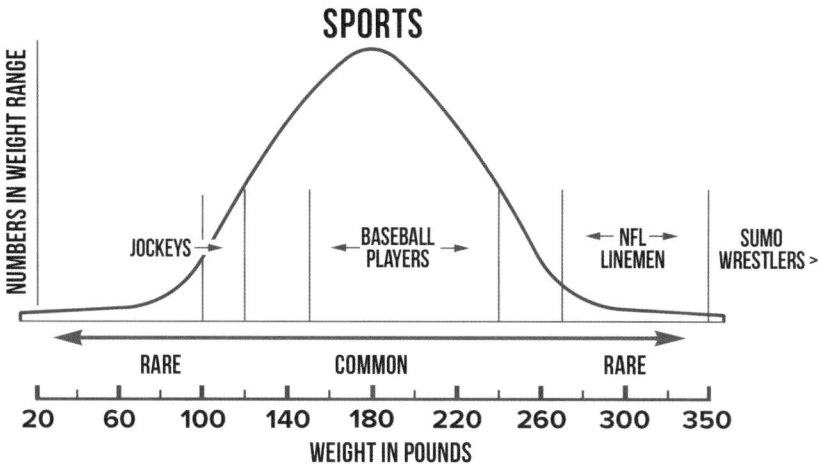

The normal distribution curve was originally derived to illustrate the occurrence of differences in nature. In World War II, this curve was used to predict how many uniforms and pairs of shoes the military would need to order in each size. Mathematicians learned that whether it's weight, height, shoe sizes, or SAT scores, they all occur on a predictable frequency distribution like the one above—very few at the extremes and an increasing number as you approach the mean/mid-point from either direction.

You can see that the weights of baseball players cover a range that is more typical of the general population. Size is not such a critical factor in that sport. However, there are important career fields at the extremes of both ends of the spectrum where size is very critical. Jockeys, who usually weigh less than 120 pounds, fall on the far left of the continuum (outliers is the current term). The good ones seem to enjoy their work and make a lot of money. On the extreme right side, we find NFL linemen, weighing on average about 350 pounds, and sumo wrestlers weighing as much as 400 pounds. You can see that they are also outliers—not many in their range either. Now, these big folks also enjoy their work and make a lot of money. So, in sports, we could say that size is a kind of talent, and there is a place for those who are light, medium, and heavy. We see that these very different talents are really neither good nor bad, but there is an advantage for certain sizes/talents in certain sports.

We chose a size to illustrate the talents from the extremes of the continuum to make it much easier to see that there can be a bad match—or a bad fit—between the person and the job. Assume for a moment that you are a sports recruiter and someone who weighs 300 pounds walks into your office and says, "Where can you use my talents?" You would not consider recommending that he or she pursue a career as a horse jockey.

Likewise, if a college student who weighs 115 pounds comes in and wants to play in the NFL or be a sumo wrestler, you would try not to laugh as you steer him or her in a better direction. These extreme and physically obvious examples illustrate the important principle for hiring and career planning that we discussed in Chapter 2—about matching the person to the role.

Unfortunately, most of our talents are not as obvious as size and we can't necessarily identify them by someone's educational degree, work experience, or interests. For instance, not all trained accountants are naturally detail-oriented and precise. Some accountants are better as generalists and excel at communicating the big picture or selling services. As in every field of work, there are a wide variety of roles in the accountancy profession, and we can't always know what's beneath the tip of the iceberg until we have experience with a person's talents/*strengths*, and *struggles*.

What's needed is a way to objectively measure talents and array them on a continuum like the normal distribution curve above. This behavioral information can be used to assist in matching people to positions so they won't struggle to swim upstream in the key elements of their work. In addition, having insight into a person's behavioral characteristics can be especially helpful for mentoring new hires and accelerating their productivity; likewise, it's a great tool for coaching individual development and managing people differently.

> *After all, when you hire you are hiring not just strengths— the struggles come with them at no extra charge—and those struggles are guaranteed to show up at work.*

This Science Is Not Soft

Moving ahead, we'll use a normal distribution curve like the one below to illustrate the distribution of individual scores on each of our eight Factors of behavior. These Factors of **DNA Behavior** were statistically developed (confirmatory and exploratory Factor analysis) and validated (strong convergent validity) and proved reliable (test-retest) using established psychometric practices (see Appendix E). Our research and development met or exceeded rigorous academic standards, and over 1.5 millions individuals worldwide benefit from **DNA Behavior** insights on an annual basis.

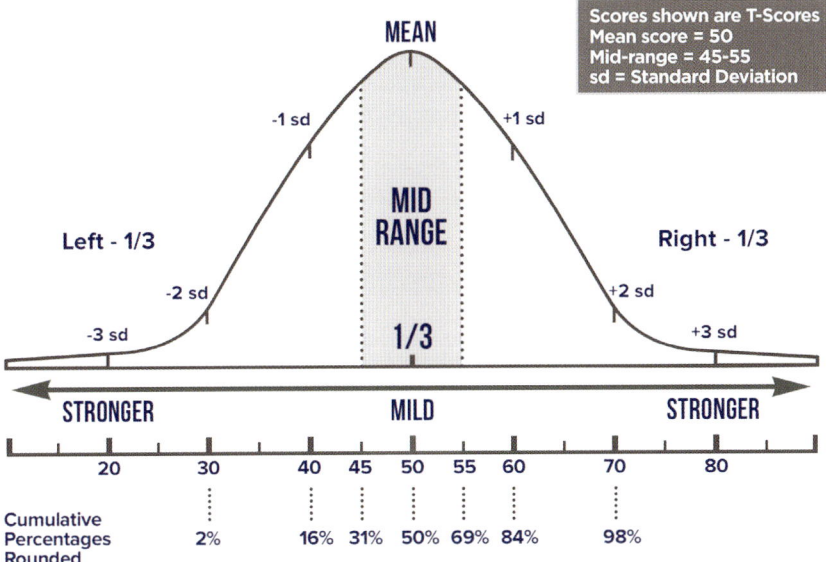

NOTE: *As shown above, approximately one-third of the population falls on the left side, one-third on the right side and one-third in the mid-range section of the distribution curve/continuum.*

The online **DNA Behavior** assessment produces a report with eight Factors of behavior that explain talents/**strengths** and the **struggles** that go with them. So, each Factor is portrayed by its own normal curve/continuum. Here's an example of Command Factor 1 its relationship to the normal distribution curve above:

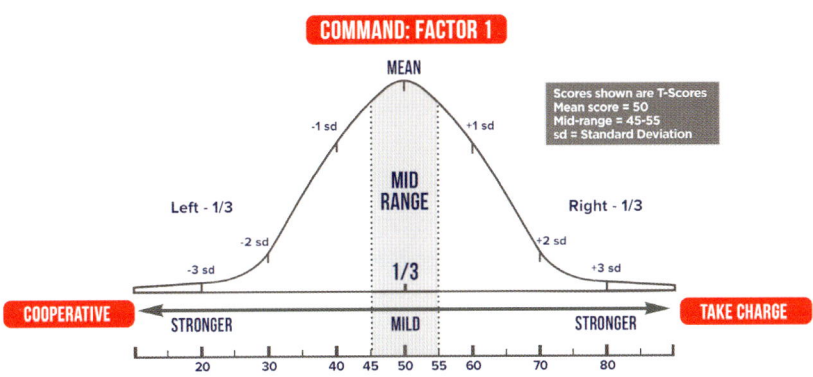

Graphically, we show each Factor on a horizontal continuum to identify the Trait (talent) associated with the left and right-hand sides (opposite behaviors as you will see later). For the sake of space and convenience, these curves are typically shown on a flat continuum like the one here:

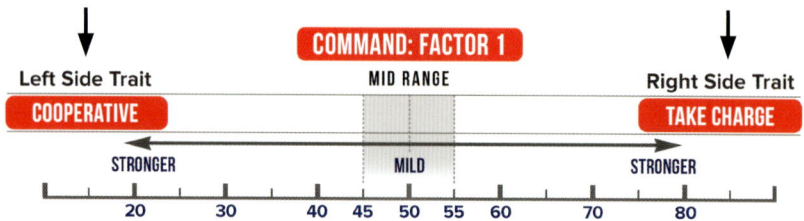

The good thing about having standardized scores laid out on mathematically defined ranges is that they allow us to see how people are different in a graphic and measurable way. If you apply the normal distribution curve insights to the Factor 1 continuum above, you can see that *no matter in which region (left, right, or mid-range) a person scores on the graph (Trait measurement), two-thirds of the world is going to be different.* For those who fall clearly on either the right side or the left side, one-third will be somewhat different (those in the mid-range) and one-third will have **strengths** and **struggles** that are their mirror opposite. This scientific, rational reality should make us pause and reflect on the implications for managing talents and connecting successfully with others. Keep in mind, this science of human nature applies worldwide, regardless of culture.

> *Whether a person's score is on the left, right, or mid-range, two-thirds of the world is going to operate differently from them in that Trait.*

Additionally, because these scores are Standard scores called T-scores, every ten points is a **Standard Deviation (SD)**[1]—simply meaning that when there is a ten-point spread in a Factor, statistically there is a measurable and likely observable difference in behavior. We (Lee and Hugh) and some of our teammates (and spouses) are as much as 20 points apart, and in a few instances, are separated by 30 points, which is three SD. That's not just different; that's more like extreme opposites. These insights have been crucial for our working together and of course, these opposites have given us great opportunities to work on applying the Platinum Rule.

You can also see that the left side of a Factor represents a Trait with **strengths** and **struggles** in equal importance to the right-side Trait, meaning that left- and right-side Traits are of equal standing. While the scores on the left side will be a lower number than those on the right side, low and high in and of itself has no significance. What does matter is the distance left or right from 50, which is the midpoint and mean score of each Factor. You'll see why this is of increasing importance as we explain each Factor in detail.

> *Though the scores on the left side will be a lower number than those on the right side, low and high, in and of itself, has no significance. It is the absolute distance from the mean of 50 that determines the strength of a Trait. To easily understand absolute, think of it as simply a negative or positive attribute to a number, meaning that -10 is the same strength as +10; they are the same distance from the mean.*

Understanding Factors and Traits

The following graphic (without any scores on it) shows the eight Factors validated in our research. If you study it, you'll see that each Factor is arrayed across a continuum (remember, each is actually a normal distribution curve) with left, right, and mid-range scoring regions. For each Factor, the left side (20-44) and right side (56-80) of the continuum depict opposite Traits.

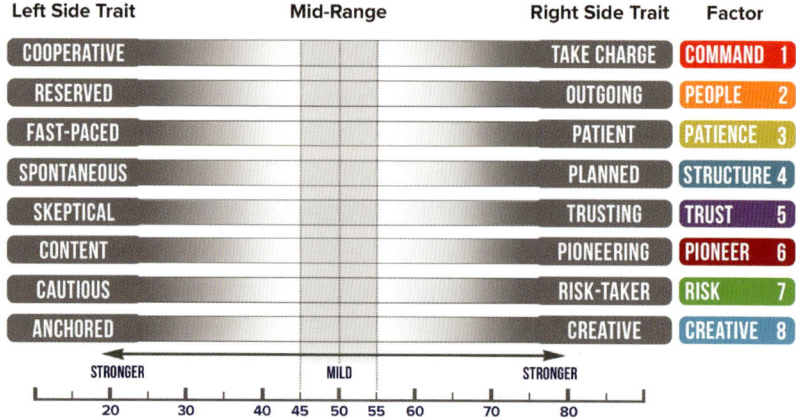

Strongest Trait

A person's *overall* strongest Trait is the one whose score is farthest right or left from the midpoint of 50 (regardless of which Factor it is). Another way of saying this is that it's the score among all the eight Factors that is the greatest absolute distance from 50. As you might expect, the "strongest Trait" will have the greatest impact on a person's behavior.

The graph below shows a person's actual **DNA Behavior** results on the eight Factors. You can see that the Factor 3 score of 26 is the strongest Trait (farthest from 50) and will have the most obvious impact on this person's behavior. (Notice it also has the longest bar on the graph, also indicating Trait strength). The strongest is also the behavior we quickly revert to under stress.

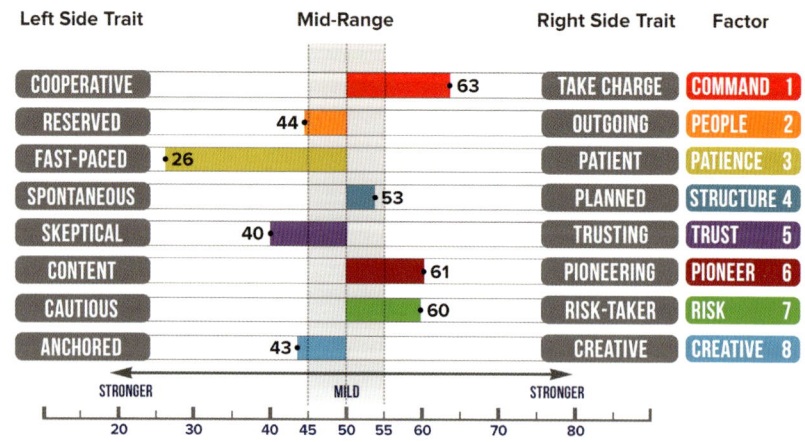

Trait Intensity

Trait intensity shown below is another important characteristic related to this type of graph. Note in the Factor 3 graphic below that as the scores move outward left or right from the midpoint of the graph (50) the behavioral Traits grow stronger. So, someone who is on the Patient side with a score of 60 may be patient and understanding, while someone with a score of 75 may be so lenient that they fail to confront when needed.

Likewise, in the opposite direction, someone on the Fast-Paced side with a score of 44 may be somewhat impatient, but the person with a score of 34 may be so fast-paced and change-oriented that others are burned out trying to keep up.

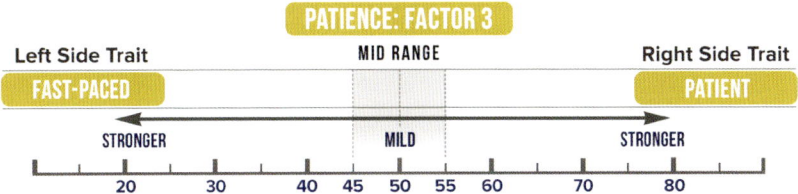

Here's one more point to remember: a person's Trait score represents their default or "home base" behavior on each of these eight Factor continua. One senior leader called it the "happy place." We sometimes refer to it as our "hangout" or "roosting place" because it's the behavior we want to go back to after we stretch or adapt; it's where things feel the most natural and comfortable.

Congratulations! Now you have the big picture showing the important role of statistical science in measuring **DNA Behavior**. And for our discussions ahead, we hope you see how the continuum graphs like the one above with its three ranges (left, right, and mid-range) can help us understand individual differences in a practical, meaningful, and very objective way.

As we walk through the eight Factors and sixteen Traits in the following chapters, we've included lists of **Strengths, Struggles,** and ways to Connect (for the Platinum Rule). Additionally, there are reflection questions intended to help you pause and think of situations where you may be required to adapt. Then, when it happens, you can become more intentional in managing your behaviors.

Mission/Results-Oriented and People/Relationship-Oriented Traits

As we have mentioned several times, 40% of the population are born with natural talents for mission/results and 40% naturally talented for people/relationships. This bent or design comes from **DNA Behaviors** and is the accumulation of our Traits. The graphic below shows you which of our Traits contribute to each. You can see that the Traits shown in Green or Results-oriented and those shown in Blue are Relationship-oriented. The weight of each going toward the overall Results/Relationship score will vary depending on the location/strength of the Trait score.

All those in green are clearly results-oriented. Though Cooperative and Spontaneous are shown in blue, their contribution toward some Relationship characteristics are not nearly so strong as Outgoing, Patient, and Trusting.

Traits from Factors 6, 7, and 8 that are not shown, as they do not carry weight toward Results and Relationships.

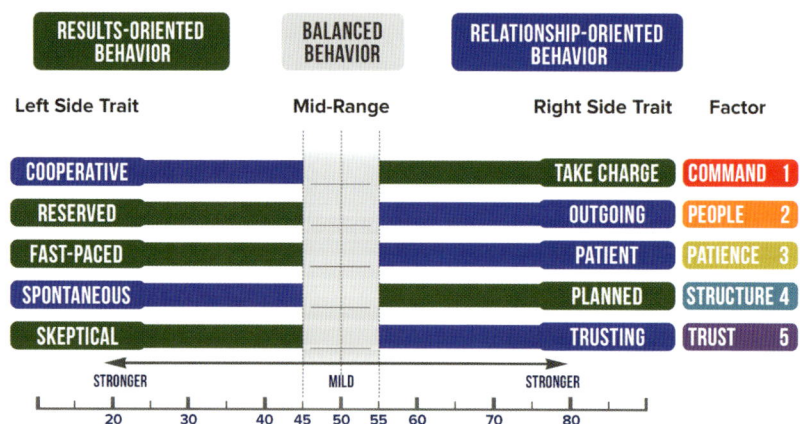

As we explore the Factors in the chapters ahead, you'll see in detail how these Traits contribute to a person's overall leadership balance as described in Chapter 4 where we shared the **Leadership Attributes Model** and the **Leadership Balance and Tilt** graphics.

DNA Behavior Style Groups

As you might suspect, some of these various Traits show up together, and combined enable a grouping that can be helpful for gaining a quick snapshot of a person's typical behaviors. We call these groupings **Style Groups** or **Styles** and they serve two important purposes. For the individual, **Style Groups** give an overall high-level summary of their natural DNA Behaviors. For the team the **Styles** give a quick way of understanding others, identifying who is similar and who is different without having to recall or explain specific scores.

From a review of the ten **Style Groups** shown below, you can see that the names give a quick picture of what to expect from someone in that particular **Style**.

Results-oriented	Both	Relationship-oriented
Strategist	Influencer	Engager
Initiator	Stylish Thinker	Community Builder
Reflective Thinker	Facilitator	Relationship Builder
	Adapter	

You can read more about each of these **Style Groups** in Appendix D.

Keep in mind that these **Style Groups** are derived primarily by using the Trait scores from Factors 1-4 to define the parameters for the ten **Style Groups**. (The mathematical possibilities compound significantly with each added Trait.) Using these first four Factors seems to work well. But keep in mind that there must be defined limits for the cluster of scores for each **Style Group** so it's possible that a person's Trait scores can be on the edge of two or even three of these **Styles**. Others might be sitting in the sweet spot (hence a better fit) for each of these Factors and strongly exhibit every characteristic of a particular **Style Group**.

Hugh is an *Initiator* but only a couple of points from being a Strategist, so he has many of the overlapping characteristics of these two Results-oriented **Styles**. Lee sits in the sweet spot of the envelope/parameters of the *Influencer*, so the description for that one matches him very closely.

At the end of each of the Trait chapters (for the first four Factors only) ahead, you'll see a listing of *Style Groups* in which that Trait plays a key role. The *Leadership Behavior DNA Report* mentioned on page 318 also uses Style Groups to help you interpret and apply your unique scores.

Learned Behaviors

Until now we have been talking about *natural **DNA behaviors***, but learned behaviors are critical for success as well. We can't always operate in our area of **strengths** and everyone must stretch and adapt to be effective in various situations. Learned behaviors surface most often in areas where we repeatedly are challenged to stretch. **Also, adapting to learned behaviors is generally the only way we can grow as leaders.**

Learning to listen better, to be more patient, to delegate and trust others are some of the very important learned behaviors that we both are still working on. Since our natural **struggles** in these areas are so strong, this learning will be a lifelong process. But just because it's not easy does not give us a pass. We have to stay in the battle to grow toward being the leaders and people we want to be.

Leaving Your Biases Behind

If you are like most people, you tend to have a bias toward your own behavioral style. For example, if you are easygoing and accommodating, then you probably value those talents more than those of someone who tends to be opinionated and aggressive. Likewise, if you are more dominant or assertive, you may tend to value those behaviors and be judgmental of those who are more compliant and passive.

Regardless of your tendency, we're going to ask you to set aside your biases and judgments to gain a more objective view of yourself and others. It won't be easy, but the rewards are huge. Ideally, you will come to understand those who are different from you and see their Traits as just as valuable as yours. After all, those who are different are your teammates. Their talents contribute to your work and life success. And more than likely some of those "different people" who can irritate you the most are living under your same roof!

Quick Coach Notes

Key Point

Talents—our natural behaviors—are measurable, so behavioral assessments can be used to identify individual *strengths* and *struggles* with a high degree of accuracy.

Questions

Before going forward, review the graphs again and make sure you grasp the technical details covered in this chapter.

1. Do you grasp that there are eight Factors of Behavior?
2. Do you understand that each Factor is a continuum with a named Trait on each side (left and right for a total of sixteen Traits) and that these two opposite sides/Traits represent opposite behaviors?
3. Does it make sense that these behaviors predict natural talents and that different people will have different talents?
4. Can you see how these talents are natural behaviors, but we do need learned behaviors to adapt and counteract our struggles, gain a balance, and be more effective in various situations and with diverse people?
5. What is an example of a learned behavior that you are using now to improve your leadership?

This understanding will help you understand the information on the Factors and Traits in the chapters ahead.

Get Your Assessment

To enhance your experience throughout this book, take the *Leadership Behavior DNA* assessment and receive your personal report in only 10 minutes. This 19-page report pinpoints your Trait Strengths and Struggles, unique Communication Style, and Results vs Relationship Balance.

Learn More at www.LeadershipBehaviorDNA.com/Book

ENDNOTE

1   There are several other standardized scoring schemes. For example, the old Scholastic Aptitude Test (SAT) used 100 points for one SD instead of the 10 points used here in T Scores. So, the old SAT scores ranged from 200 to 800 and a score of 500 would be the mean and mid-point, and 800 is the max on either Verbal or Math. On the newer SAT where the max score is 1600, you would double each of these scores, so one SD becomes 200 points and the mean would become 800.

THE COMMAND FACTOR

This Factor indicates a person's desire to control the agenda, willingness to assert, and need to make decisions.

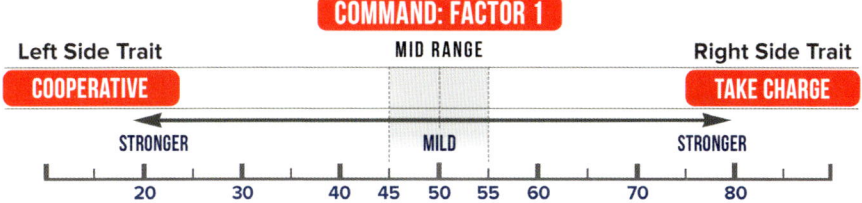

Cooperative Leader Qualities

[Process-oriented]

- Desire to fit in
- Here and now thinking
- Follow agenda
- Flexible in approach
- Cooperation

Take Charge Leader Qualities

[Results-oriented]

- Desire for control
- Visionary thinking
- Set agenda
- Definite in approach
- Confrontation

— The Command Factor —

Is it in your nature to take control and set the agenda at work? Or, is it more your natural style to collaborate and follow an established agenda? The Command Factor illustrates your natural DNA inclination on a continuum where "Cooperative" and "Take Charge" are opposites. If you fall on the right and naturally take charge, your natural drive is to take control of the agenda and direct others toward achieving your goals. If you fall on the left side of the scale above and are primarily cooperative, you are naturally motivated to fit in with someone else's established agenda.

What about the Mid-Range?

If your Command score falls in the mid-range, congratulations! That means you have natural flexibility that allows you to operate more easily with either left- or right-side behaviors, depending on the situation. This does not mean that you will be wishy-washy but that you can more easily adapt to left- and right-side behaviors depending on the occasion. For example, in leading your team or work group, you are comfortable being "in charge," but when operating with your manager and peers, you can be comfortable playing more of a support role. So, if you are in the mid-range on the Command Factor, you probably relate to some of the *strengths* and *struggles* from both sides. However, typically neither your *strengths* nor your *struggles* will be as strong as those on the left or right side.

One-third of the population will score on the left side, one-third on the right side and one-third will score in the mid-range.[1] *There are no bad ranges or scores. All have strengths and struggles.*

Chapter Format

As with the other seven behavior Factors in the following chapters, we'll take an in-depth look at both sides of the continuum, beginning with the right side first.

CHAPTER 6 ▶ The Take Charge Trait

FACTOR 1: RIGHT-SIDE TRAIT

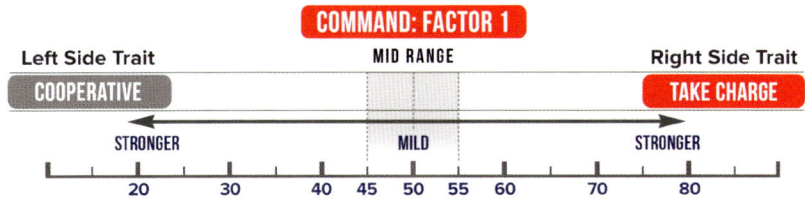

*Inaction breeds doubt and fear. Action breeds confidence
and courage...Go out and get busy.*

—Dale Carnegie

As you would expect, Take Charge personalities naturally are driven to control their environment. They naturally assume authority, and they are comfortable giving direction to others. They especially like to get results—the quicker the better. They are self-assured, often expressing their strongly held opinions in a very confident and direct manner.

Here is a list of the **strengths** and **struggles** associated with the Take Charge Trait (scores that plot on the right-hand side of the scale above). Note how **strengths** can become **struggles** when pushed to the extreme. Understanding these insights will not only help you connect with yourself but assist you in connecting with others who are different from you.

Take Charge – Strengths and Struggles

 **Strengths in Leadership**

1. Results-oriented
2. Initiating, want to set the agenda
3. Decisive, speak directly
4. Act with assurance and confidence
5. See the strategic/future potential

 **Struggles in Leadership**

1. Opinionated and may ignore outside input
2. Can assume control without realizing it
3. May not listen well to others
4. Uncomfortable taking direction from others
5. May underestimate work needed to achieve goals

Take Charge Trait examples [2]

For a better picture of this Trait, consider the following well-known people who exhibit behaviors representative of this group. Examples include media personalities Dolly Parton, Simon Cowell, Oprah Winfrey, and psychologist Dr. Phil McGraw. In the military, of course, we've had generals like Patton, MacArthur, Schwarzkopf, and more recently Secretary of Defense (General) Mattis. Take Charge personalities in government would include Prime Minister Margaret Thatcher and Presidents Teddy Roosevelt, Harry Truman, Barack Obama, and Donald Trump. There are many prominent ones in sports as well and good examples are Michael Jordan, LeBron James, Coaches Bill Belichick, Nick Sabin, and the legendary Tennessee basketball coach, Pat Summit.

 ## Take Charge – Leadership Strengths

Results-oriented

These people are energized by making things happen and the sooner, the better! If they are in charge, they don't hesitate to make decisions and get things moving. They use their strong will and directing nature to push ideas and projects along toward a "quick victory." If they are not in charge, and progress is lagging, they create pressure for decisions and action. If continually frustrated by inaction, they may disengage or look for another opportunity where they can more easily create results.

Confident, bold, and in control

Take Charge personalities are rarely short on confidence. They typically assume that they see the best solution and that they will prevail in any undertaking. If you look back at the list of examples above, you can see these *strengths* quite easily. Whether you like them or not, you can see that they attract followers because they come across as knowing what they are doing, where they are going and how they are going to get there. They expect to win, and everyone wants to be on a winning team.

Visionary, multi-taskers, and confident in their strong opinions

They are outward focused to assess the environment for issues related to their power, control, and solutions, (but not necessarily for relationships) and seem to have an extraordinary strategic or visionary talent—to see over the horizon and connect the dots. They love to develop or build, and this strategic view allows them to envision what the finished product will look like. Their minds work quickly, so they prefer having multiple projects to keep them engaged.

Primarily generalists, they are ready with an opinion on any subject. If you ask them a question, you are going to get an answer that they feel strongly about, although they may not have talked about it before. No doubt, the expression "sometimes wrong, but never in doubt" describes this group quite well.

Leadership-oriented and power-sensitive

People with attributes from the Take Charge Trait have a keen sense of awareness in areas related to leadership, money, and power structures. They naturally feel most secure when they are leading because they trust themselves and tend to be somewhat distrusting of others. They also know how to use their power to protect their territory. They abhor a power vacuum and if there is one in their environment, they will naturally fill it with their own influence.

 ## Take Charge – Leadership Struggles

As pointed out in Chapter 3, *struggles* can comprise weak or missing *strengths* and *strengths* that are overused or pushed to the extreme. See how well these qualities describe the Take Charge people you know.

Egotistical, self-centered and insensitive to others

Sounds rather harsh, doesn't it? But read on and see how to understand and best connect with these people.

In team development sessions, we separate people into groups sharing the same Traits for the "Amazing Traits Exercise." The assignment is for each group to present their Trait as the most amazing for success in their role. This is a powerful experience for everyone because there is nothing so insightful as experiencing these different *DNA Behavior* Traits in the flesh.

The "amazing" ego of the Take Charge group is sometimes attention-getting due to their cocky attitude. In what was couched in humor, one Take Charge group actually said: "We are the best and most amazing because we are the ones who tell you little people what to do." Most people laughed in disbelief, and some even tossed something at them. But we all knew that this is not far from the way many Take Chargers see the world. It's also typical for them to claim the *strengths* of other Traits that they really don't have. That's not unexpected because their strong ego tells them that they are good at everything.

This exercise also brings self-awareness that this group (and all groups) desperately needs because it requires them to share some of the common *struggles* of their group. They typically admit to being self-centered, controlling, impatient, and opinionated. However, without even noticing it, Take Charge people will sometimes deflect their issues to make them the problem of others. Like a giant magnet, they often pull from others to meet their own needs. It's hard to admit, but we personally understand these **struggles** all too well.

Those who have real courage begin to gain self-awareness and grow in humility. They accept that too much ego is a serious **struggle** and address the problem by shifting their focus from self to others. They learn to observe the body language of others to see whether their spirits are being lifted or burdened during their interactions. They also enlist confidants who will give them honest feedback on how they are affecting others and learn to show empathy that may not feel natural.

Unwilling to be wrong – Look out for the "Progression in D Major"

One of this group's best talents is their ability to operate decisively and with confidence. They typically build a track record of successes, and these further stroke their ego, which in turn add to their already high confidence. But no one can be right all the time and when they are confronted with being out of step, Take Chargers often have great difficulty accepting it.

When these **struggles** are taken to the extreme, it can be ugly. Perhaps you have heard it said about a powerful leader, "There's a graveyard just outside his/her office for those who dared to confront them with the truth." Of course, if you continually shoot the messenger, pretty soon there will be a stack of dead messengers— and no more feedback. A good indicator of the dysfunctional dominating personality is that they keep their non-challenging people and run off their best.[3]

Observing this a few years ago, it occurred to us that what we were seeing, to borrow a musical term, was a "Progression in D Major." How far the progression goes depends on the level of dysfunction of the individual. You can probably think of bosses, famous politicians, high profile coaches, and religious leaders who went down this scale. Note the progression below.

Step 1. **Deny.** "That's not true. It never happened." "They're wrong."

Step 2. **Defend.** "They just don't understand the situation. It was the right thing to do."

Step 3. **Demonize.** "They are out to get me. They are disloyal, jealous, etc."

Step 4. **Destroy.** At this point the evidence is so strong the only tactic left is to try to eliminate the opposition.

A dominant and controlling person is most likely the one to be caught in this progression. For all his great achievements, this parallels the behaviors observed during the fall and firing of the great basketball Coach Bobby Knight at Indiana.

After watching many leaders over the last thirty years, we've observed that they may be outwardly confident while being inwardly insecure.

Regardless of the person or Trait, to the degree that we are insecure the more likely we are to exhibit unhealthy behaviors in our leadership. None of us are completely secure so we all are vulnerable to this principle.

The main defense for anyone, regardless of their DNA dictated behavior, to prevent this progression is humility based on a true comfort and acceptance of ourselves and concern for others.

Humility does not imply weakness; rather, it indicates true confidence and self-worth that is strong enough to openly admit, "I'm not perfect, I made a mistake," or "I know I can be wrong and I respect you enough to listen to what you have to say."

Poor listeners

A common **struggle** shared by this group is that, when it comes to listening, they are more "awful" than awesome or amazing. Of course, this revelation is no surprise to everyone else because they have been on the receiving end of this flaw many times. It's not easy, but when they are honest, Take Chargers admit that listening is a problem. It's not that they don't have good intentions; it's just that there are several overriding issues.

First, listening presents a tough challenge for this group because they must yield both control and direction of the conversation, as well as precious time. After all, why listen if you already know the solution and have charted the correct course?

In the "Amazing Traits" exercise, people tend to be honest and transparent. For example, one senior leader commented for the rest of her Take Charge group: "You don't understand how hard it is for us to listen. Our minds just can't slow down enough to stay with you." Another typical response is "Sometimes I have a hard time hearing what you are saying because my mind has jumped ahead to my response. Or: "If I disagree with you, I'm thinking about how I'm going to convince you that I'm right and you are wrong."

Take Chargers love a big challenge and becoming a good listener will challenge every ounce of their being. That's because it will require some degree of mastery over all the other **struggles** of this Trait.

Becoming a good listener requires humility, patience, setting aside strongly held opinions, and being sensitive to the thoughts, feelings, and perspectives of the other person. The task is difficult, but the payoff (Results) will bring dividends that are truly "amazing."

Learning to Listen

Several years ago, Hugh's team had trained a strong Take Charge leader of a fast-growing wealth management firm on the principles of understanding people before numbers. The idea being that if he could better understand and manage the unique talents of his team members' then productivity and workplace engagement would improve. In one post-training instance he reported back that he had a very energy-draining brainstorming session with his COO.

The COO was far more Cooperative in style and very Planned. What the Take Charge leader did not realize was the length of time that the COO needed to process the new concepts and strategies being thrown out for discussion. So, the leader felt like he was being contradicted and that the COO did not get it. Likewise, the COO felt he was being bombarded and unnecessarily put on the spot.

Both parties sensed there was something energetically wrong in the conversation, and the leader stepped up the next morning and asked his COO how he felt about the conversation. When both admitted they were drained, the leader made a commitment that he would never again just throw ideas out to the COO and expect an immediate response. Rather, the leader promised to provide digestion time. The great thing is that the leader recognized what he had done and adapted his behaviors and expectations to build a very sound, long-term working partnership with his COO.

Whom do you know with the Take Charge Trait?

1. _____

2. _____

3. _____

Quick Coach Notes

Ideal Work Environment

Take Charge personalities work best when they can build, direct, develop, create, lead, conceptualize, decide, control, and initiate solutions.

Connecting with the Take Charge Trait

1. Remember their need for control.
2. Give direct answers; get to the point.
3. Move quickly to the bottom line.
4. Offer options so they can decide.
5. Don't contradict them; let some time pass.

Managing the Take Charge Trait

1. Clarify roles, what they own and do not own.
2. Don't micromanage, give them authority.
3. Speak with confidence and authority.
4. Let them know you will use power if needed.

Take Charge people should keep in mind that success is a team effort and that it is important to hear what others have to say. Listen up and give more respect to others' opinions.

DNA Behavior Style Groups with the Take Charge Trait

Note: See Appendix D for more information on the ten Style Groups.

- Initiator
- Strategist
- Influencer
- Facilitator (sometimes)

ENDNOTES

1 Technically, the mid-range of the normal distribution (and thus our continuum) is slightly more than a third and the left and right are slightly less. For convenience of expression and to communicate the basic concept, we round up or down to a third for each range.

2 Well-known personalities mentioned throughout the book have not taken the *Leadership Behavior DNA Assessment*. But in our observations of their behavioral strengths and struggles, they do exhibit specific Factors and Traits identified in the DNA Behavior Discovery Process.

3 For more insights into the impact of these leaders on their companies, see *Good to Great*, by Jim Collins, (chapters 2 and 3).

CHAPTER 7 ▶ THE COOPERATIVE TRAIT

FACTOR 1: LEFT-SIDE TRAIT

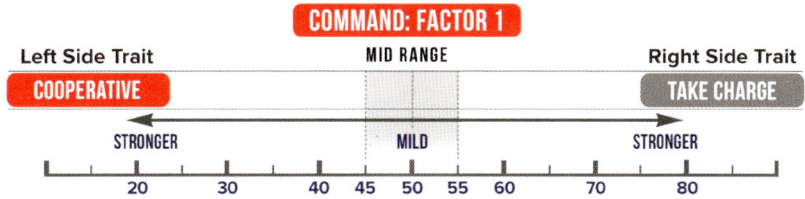

Cooperation is the thorough conviction that nobody can get there unless everybody gets there.

—Virginia Burden

Now we move to the other end of the Command spectrum and look at those who are much more willing to accommodate someone else's agenda.

As you will see from the list of typical ***strengths*** and ***struggles*** below, the Cooperative ***DNA behaviors*** are basically opposite from the right-side Take Charge Trait group. They are much less concerned about power and who is in control and more interested in fitting in with and supporting the established agenda.

Cooperative – Strengths and Struggles

 **Strengths in Leadership**

1. Follow the established agenda
2. Process-oriented
3. Speak diplomatically, promote stability
4. Like to focus on one thing at a time
5. See the practical in the present

 **Struggles in Leadership**

1. Can be unassertive or timid
2. May be hesitant to speak out
3. Can underestimate own abilities
4. May first consent but later disagree
5. May not see the strategic/future potential

Cooperative Trait examples

Prominent examples of this group might include well-known personalities: Halle Berry, Christopher Walken, Kanye West, Rosa Parks, Mr. Rogers; government leaders Presidents Abraham Lincoln, Gerald Ford, George H. W. Bush (41), and Chancellor Angela Merkel; business leaders Warren Buffett and Indra Nooyi; military leaders, General Omar Bradley; Baseball Hall of Fame catcher and manager Joe Torre, and baseball great Derek Jeter; coaches Dean Smith, and Tom Landry.

 ## Cooperative – Leadership Strengths

Process-oriented and likes to focus on the practical, here and now

One of the key *strengths* of this group is their ability to see practical steps that need to be executed. A good way to look at this talent is to compare it with their right-side teammates. The results-oriented and visionary Take Charge person may be touting that "We can double our revenues in three years." The Cooperative person looking at the exact same circumstances might say, "That sounds great, but how are we going to make payroll at the end of this month?" Their realistic and practical insights are critical to success for any team.

Team players who follow the set agenda

Rather than come out the gate trying to project power, this group would much rather cooperate and collaborate. They are typically very loyal to their teammates and leaders and enjoy helping them be successful.

Since they are Cooperative, they can accept and operate from an already established agenda without having to put their own unique stamp on it. They excel at maintaining or operating an established program that needs consistent execution.

Good listeners and non-confrontational

Their combination of talents makes it natural for this group to be good listeners. Listening was the number one rated leadership attribute in our poll of over three hundred supervisors and managers. Cooperative people typically find it easy to apply the wisdom of Saint Francis of Assisi that has been institutionalized as Stephen Covey's habit number five, "Grant that we may not so much seek to be understood as to understand."

This group generally relates well with others and prefers to cooperate rather than cause a confrontation in order to get exactly what they want or to convince you of their opinion. Because they are not so personally invested in their own ideas, they find it easy to look for win-win alternatives. Their tendency to speak tactfully using mild tones can have a calming effect on what otherwise might be a hectic and stressful environment.

Team-oriented leaders

Cooperative personalities exhibit many excellent leadership characteristics. A good sense of humility enables them not to worry about who gets the credit. Rather, they just want to see things run smoothly and achieve team goals and success. The value of these Traits was often overlooked in many leadership discussions until the appearance of Jim Collins popular book, *Good to Great: Why Some Companies Make the Leap and Others Don't.*

In describing some of the characteristics of what his research team called the "Level 5" leader, Collins points out, "Those who worked with or wrote about the good to great leaders continually used words like *quiet, humble, modest, reserved, shy, gracious, mild-mannered, self-effacing, understated, did not believe his own clippings;* and so forth."[1]

Remarkably, the leaders in all eleven good-to-great companies showed no interest in self-promotion. They were not ego driven, yet highly competitive about the mission. Of course, Collins and his team also identified several key Take Charge Traits in these "Level 5" leaders indicating that initiative and drive for results are always needed in a well-balanced leader.[2]

Cooperative – Leadership Struggles

Hesitant to challenge or speak up

We mentioned the Amazing Traits Exercise earlier as a way to see and experience *strengths* and *struggles* straight from the different behavioral Traits. One of the most consistent *struggles* that Cooperative people share is that they hold back, which may communicate to others that they lack confidence. Whatever the cause, in looking over the full list of their *struggles*, it would appear that hesitancy frequently limits their contributions and productivity. Thus, connecting with Cooperative personalities may include inviting, even coaxing them to share their thoughts and ideas.

As part of our team development sessions, we sometimes throw out a simple but tricky math puzzle for the group to solve. The Cooperatives are often the first to get the right answer, yet they typically just say it once softly and then sit back. In the meantime, two Take Charge teammates (both with the wrong answer) may argue until time expires while the Cooperative people just listen. Their reticence to speak up can also add to the problem because, as we learned earlier, the Take Chargers tend to be poor listeners.

During the exercise debrief we point out what happened and then show how it parallels reality on their team. The hesitancy of the Cooperative personalities to fight for their ideas is usually an ongoing issue.

To overcome these *struggles*, they have to believe in themselves enough to risk speaking up. It will require getting out of their comfort zone. By choosing their battles carefully, they can gain success and further confidence for bigger challenges. Of course, their teammates need to be intentional about encouraging their input as well.

Slow to make decisions, initiate, or take action

Typically, this group is hesitant to take ownership for decisions, preferring to get everyone's buy-in first. Leadership by consensus has some good points, but it's not always appropriate and can delay

84

action and preclude timely results. In working with some Cooperative leaders, we've seen them stagnate because of indecisiveness, usually accompanied by too much discussion in too many meetings. When this happens, people start to lose their enthusiasm for the project or goals.

In a team Hugh facilitated, the leader was an extremely Cooperative person. He had achieved success in the business by being very well liked and consensus-oriented. As a leader, no decisions would be made without consulting the team and the vast array of people he had as his "sounding board." Such a collaborative approach allows good thinking to be put on the table. However, what comes with that is a natural hesitation to make decisions quickly when they are needed. Like most areas of leadership development, courage is required.

Overcoming this *struggle* also requires confidence and risk-taking. An experienced mentor or coach who is a little more to the right on this scale—maybe even mid-range—can provide insights and suggestions on how to handle specific situations. This type of coaching is ideal because it reduces the "all alone" feeling and provides the Cooperative person an opportunity to gain knowledge, experience, and confidence.

May lack strategic vision

This group is typically so focused on the potholes and curves in the road ahead that they don't think about looking out over the horizon. And even if they did, it's usually not their talent or passion to keep up with all the trends and possibilities that could come together.

Cooperative people can overcome this *struggle* through several actions. To begin with, they likely need to become more aware of the trends in the current environment. Expanding their information sources and subjects to cover a broader perspective on events in business, technology, politics, medicine, and similar subjects can do this. Beyond that, there are usually plenty of visionaries in most organizations and industries. The challenge will be to pick which strategic horses they want to ride with.

Whom do you know with the Cooperative Trait?

1. _____

2. _____

3. _____

Quick Coach Notes

Ideal Work Environment

Cooperative personalities work best when the goals are clearly defined and there is a consistent work process. They are usually more productive when their tasks focus on maintaining, rather than launching.

Connecting with the Cooperative Trait

1. Remember their need to fit in.
2. Invite and encourage their input.
3. Be an active listener.
4. Remember to focus on the practical.

Managing the Cooperative Trait

1. Believe in them.
2. Let them know they are important; highlight their value to the workplace/team.
3. Capitalize on their focus on the process—it's how they get results.
4. Focus their work on their *strengths*.

Cooperative people need to realize they tend to hold back and that many of their best ideas never get heard. Speak up!

DNA Behavior Style Groups with the Cooperative Trait

Note: See Appendix D for more information on the ten Style Groups.

- Adapter
- Relationship Builder
- Community Builder
- Reflective Thinker (sometimes)
- Stylish Thinker (sometimes)

Take Charge, Cooperative, and Mid-Range—
we need them all

From a leadership and management perspective, this first Factor dealing with control and assertiveness seems to have a bias toward the right-side Take Charge Traits. There is no denying that the characteristics that go with the right side such as decisive, assertive, independent, and visionary are strong leadership attributes for getting results. However, keep in mind that supervisors and managers typically identify the key attribute of their greatest leader as "a good listener," clearly a left-side behavioral talent.

Our research found an interesting balance between the left and right sides of this Factor in terms of valued leadership attributes. Of the top fifteen, five were related to left-side Traits and five were right-side Traits. (Five were more related to other areas.) So, you see, Traits from both sides are required for success as a leader or follower.

If you are on the left or right, learn to recognize and encourage the unique talents of your opposite side teammates. Understand their needs and expect their *struggles*. Let them know how much you value them because of who they are and don't be offended or take it personally when they act like themselves instead of you.

— Self-Assessment Application —

Based on the behavioral Traits described in this chapter and the previous chapter (or based on your actual **DNA Behavior** assessment results), what is your default **DNA Behavior**? Is it more right side, left side, or clearly in the middle?

Place an "x" on the "Cooperative to Take Charge" scale below that best describes you. You may also use the free Self-Assessment Worksheet to capture your strengths and struggles for this factor. Download a copy at www.LeadershipBehaviorDNA.com/Book.

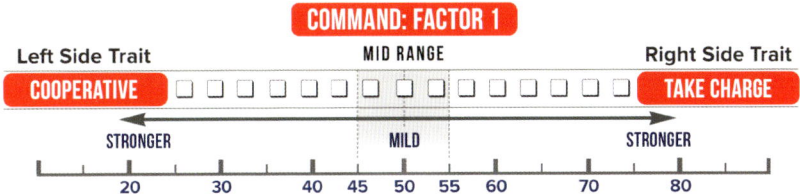

1. Looking back at the **strengths** and **struggles** for these Traits,
   a. What are some of your key **strengths** for leadership?
   b. Looking at your **struggles**, what is one area where you could adapt and become a better leader?
2. How can you apply the *Quick Coach Notes*?
3. With whom will you share this information for more insight, discussion, and accountability?

Calculate your specific Factor score by taking the *Leadership Behavior DNA* assessment. It only takes 10 minutes to receive your personal report.

Learn more at www.LeadershipBehaviorDNA.com/Book

ENDNOTES

1 *Good to Great: Why Some Companies Make the Leap and Others Don't*, Jim Collins, Page 27, 2001, HarperCollins Publishers Inc, New York, NY.

2 Ibid. pages 22-35.

THE PEOPLE FACTOR

This Factor indicates a person's openness in expression, transparency, and ease in relating to strangers.

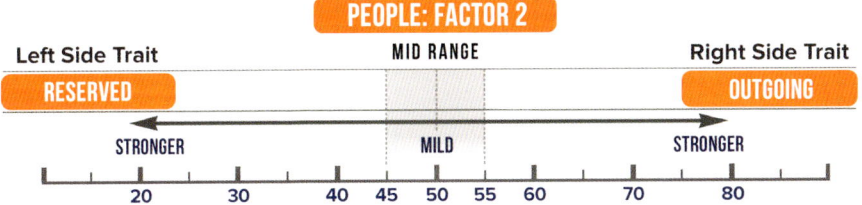

PEOPLE: FACTOR 2

Left Side Trait	MID RANGE	Right Side Trait
RESERVED		**OUTGOING**

STRONGER — MILD — STRONGER

20   30   40   45   50   55   60   70   80

Reserved Leader Qualities

[Motivated to Reflect]

- Like to think
- Consider, analyze
- Work well alone
- Minimize emotions
- Reservation about new ideas

Outgoing Leader Qualities

[Motivated to Connect]

- Like to express
- Think out loud
- Engage, network
- Open, public
- Enthusiasm for new ideas

— The People Factor —

Since these Traits are obvious in relationships, most people will have a general knowledge of these concepts. At some level, you already know that some people are outgoing, and some are reserved. But we need to go much deeper because this Factor is rich with insights that can revolutionize your approach to work and team relationships.

Before launching into the People Trait, we need to clarify the most basic difference between the ways individuals respond to other people. You have likely used the terms extrovert and introvert to describe how people relate to one another. Those labels are applicable here as well if we clarify them. Some assessments use Extrovert and Introvert to mean outward focused and inward focused. However, whenever we use the terms Outgoing/extrovert and Reserved/introvert, we are referring to how an individual responds to others, primarily in two ways—how comfortable they are in meeting and engaging with strangers, and what happens to their energy when they engage with people.

Generally, extroverts are eager to meet people and they are energized by interacting with them; while introverts are less interested in meeting people and are de-energized by social engagement. Thus, the Outgoing/extrovert will eagerly anticipate a large social event while the Reserved/introvert will typically dread it. This focus of energy is at the core of understanding the People Factor. As with all the Factors, there is no good or bad side of this continuum; rather, they are just different.

What about the Mid-Range?

Someone whose People Factor score is mid-range (45-55) will operate with flexibility in their work setting that will allow them to be Outgoing in some situations yet Reserved in others. As a result, they will likely relate to some of the *strengths* and *struggles* of each of the Traits. As with all the Factors of *DNA Behavior*, one-third of the population will score on the left side of the scale, another third on the right, and the final third in the mid-range. There are no bad scores and all Traits have *strengths* and *struggles*.

CHAPTER 8 ▶ THE OUTGOING TRAIT

FACTOR 2: RIGHT-SIDE TRAIT

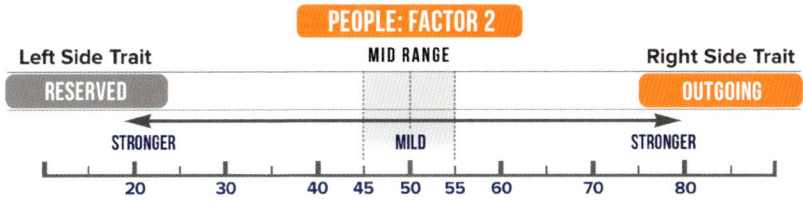

I'm a nonstop extrovert, a people person who loves mingling and gabbing and getting out in the world.

—Meghan McCain

The expression "two are better than one" has special meaning for those who have Outgoing behaviors. For them, being alone is not much fun. They love to interact with others regardless of where it is. They will talk to strangers on the elevator, in the ticket line, even in other cars while sitting at traffic signals.

Outgoing folks are so expressive that they are easy to recognize. If you observe someone who smiles often, laughs easily, and enjoys talking in a group, then it's likely that their natural "happy place" is on the Outgoing side of this continuum. These bubbly, high-energy folks are hard to miss because they naturally want to "go public" and usually maneuver their way into the limelight. Let's put them at the center of attention now.

Outgoing – Strengths and Struggles

 **Strengths in Leadership**

1. Good at meeting new people
2. Lighthearted, optimistic, and enthusiastic
3. Make a good impression, thrive in the limelight
4. Like to promote, advocate, and sell
5. Work will with open-ended situations

 **Struggles in Leadership**

1. Strong need for approval of others
2. May be overly verbal or dominate conversations
3. Can be overly optimistic
4. Often struggle working alone
5. May display strong emotions

Outgoing Trait examples

As you would expect, there are many well-known public figures that display characteristics from this group. In the entertainment and media arena consider Kelly Ripa, Goldie Hawn, Jim Carrey, Reba McIntyre, Wendy Williams, Kathie Lee Gifford, and Al Roker. Government leaders would include former Prime Minister Tony Blair, former Presidents Bill Clinton, Ronald Reagan, and Dwight Eisenhower. Generals Patton and Schwarzkopf would fit in this group as well. Sports figures include gold medal skaters Tara Lipinski and Sarah Hughes, gymnast Mary Lou Retton, and competitors turned broadcasters Terry Bradshaw, Dion Sanders, and Darrell Waltrip.

Several strong underlying motivations relate to the Outgoing person's drive to relate to others. Foremost, they are outwardly focused on connecting with people. Their attention is outward, and they search for others with whom they can connect and share their thoughts. This is a very important concept because they do much of their best thinking and analyzing as they are talking. As strange as it might sound to a Reserved person, Outgoing people often don't know what's coming out of their mouths until it "hits the street." In a sense, listeners are the midwives that assist them in giving birth to many of their best thoughts and ideas.

Whereas Take Charge individuals are outwardly focused to assess who has power and determine its impact on their control, the Outgoing person is outwardly focused to connect with others—to express, to recognize and be recognized.[1]

Of all the Traits, Outgoing people have the greatest need to be popular and admired. This need to be acknowledged (even just speaking to them acknowledges their being) explains some of their dependence on connecting with others and why they want to engage other people at every opportunity. Social activity is crucial for them because it meets so many of their needs. When they are required to work alone for extended periods of time, they become like a fish out of water searching for their survival environment.

There are two special considerations when you are evaluating someone's "people needs." First, age and maturity matter. Adolescents typically go through a socialization period that causes them to exhibit higher than normal Outgoing Traits, regardless of where they are on this continuum. During this period, even those with the Reserved Trait may place high importance on friends and fun. However, as they become adults, their social needs begin to fade back toward the Reserved side of the continuum. Also, as you would imagine, Outgoing extroverts who have extremely high public exposure may become saturated and withdraw somewhat to have some private time to recharge.

 ## Outgoing – Leadership Strengths

Good at networking, making good first impressions, and open to almost anything

If you want to know whom to call on for help, or who knows something about a particular subject, then ask an Outgoing person. If they don't know, then they likely know someone who does know. Networking comes naturally to them and is a powerful asset in many career fields. They maintain an ever-expanding mental (and electronic) database of contacts with which they "touch base" on a regular basis. Even discarding a business card of someone they met casually on a flight two years ago can be a painful decision.

If you want someone to greet and welcome people at a social function, or someone to host the international group that is coming to town, then look first to this group. They smile easily, excel at hospitality, and they are so genuine in their enthusiasm for strangers. All their talents collectively enable them to make good first impressions.

Openness is also an important asset for this group. They tend to be transparent and willingly share their inner thoughts openly with others. Once when Lee was conducting an ice-breaker exercise to kick off a team building session with the leadership team at an engineering plant he asked each person to share something about themselves that no one else at the table knew. When it came to be her turn, the very outgoing lead engineer gleefully shared, "I have something to share that no one knows. I had a ring put in my navel last weekend." And at the break, she took the one other female in the group to the ladies' restroom to proudly show her this new addition. It was a classic illustration of how Outgoing people are extremely transparent, sometimes sharing more than you may want to know. (As a side note, engineers are mostly Reserved.)

They also have an openness to make new friends. And, they rarely encounter an idea that they are not open to trying. A closely related attribute is optimism. Perhaps they are open because they believe that everything is going to work out fine.

Strong verbal skills, good at promoting, enthusiastic, upbeat, positive, and humorous

Outgoing persons can talk about anything, anywhere on a moment's notice. They are usually very good at sales and promoting because their natural Traits are powerful tools to connect and engage our emotions. A classic representative of this group is the likable boxer, George Foreman. You may recall that George was twice the heavyweight-boxing champion of the world who converted from puncher to preacher and has now turned pitchman.

Outgoing – Leadership Struggles

As pointed out in Chapter 3, *struggles* can comprise weak or missing *strengths* that are pushed to the extreme. See how well these qualities describe the outgoing people you know.

Too much talk (not enough action), overly optimistic, procrastinate on tasks, and have difficulty working alone

Not all work can be done through talk, so there comes a time when our fun-loving friends must actually do some non-talking work. If it means shutting the door and performing a solitary mental task, expect them to procrastinate.

Of course, they don't see this as a problem because their strong optimism is saying, "No problem." right up until the last hour before the project is due. If you are in their network and you know they are up against the wall, you can expect to see them show up on your caller ID; they'll likely be reaching out for a little help on the pressing deadline.

Hugh had the good fortune to coach a CEO who was very Outgoing. He had a gift of engaging his team in conversations and always created a good impression with customers. Nevertheless, his team members did not walk away feeling heard because in reality the CEO was not truly listening. This eroded trust in the business and eventually the team gave up on having substantive discussions. However, once the CEO curbed his own need to talk all the time and was more inclusive in the way he listened, the team responded with more cohesion that led to better execution.

All behavior groups must learn to observe the effect of their interactions with others. It's easy for the Outgoing's verbal energy to get out of control, talking *at* people without noticing that they are not connecting. Then, they wonder why there is no action. In one such case, we learned that the CEO had been trying unsuccessfully to inspire the operations team on the future of the business. Through coaching, we discovered that this Outgoing leader was talking to a team full of Reserved and Planned people. So, when he got blank faces, the CEO doubled down and increased his emotion to get a response.

What this CEO did not realize was that his intense verbal emotional expression drove the Reserved people even more inward into their shell to the point of not trusting the leader. The lesson for this Outgoing leader was that he needed to keep his stories factual and pointing to data and logic. The operations team did not need an inspiring motivational talk; they wanted to know specifics on how the CEO was going to implement change. For Outgoing personalities, gaining "in the moment feedback" by noticing the expressions of others will alert them when their talking is out of control.

Unfocused, overcommitted, and overwhelmed

The downside of their openness is that they want to do everything—especially if it's something new, exciting or fun. In addition, they crave approval; and one more commitment is another opportunity to look good. But then the other shoe falls, and they can exhibit near manic behaviors when they suddenly discover they have ten balls in the air and can only catch six. In this overwhelmed state, quality/standards start to slip toward the "just get it done" level and well-intended promises can be completely forgotten.

The balancing mantra of most Outgoing/extroverts needs to be *focus, focus, focus, no, no, no*, and then *prioritize, prioritize, prioritize*—and when that is finished, repeat it a few more times. They will do well to prioritize and then fight with the viciousness of a wounded tiger to stay on task. Additionally, successful ones know that they must pay attention to schedules, learn to say "no" and develop plans that will allow them to meet deadlines.

Observing an opposite Trait (Reserved) mentor and constant self-coaching can be a powerful tool for those with the Outgoing Trait to help them deal with their *struggles*. Of course, that's true for all other Traits as well.

Emotional and uninhibited

Outgoing people are not very good at hiding their emotions, and this can get them in trouble. Also, their personal/relational outlook and the fact that their ideas are tightly bound to their egos makes it almost natural for them to interpret disagreement in very personal terms. This can make team problem-solving a volatile encounter.

Think about it. Strong, emotional expression would be an expected behavior from someone who tends to be verbal, open, uninhibited, and naturally expressive in other areas. Emotional expression is a good news/ bad news situation. The good news is that Outgoing folks express their anger and get over it very quickly. The bad news is that they express their anger and it sometimes gets them in deeper trouble.

Recently one of our clients, an Outgoing and highly successful senior manager whom we'll call Jack, called for advice. Jack said he was thinking about leaving the company. He shared the events that began his downward spiral, the root cause being a meeting in which he made some emotional and cutting remarks to his boss in front of others. This event soured his boss and began the decline in their relationship.

Our consultant reviewed the facts and helped Jack see that his emotional remarks had really been the cause of the problem. He suggested that Jack sit down, write a letter to his boss, apologize, and ask for his forgiveness. Jack wrote the letter and dropped it off at the boss's office in the morning. That afternoon, the boss called with a totally different tone, and asked Jack to come over for a meeting.

It's very important for Outgoing people to learn to depersonalize conflict and view it more objectively—as just a different viewpoint or the other person's problem—but not necessarily as a personal affront. With maturity they learn to coach themselves to behave and respond in the most effective way. However, until that point, most will need to express their emotions and will need a plan that allows them to do it without damage. A good technique is for them to have a friend to whom they can safely vent, someone who can serve as a sponge or a punching bag—someone to absorb their emotions without damage to anyone.

The bottom line for these Outgoing and engaging extroverts is that emotions are like dynamite. In the right amount and at the right time, dynamite can be used to make a tunnel through the mountains. But an out-of-control blast can destroy the entire mountain and injure many people in the process.

Whom do you know with the Outgoing Trait?

1. _____

2. _____

3. _____

Quick Coach Notes

Ideal Work Environment

The Outgoing Trait is best suited for a fast-paced, fun-oriented environment where their primary work centers on engaging people. They need variety, mobility, and the opportunity to influence, impact, train, and encourage others as well as promote ideas, products, and services by using their enthusiasm and strong verbal skills.

Connecting with the Outgoing Trait

1. Accept their need to gain recognition and express.
2. Remember their need for fun and/or excitement.
3. Invest time in building the relationship.
4. Tell them who is involved.

Managing the Outgoing Trait

1. Remember their best talents relate to connecting with others—working alone sets them up for failure.
2. Help them transfer their talk to an action plan.
3. Stay involved with them, listen to their ideas, and don't ignore them.
4. Give frequent affirmation for specific work.

Outgoing extroverted people should remember that an effusive nature can be offensive to introverted friends. Button up, tone it down and give your opposites some room.

DNA Behavior Style Groups with the Outgoing Trait

Note: See Appendix D for more information on the ten Style Groups.

- Engager
- Influencer
- Community Builder
- Stylish Thinker

ENDNOTES

1 Contrary to what many people think, there is no correlation with this Outgoing Trait and the Take Charge Trait of Factor 1. There are as many Take Charge people who are Reserved as Outgoing.

CHAPTER 9 ▶ THE RESERVED TRAIT

FACTOR 2: LEFT-SIDE TRAIT

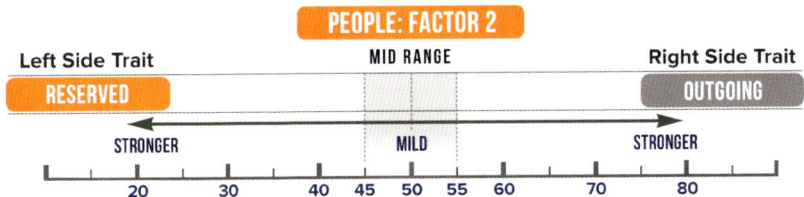

We are drawn to ideas, we are passionate observers, and for us, solitude is rich and generative. Think of all that goes on in the playground of solitude: daydreaming, reading, composing, meditating—and just being, writing, calculating, fantasizing, thinking, praying, theorizing, imagining, drawing/painting/sculpting, inventing, researching, reflecting. You get the idea.

—Laurie Helgoe[1]

In a society that is fed by television and the entertainment industry, it often appears that the important people are all highly Outgoing and extroverted. How misleading, because stage presence is very much about "performing." Additionally, underneath the hype, the Reserved people are often the ones calling the shots and reaping the cash. There is a saying that still waters run deep, and this is usually true of those whose "happy place" is on the quiet, reserved, almost un-public end of the people continuum.

From experience, we can predict that the Reserved who are reading this are starting to feel uncomfortable with this exposé of their nature. If they were here, they would say, "Let's just skip over this section, and move on to the next chapter."

You see, Reserved people much prefer to keep personal information private. If that's you, then we ask your indulgence for two reasons. First, your Outgoing teammates need to know you better, so they can understand you, quit trying to change you, and learn to value your Reserved nature. Second, by understanding yourself better, you will be able to better manage yourself and coach others.

Let's put the spotlight (if that makes you uncomfortable, think of it as a candle) on Reserved introverts and learn more about this Trait.

Reserved – Strengths and Struggles

 **Strengths in Leadership**

1. Prefer working with tasks
2. Good at working alone
3. Serious, realistic, and modest
4. Set boundaries to stay focused
5. Persistent to get closure

 **Struggles in Leadership**

1. May appear withdrawn or unfriendly
2. Tend to see the downside first
3. May seem quietly self-righteous
4. May resist collaborative work
5. Drained by extensive interaction

Reserved Trait examples

Although they usually don't seek public attention and fame, many famous people are Reserved. They just learn to adapt their behaviors to accomplish their "up front" or on-camera responsibilities. To readily recognize Reserved Traits, it can be helpful to think of them alongside an Outgoing contemporary.

For example, compare the following Reserved individuals with the Outgoing in parenthesis. Consider these examples from television news and talk shows: Trevor Noah (Jay Leno) Barbara Walters (Wendy Williams), and George Will (George Stephanopoulos). In politics: President Jimmy Carter (President Bill Clinton), and Senator Bob Dole (Elizabeth Dole). In sports: skaters Dorothy Hamill (Tara Lipinski), basketball stars Larry Bird (Magic Johnson), NASCAR drivers the late Dale Earnhardt (Darrell Waltrip), broadcasters Ron Gant (Dion Sanders) Frank Gifford (John Madden), baseball pitchers Greg Mattox (Don Sutton). Others include Mother Teresa (Billy Graham), Bill Gates (Steve Jobs), Warren Buffett (Jack Welch).

Reserved – Leadership Strengths

The greatest **strength** that Reserved people offer is that they are task-focused. They are not distracted with concerns about who else is involved or what other people are saying. They're busy getting their own work done.

We have seen some unique and creative illustrations of this Trait as part of the Amazing Traits Exercise. During team-building sessions, one group stood out above all the rest. When it was time for them to present, the Reserved group stood beside their flip charts and lifted the cover sheet to reveal what they had written during the 10-minute prep time. The spokesperson said nothing but used a pointer to deliver their brief message. In great big letters they had written: "We don't talk it, we walk it." Then, they all sat down without saying a word. The audience was initially stunned, then cheered at this powerful illustration of Reserved Traits.

Work well alone, focused, stay on task, and finish what they start

Reserved people are usually quite comfortable working alone and even prefer their own inner world to constant interaction with others. This more solitary approach complements their desire to avoid the interruptions and distractions that come from having others around. In fact, one of the most common complaints of this group is that other people come into their offices and talk when they have work to do. They prefer to stay focused on their tasks in order to finish what they start.

Quiet, reflective, and deliberate

Since they typically process internally, Reserved persons find it quite normal to not express everything that's on their mind. Rather than talk, they prefer to reflect, play out, or mull over their thoughts and ideas. This explains why they often respond to a question with "Let me think about it." When they do give their answer, it's going to be a well thought-out, reasoned approach.

Lee remembers the day he asked his associate Bob a question

about marketing. Bob had many years in business and lots of exposure to marketing and advertising, so when he responded: "Let me think about it," it got his attention. Since Lee knew that Bob had ten times the knowledge that he did, it was difficult for him to comprehend why he needed to think about it. Bob came back later in the day and provided a brilliant answer that was exactly what was needed. Noticing this pattern on repeated occasions, this became Lee's aha moment about the discomfort caused by putting Reserved folks on the spot with an off the cuff question. He learned that it's much better to give them a heads up and time to reflect—another example of the Platinum Rule paying off.

Unemotional, matter of fact, and realistic

Since this group tends to be low-keyed, it's quite unusual to see them respond emotionally—either to problems or successes. And to their credit, they are much less likely than those on the Outgoing side of the continuum to get in trouble with emotional outbursts. This may be in part because they just don't express their feelings as much and partly because they don't take things as personally.

We suspect that most good card players are Reserved. In a crowd of people, you can usually identify them because of their "poker face" expressions. In addition, they typically communicate in a straightforward, matter-of-fact style. Whether asking or responding, they like to use a minimum of words and little emotion.

People from the Reserved side also like to be very realistic in giving appraisals, estimates, and making commitments. Their tendency is to be conservative and minimize in order not to overstate. They much prefer to say no than to overcommit what they think they can do. And they often will downplay their capabilities (sandbagging) in order to under-promise and over-deliver on their obligations.

Reserved – Leadership Struggles

Drained by social contact, can come across as shy or unfriendly or closed to others

During a session with a leadership group, we were discussing individual Traits and sharing *strengths* and *struggles*. One senior engineer underscored this *struggle* saying: "I'd rather have a root canal than go to a party where there's a bunch of people I don't know." Those who have a reserved nature echo this general sentiment in virtually every training workshop.

In most lines of work, some degree of socializing is necessary, and so people do learn to adapt—some even become very good at it. When reviewing his profile report, one entrepreneur friend was relieved to see that he came out on the introverted Reserved side of this Factor. He said that because he had worked in sales and learned to socialize, most people thought he was Outgoing. His relief came in knowing that he was not being a phony but a Reserved who had adapted to meet the needs of the situation.

Gary, one of our good friends, is a consummate presenter, having trained more than 100,000 people in corporate America. When he's facilitating, his enthusiasm and verbal energy give the impression that he might be Outgoing. But when the day is over, he prefers to retreat straight to his hotel room, order dinner from room service and sequester himself in order to recharge his batteries for the next day.

Putting Reserved people in roles that require extensive meeting and greeting is an exceptional challenge that only a few of them can survive. We recall a young lady who was about to lose her job as the front desk receptionist. When she was hired, no one considered that as a Reserved introvert she would be severely stressed by having to interact with strangers all day, every day. To make matters worse, she was expected to multitask by answering the phone and greeting people while recording data into a spreadsheet. She called in sick at least one day almost every week until finally someone realized it might be a bad job match for her. She was moved to another job where she could work alone and be more focused. Her attendance and performance improved dramatically; she became a valued contributor and loved her work.

Still, at times, Reserved folks do need to push themselves to meet the social needs of work and their families. However, they should be realistic about their needs for time alone in their job choice and plan for extra rest when they have extensive people exposure.

Here's an important reminder about taking time to recharge:

Everyone must stretch as part of their roles and responsibilities—in life and work. This means there needs to be a plan to recharge and that will be different for each Trait and to some degree for each individual. Reflect and become aware of how you recharge. Also, consider this concept as we work through the various Traits.

Pessimistic, negative, skeptical, closed, and unenthusiastic

If Reserved people are not careful, their **strength** of being "very realistic" can easily slide into pessimism. As one highly reserved person put it, we sometimes tend to see the roadblocks rather than the finish line. Reserved people can get uncomfortable and turn negative when the environment gets to be what they consider out of control with enthusiasm.

These Reserved people should keep in mind that they can play a very important role by using their natural skepticism to bring reality to a dialogue. At the same time, they need to remember that optimism and a positive attitude are essential for progress and resilience.

Tend to isolate, may not communicate, and slow to respond

By their nature, Reserves drift toward isolation from the group. Additionally, their words and body language can send a message that says: "Leave me alone." When a DNA Team Performance Report[6] shows most of the people as Reserved, we can predict with a high degree of accuracy that they have insufficient communications. Getting them to talk and share needed information can be like herding cats. They may say, "Yes, we need to talk more." But usually they go right back to their old (natural behavior) ways, which is to keep things to themselves.

Being careful with information in an organization is often a good thing, particularly in managing people's expectations. However, we recently worked with a very Reserved leader who was destroying company culture by being too withdrawn, private, and secretive. He was far too guarded in the release of critical information to the board and key executives. This was causing people to work around the company systems and also filter information when sharing. In some cases, the team made mistakes because they were not adequately informed.

The best solution to this *struggle* is about the same as the solution to most other *struggles*—adapt your behaviors to the point where you start to feel out of your comfort zone. At that point, you are probably starting to make progress in overcoming the *struggle*, at least to an acceptable level. Remember, even a little change can pay big dividends.

Whom do you know with the Reserved Trait?

1. _____

2. _____

3. _____

Quick Coach Notes

Ideal Work Environment

Reserves work best in a quiet environment where they have time and space to work alone for extended periods. They are usually more productive and less stressed by working task assignments with data, rather than engaging people and people problems.

Connecting with the Reserved Trait

1. Honor their need to avoid attention and reflect.
2. Allow them to process their responses.
3. Present the facts; minimize emotions.
4. Do not mistake their lack of response for inattention.

Managing the Reserved Trait

1. Avoid overly animated and embellished explanations.
2. Respect their privacy.
3. Try not to interrupt their work.
4. Encourage and affirm them in private.

Reserved introverted people need to remember that extroverted Outgoing friends take it personally when you are unresponsive, distant, and closed to their enthusiasm and craziness. Open up, lighten up, and give others some attention.

DNA Behavior Style Groups with the Reserved Trait

Note: See Appendix D for more information on the ten Style Groups.

- Initiator
- Reflective Thinker
- Strategist
- Facilitator
- Relationship Builder (Sometimes)

Outgoing, Reserved, and Mid-Range—
we need them all

After observing and participating in many discussions with Outgoing and Reserved groups, we're convinced that it is almost impossible for each side of this continuum to ever fully understand the other side. They are wired so differently that they can irritate each other just being who they are. If each side can just make small efforts to adapt to the other, it will draw everyone sufficiently closer to make a huge difference. And as is the case with all the opposite Traits, learn to coach yourself to value the ***strengths*** of the other side and accommodate or minimize their ***struggles*** as much as possible.

— Self-Assessment Application —

Based on the behavioral Traits described in this chapter and the previous chapter (or based on your actual *DNA Behavior* assessment results), what is your default *DNA Behavior*? Is it more right side, left side, or clearly in the middle?

Place an "x" on the "Reserved to Outgoing" scale below that best describes you. You may also use the free Self-Assessment Worksheet to capture your strengths and struggles for this factor. Download a copy at www.LeadershipBehaviorDNA. com/Book.

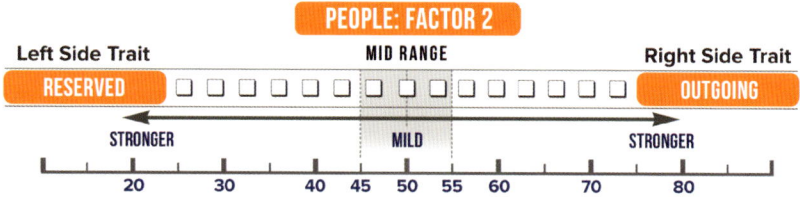

1. Looking back at the *strengths* and *struggles* for this Trait,
   a. What are some of your key *strengths* for leadership?
   b. Looking at your *struggles*, what is one area where you could adapt and become a better leader?
2. How can you apply the *Quick Coach Notes*?
3. With whom will you share this information for more insight, discussion, and accountability?

Calculate your specific Factor score by taking the *Leadership Behavior DNA* assessment. It only takes 10 minutes to receive your personal report.

Learn more at www.LeadershipBehaviorDNA.com/Book

ENDNOTES

1 A graphic depiction of the team showing where each person falls in the eight Factors. Look for an example in chapter 23.

THE PATIENCE FACTOR

This Factor indicates a person's natural pace, desire for stability, and need for harmony.

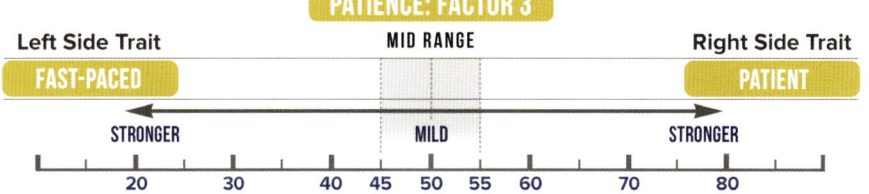

Fast-Paced Leader Qualities

[Motivated by Action]

- Impatient, Change-oriented
- Challenge, confront
- Objective, emotionally distant
- Results driven
- Rational, logical

Patient Leader Qualities

[Motivated by Stability]

- Steady, maintain, preserve
- Like harmony, tolerant
- Sensitive to feelings
- Priority is peace and calm
- Sensitive, empathetic

— The Patience Factor —

Do you prefer steady, predictable routines in your life or more of a dynamic, fast-paced environment? The Patience Factor predicts a person's desire for steady or Fast-Paced work and the need for harmony or challenge in their world. The right side of the scale prefers a more patient and consistent pace.[1] The left side likes a fast pace and quick action in daily activities. Closely tied to these opposite characteristics is the way that each group deals with stability and change. The right side protects and promotes stability and resists change. The left side instigates change and becomes quickly bored if things stay the same. In the discussions that follow, right-side people are considered Patient and left-side are considered Fast-Paced.

Interestingly, another very important aspect of this Factor is how a person responds to the feelings of others around them. Those who score on the Patient (right) side are very compassionate and have a radar-like sensitivity to the feelings and needs of others. The Fast-Paced group, those who score on the left side, are more emotionally detached and naturally focus on logic to make rational choices. At full *strength*, they have little to no natural radar for the feelings of others and may even shrink from the idea of feelings. Ironically, they often have strong feelings of aversion about feelings.

Obviously, since both the feelings of others and the logic of the situation are very important, this is a good time to reiterate an important point on the nature of behavioral Traits. There are significant advantages (and disadvantages) of being on either side (or any point) of the continuum for any of the eight Factors that we are discussing.

CHAPTER 10 ▶ THE PATIENT TRAIT

FACTOR 3: RIGHT-SIDE TRAIT

*Without patience, we will learn less in life. We will see less.
We will feel less. We will hear less…*

—Mother Teresa

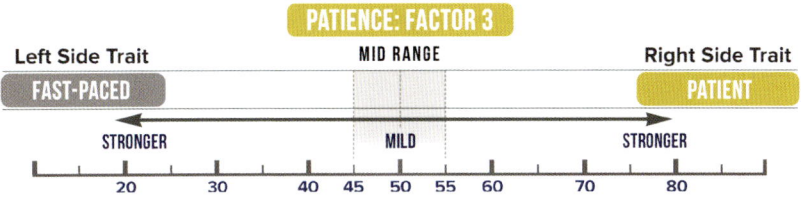

As we have already seen, those whose behaviors default to the Patient side of this continuum naturally exhibit many of the characteristics that we commonly think of as being peaceful, patient, and supportive. Their strong drive for harmony usually translates into a "go along" demeanor that enables them to work well with others. Like the Outgoing group, these people are typically relational but for different reasons and in different ways. Whereas the Outgoing Trait tends to relate out of a need for interaction and attention, the Patient person is relational out of a strong need to support and care for others. Let's examine their typical ***strengths*** and ***struggles***.

Patient – Strengths and Struggles

Strengths in Leadership

1. Compassionate, warm, and sensitive
2. Listen well, receptive to others
3. Patient, willing to wait
4. Loyal, promote harmony
5. Consistent, steady, and even-paced

Struggles in Leadership

1. May compromise too much
2. Do not like to challenge or confront
3. May be too trusting
4. Can be resistant to change
5. May not share true feelings

Patient Trait examples

Well-known examples from this group include: Christopher Walken, Halle Berry, Kanye West, Joanna Newsom, Sufjan Stevens, Shirley Temple Black, Rosa Parks, and Shakespeare, government leaders former Presidents George H. W. Bush, and Gerald Ford, and the often voted most admired president of all time Abraham Lincoln and Chancellor Angela Merkel. Also, in this group are businessmen Warren Buffett, Indra Nooyi, and Truett Cathy; sports figures like former Cowboy coach Tom Landry, San Antonion Spurs assistant coach Tim Duncan, New York Yankee manager Joe Torre, and Hall of Fame shortstop Derek Jeter.

 ## Patient – Leadership Strengths

Compassionate, supportive, and understanding

Those on the right side of the continuum seem to have a natural ability to come across as being "nice." They can be very competitive, but they are not driven to be number one in everything, and they don't have a great need to be in the limelight like the Outgoing folks. Rather, what the Patient person wants most is to be friends and just have everyone "get along." In many ways, they are the antidote to today's fast pace, high stress, and "in your face" lifestyle.

The Patient person truly has both a natural desire and ability to support others. Unlike any of the other Traits, they can actually be more concerned about making others look good than in doing the same for themselves. Consequently, they often are very content to remain in the background doing the quiet but necessary things that make the gears in an organization turn smoothly. This low concern for attention often means that they get little recognition for the important work they do.

The Patient Trait is very powerful in any situation where building deep relationships and giving support and encouragement are involved. They can be excellent leaders when they learn to adapt and do the "tough love" behaviors required of all leaders. As you would suspect, counselors and therapists typically score in the Patient range of this continuum, as do many pediatricians, teachers, and successful coaches.

As businesses try to regain a focus for customer service, Patient Traits are in high demand. More and more people are realizing that matching people to their work can have great benefits. An article on this subject quoted a manager from one of the Ritz Carlton hotels saying: "Almost everyone was hired here based on personality, not on experience. 'We made a real effort to hire people who had compassion for guests' concerns. When people come to a hotel, they bring more baggage than what's under their arm.'"[2]

Kind, peacemakers, tolerant, and team players

One of the best contributions from the Patient folks is that they tend to say nice things or nothing at all. Their sensitivity seems to help them avoid being critical or harsh in their comments about others. They seem to be much more interested in promoting peace and harmony than arguing with others' viewpoints. They also tend to ignore or downplay negative and inflammatory comments, whereas their left side (fast-paced) opposites would be more likely to respond in kind by escalating the intensity.

You can learn a lot about a person's Traits from the media when they do objective and fair in-depth reporting. Such was the case when CBS's *60 Minutes II* featured the highly successful (Baseball Hall of Fame) NY Yankee manager Joe Torre. The segment turned out to be an excellent presentation of the characteristics of a Patient leader.

The host described Torre as "understanding", "a loyal father" and said, "he treats them [his players] like his own kids." (In a written article, Brian Jordan, a former Braves outfielder, referred to Torre as "my father figure."[3]) In talking about his own leadership style, Torre used a number of keywords that are also indicative of his Patient talents saying:

> *"I hate that confrontational stuff.… I try to see it from their side.… I feel for them.… You blame yourself.… The subway series was war [indicating painful conflict]."*[4]

Joe Torre's ability to promote harmony among his highly paid players certainly contributed to the Yankees' tremendous success while he was their manager. Likewise, his ability to work for an owner that frequently fired managers gave the team continuity in leadership and contributed to four World Series championships in five years.

The Patient Trait group offers two other interesting characteristics. Family relationships seem to take a higher priority for them than any other group. They seem to have a natural ability to nurture and care for others. In fact, they may attempt to create a "family" atmosphere at work. (It's very consistent that a Patient person like Joe Torre would be referred to as a father figure.) Author and counselor, Dr. John Trent calls this group the Golden Retrievers because they are so loyal about staying close to home and protecting the family.

Over the years, we've also noted that this group has another common attribute: a great need for stability at work. They are among the best for working in one place for an extended period of time. They like to go to work in the same office every day and go home to sleep in their own bed at night. Typically, they are not as comfortable as road warriors.

Persistent, dependable, and steady

A helpful analogy to understand the Patient group comes from the world of mechanics: the flywheel. The function of the heavy wheel is to provide inertia and keep the engine purring at a constant speed in spite of the gaps in the firing of the cylinders. Another similar analogy is the massive mill wheel, which does not accelerate or slow down quickly, but once up to speed, it just keeps on turning. Patient people tend to operate similarly. They don't change speeds easily; they just keep on producing at a dependable steady pace.

Given a stable situation, they are not likely to miss school or work and often are the ones that set attendance records. These natural tendencies give them an advantage in projects that require steady dependable production and long-term commitment.

 Patient – Leadership Struggles

Sensitive, naïve, and may compromise too much

Underneath their genuine concern and sensitivity for others, there is often an ego that tends to *struggle* with its own self-worth. It doesn't take much criticism to injure the feelings of those who have a Patient bent. Their sensors are so acute that even someone's unspoken anger can cause them significant stress or discouragement. Of course, this sensitivity can make it difficult for others who are not so Patient because they end up having to walk on eggshells to avoid hurting the Patient person's feelings.

The Patient person naturally sees the best and wants to believe the best in others; however, they tend to trust when trust may not be warranted because they do not naturally take a critical and skeptical perspective. They are more likely than other groups to be taken in by deception. Balancing sensitivity and kindness with a good dose of skepticism and discernment will help Patient people avoid some of the pains and problems that come when trust is betrayed.

Patient workers also have a tendency to compromise too much. They often give away too much of themselves, their power and especially their time in an attempt to please others. They need to be objective about what is reasonable and then set boundaries on what is appropriate for themselves and others.

The easiest cure for these boundary *struggles* is to "just say no." Of course, this can be very difficult to do because if people have been accustomed to a "yes," they may become angry when they hear "no." But it must be done because, in the end, it's the right thing to do, and it's the only way for the individual to preserve his or her dignity.

Saying "no" requires personal courage and confidence that what you are doing is right; and even then, it takes practice. Managers can also assist in this step by giving their Patient people explicit permission to say "no" and by regularly reviewing workloads to make sure they don't get overloaded.

Avoids conflict, slow to confront, and doesn't verbalize true feelings

The biggest issue for Patient leader is that they resist engaging in healthy conflict and are hesitant to confront when confrontation is needed and appropriate.

It shouldn't be a normal thing to enjoy conflict, but conflict is normal, and so they would do well to learn how to operate in it with some effectiveness. As an Air Force commander, Lee had to replace a good friend in a leadership role because he consistently failed to confront poor performance.

One of the most successful entrepreneurial leaders Hugh's team coached was very Patient in his style. Craig had built from scratch a technology business serving accountants with revenues of more than $100 million in a fairly short period of time. His key *strength* was being able to create a supportive environment and work collaboratively. He was also extremely creative and that is why he could design new technology for accountants.

Craig's challenge came about 10 years into the business when he needed to reorganize some of the divisions for the next level of growth and also cut costs. His board, dominated mostly by logical Fast-Paced leaders, pushed him to lay off some people who had been in the company from the start. Of course, this idea was painful to him and he procrastinated for a long time over the decision. Eventually, Craig saw that the changes needed to happen. And, of course, he handled it with a relational bedside manner by providing relatively generous separation packages.

Many times, we have watched meetings in which Patient people sit quietly and let a decision be made without expressing their true feelings. This was especially puzzling when we knew they didn't agree with the direction that the decision was heading. It apparently goes back to those same issues of needing harmony, avoiding conflict, and perhaps lacking confidence in their personal power, especially in taking a stand against someone in power or authority over them.

Also, as Pat Lencioni points out so well in his widely-used leadership books that healthy conflict (think judicious debate) is essential in order to make sure all perspectives are considered when an important decision is made. Airing out different opinions can be very healthy and an excellent step to get buy-in and full-hearted support for decisions. But the natural behavior of the Patient person is to shut down during these debates, and that's a big mistake. The team needs them to speak up with the full weight of their knowledge, ideas, and opinions. Anything less is holding back, which is detrimental to the team effort.

Whom do you know with the Patient Trait?

1. _____

2. _____

3. _____

Quick Coach Notes

Ideal Work Environment

Patient workers are typically very versatile and can work in almost any field where they have an interest as long as harmony and stability prevail. They will be the most satisfied when they can see their efforts directly contribute to the overall growth, development, and success of others.

Connecting with the Patient Trait

1. Remember their need for stability, harmony, and compassion.
2. Soften the tone/volume of communication.
3. Slow down the pace of communications.
4. Show an interest in them. Draw out their feelings.

Managing the Patient Trait

1. Use written policies and procedures.
2. Lower your intensity.
3. Build trust and create a safe environment so they will share their true feelings.
4. Provide training and support when dealing with change.

Patient people must remember that a sensitive nature and patient style does not always yield the best results. Toughen up, speed up, and speak up.

DNA Behavior Style Groups with the Patient Trait

Note: See Appendix D for more information on the ten Style Groups.

- Relationship Builder
- Community Builder
- Facilitator
- Reflective Thinker (sometimes)

ENDNOTES

1   For a person scoring in the Patient range, this need for patience and stability may be somewhat offset or modified when accompanied by the Outgoing Trait, which likes to move quickly and randomly. For example, someone who also has Outgoing traits will enjoy a faster pace and more change than a Patient person who is also Reserved.

2   "When something is wrong, those who care make it right." *USA Today*, Page 11E, September 12, 2000.

3   "Joe Torre's Secret for Success," CBSNEWS.com, December 13, 1999.

4   "Heading for Home," *60 Minutes II*, May 8, 2001 and CBSNEWS.com, New York, May 8, 2001.

CHAPTER 11 ▶ THE FAST-PACED TRAIT

FACTOR 3: LEFT-SIDE TRAIT

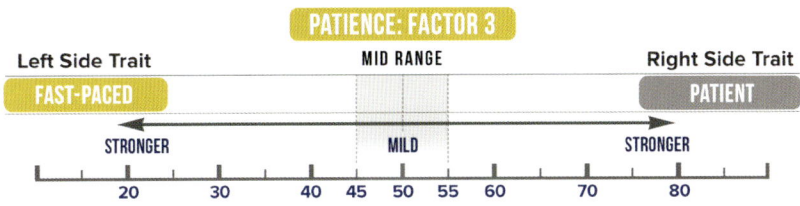

If everything seems under control,
you're just not going fast enough.

—Mario Andretti

As we have seen with the first two Factors and will be true on all the Factors, the left side characteristics are the mirror opposite of the right side. The Patience Factor is one of the most defining and impactful in terms of relationships. As mentioned earlier, the right side needs patience, stability, harmony, and low intensity. Well, guess what? The left side, Fast-Paced folks love speed, intensity, and challenge to the point of creating conflict. While the Patient side is sensitive to feelings, the Fast-Paced often has little or no radar for feelings and could be crushing others emotionally under their heels and never even know it. Let's examine the talents of the Fast-Paced Trait.

Fast-Paced – Strengths and Struggles

 **Strengths in Leadership**

1. Will challenge others, not afraid of conflict
2. Logical, objective and detached
3. Action-oriented, work at a fast pace and respond quickly
4. Comfortable making difficult decisions
5. Welcome change, stir the pot

 **Struggles in Leadership**

1. May not notice others' feelings
2. Can be judgmental and critical
3. May lack patience and speak harshly
4. May tend toward overactivity
5. Prone to discontent

Fast-Paced Trait examples

Fast-Paced people are usually easy to spot because they don't hesitate to tell it like it is. It's easy to find public figures that seem to be perfectly comfortable doing just that. We've seen this in Presidents Teddy Roosevelt, Harry Truman, Lyndon Johnson, and Donald Trump. Other government leaders who exhibit this Trait are Senators John McCain and Chuck Schumer; former British PM Margaret Thatcher; generals George Patton and Norman Schwarzkopf; personalities like Ted Turner and Dr. Phil McGraw; media hosts Wolf Blitzer and Laura Ingraham; basketball player Charles Barkley, golfer Jack Nicklaus, coaches Nick Saban and Bill Belichick. They all have strongly held views and don't hesitate to confront those with whom they disagree. Let's analyze them more closely.

Fast-Paced – Leadership Strengths

Logical, detached, make the difficult calls, and tough-minded

This left-side group typically operates unfettered by feelings and makes decisions primarily on a logical, rational and objective basis.[1] This can be a very important talent in many situations because the best long-term course of action may be painful and unpopular at the time.

The reality is that leaders, teammates, coaches, and parents face difficult and sometimes unpopular decisions every day. Whether it's initiating a corporate layoff, telling someone you can't do what they want you to do or employing "tough love" with a teen, the Fast-Paced person has the edge in natural talents for handling these difficult decisions.

Confront easily, comfortable in conflict, and thick-skinned

Fast-Paced people are naturally wired to confront wrongs in order to correct them before they get very far off track. The story of our friend Gary's young daughter illustrates this very well. Gary is a very Patient person who can just ignore many of the little irritants of everyday life. But his daughter is very different, and this was evident at an early age.

Gary's family had stopped at a fast food store to pick up some burgers. As they were discussing the order, his daughter said, "Dad I don't want any mustard." In an effort to teach her how to order, he suggested she tell the person taking the order. She turned and looked him straight in the eyes and said: "No mustard." They took their burgers and went back to the car. As Gary was about to drive off, he heard the back-seat car door open and saw his daughter walking back into the store. When he caught up with her, she was confronting the person behind the counter for putting mustard on her burger. As Gary extracted his six-year-old daughter from the store he asked, "What were you doing?" and she replied, "Dad, they have to learn."

Now fast-forward 22 years later. Gary's at his daughter's home and she has just come home with the groceries that included a box of doughnuts. Opening them, she expressed her disappointment at their size and freshness. Using the toll-free number on the box, she immediately called the headquarters of this nationally-known brand to register her strong complaints. When she hung up the telephone and looked over at Gary, she said, "Dad, they have to learn." The light clicked in Gary's head, and he flashed back to the "no mustard" incident of her childhood. His daughter, of course, did not remember that event, but it was clear that her natural DNA had not changed a bit. She still "had to confront" an obvious wrong.

Now that you are getting the picture of these Fast-Paced Traits, let's go a bit further in looking at how they can be comfortable in conflict. Several years ago, Lee was conducting a team session for an auditing firm. During the discussions, two people who had scored in the Fast-Paced range (one male and one female) got in a debate about how the work was scheduled. Their voices got louder, and their jaws tightened a bit, but it was obvious that this was normal behavior for them. In fact, they seemed to be enjoying it so much that they failed to notice how uncomfortable their Patient teammates were with their game of conflict. This exchange evidently was beneficial because the man later told Lee that their relationship had improved steadily since that day. A good debate increased their trust and respect for each other.

Fast-paced, action-oriented, and promotes change

Fast-Paced people thrive on quick action and change. They walk fast, they usually talk fast, they think and respond fast, and they definitely want fast action. When they have to sit still, they are like a coiled spring just waiting for an opportunity to uncoil and get moving again. We've made observations about their body language. In one-on-one situations, about seven minutes seems to be the threshold when they start to get noticeably restless. So, if you are presenting to them, keep it moving and keep it short.

This group also excels in rapidly changing situations. They can quickly shift their focus from one priority to another, a talent that helps them excel in chaos.

The Fast-Paced are energized by change. They have a penchant for action and a low threshold for routine. They quickly adopt new systems and adapt to situations and then move on as though the old never existed. Their drive for change is so strong that it can be difficult for them to do something the same way twice. When driving regularly to the same place, they may take a different route. If speaking, they will make some changes in their presentation each time they give it.

Their comfort with and even preference for change is likely rooted in their love of a challenge. Is there a problem to solve, a change needed, an obstacle in their way? Not to worry! They are attracted to a challenge like a bear is to honey. They respond aggressively when someone lays out a problem. Expressions like, "That's probably too difficult" or "No one has ever done it" pull them in like a magnet.

 ## Fast-Paced – Leadership Struggles

Insensitive, can seem cold-hearted, and deny feelings

As you have probably guessed by now, the Fast-Paced people don't hide their struggles very well and unfortunately, they often don't care because they are so keen on following logic. This group can be very insensitive to others and never know it. Also, most Fast-Paced people have Take Charge Traits and, when you put these two Traits together, their struggles compound.

When Fast-Paced/Take Charge individuals are really focused on their results, they may unknowingly work people until they drop. It was said that "[General] MacArthur seemed unaware of the fact that he caused inconvenience to others."[2] Eisenhower said of him, "MacArthur could never see another sun, or even a moon for that matter, in the heavens as long as he was the sun."[3] This speaks to *struggles* from his Take Charge (high ego) and Fast-Paced (insensitive) nature.

Since they don't naturally think about feelings, Fast-Paced people sometimes treat people in a very cold-hearted fashion, as though they were inanimate objects. Corporate America is rife with horror stories of senior leaders and CEO's who treat people like sticks of wood—they grind them into sawdust and toss them on the heap out back.

We had the challenge of coaching a brilliant COO who was a great systems implementer and business problem fixer. The solutions brought to the table were very orderly and executed in a straightforward manner. The problem with this hardline, rational approach was that it was out of balance—all results and no concern or support for people. Eventually, morale crashed and performance fell. With no bad intention, the team culture was destroyed as the strictly rational approach killed the team relationships. Ultimately, the team productivity faltered because no one was willing to bring any problems forward. Fear kept them from adapting to meet the needs of client cases that did not fit the rigid process.

Judgmental and critical

The Fast-Paced group seems to have a radar for identifying the *struggles* of other people, and they can easily fall into the trap of "just being honest." Their impatience and their low tolerance for being irritated, along with their confronting nature, make it easy for them to bring out the "truth" by judging and criticizing. The Fast-Paced folks may think they are just being honest and "telling it like it is," but this candor can be very discouraging and even painful to their teammates.

Not only does this critical nature affect teams at work, but it can also lead to serious problems at home. We all need encouragement at a much greater ratio than criticism, and home should be a place where everyone gets much more positive than negative feedback. Unfortunately, the self-confidence of many children is undermined by too much criticism from highly Fast-Paced (Take Charge/controlling) parents. This same problem can be the cause of strife between mates who actually care for each other very much.

Impatient, restless, and too many changes

At some point, impatience with others also can send a strong message that "I'm more important than you." When you think about it, showing patience is in effect giving up some control and deferring to others. The Fast-Paced and Take Charge person is likely to exhibit behaviors that say, "By being patient, I'm allowing you to control me and I don't like that. I've got to get back on my own agenda—so your time is up." The solution to impatience usually comes from a willingness to *give* to the other person rather than *take* for yourself. It's as simple as that, but to actually offer patience can be about as difficult as re-directing a river.

As in most behavior adaptations, our values and concern for others must override our natural DNA. Intentions are good, but without internal motivation, they tend to fall by the wayside.

The struggle of being restless and wanting to always change things can put enormous stress on others. As we have already seen, the right side of this Factor does not adapt to change easily. Beyond that, change generates extra work and additional problems that can lead to chaos. Fast-Paced people can actually enjoy a crisis and unconsciously this may be part of their desire to make changes, but change does not come without a price. And so, the solution really is to step back and count the cost. Are the real costs of the changes worth the expected benefits? If not, maybe it's a good time just to let the urge to change pass.

Whom do you know with the Fast-Paced Trait?

1. _____

2. _____

3. _____

Quick Coach Notes

Ideal Work Environment

Give them problems to solve, and freedom to work at a fast pace. They thrive on change and usually do well in crises. Since they are naturally confrontational, make sure they have significant challenges to absorb their combative energy.

Connecting with the Fast-Paced Trait

1. Remember their need for quick action and logic.
2. Anticipate their immediate responses and quick fixes.
3. Speak/move at a quick pace.
4. Use logic, summaries, and key points.

Managing the Fast-Paced Trait

1. Expect them to confront you to provide logic. Don't be turned off by their pushbacks. They often push back/fight you in order to understand your logic and learn.
2. Help them understand that they must respond to others based on others' behavior style. And especially, they must learn to tone it down with their Patient opposites.
3. Provide them a big challenge. Since they hate boring work and routines, make those a challenge.
4. Be very clear and be direct. They have strong opinions and subtlety typically will not work with them.

Fast-Paced detached people should remember that people are not machines; they do have feelings, and feelings are important. Also, quick action is not always the best policy or, as General Eisenhower often said, "Don't hurry to a mistake." Soften up, show more patience and kindness, and don't be so critical.

DNA Behavior **Style Groups with the Fast-Paced Trait**
Note: See Appendix D for more information on the ten Style Groups.

- Initiator
- Influencer
- Strategist
- Stylish Thinker (sometimes)
- Engager (sometimes)

Patient, Fast-Paced, and Mid-Range—we need them all

The Patient and the Fast-Paced people should learn to honor those who are different, even when their ways seem so irritating. Remember, to turn the coin over and focus on the person's **strengths**. Learn to value the unique attributes of the other and try to adapt their own behaviors rather than trying to change someone else's.

Learn to recognize and encourage the unique talents of your opposite side teammates. Understand their needs and expect their **struggles**. Let them know how much you value them because of who they are and don't be offended when they act like themselves instead of you.

— Self-Assessment Application —

Based on the behavioral Traits described in this chapter and the previous chapter (or based on your actual **DNA Behavior** assessment results), what is your default **DNA Behavior**? Is it more right side, left side, or clearly in the middle?

Place an "x" on the "Fast-Paced to Patient" scale below that best describes you. You may also use the free Self-Assessment Worksheet to capture your strengths and struggles for this factor. Download a copy at www.LeadershipBehaviorDNA.com/Book.

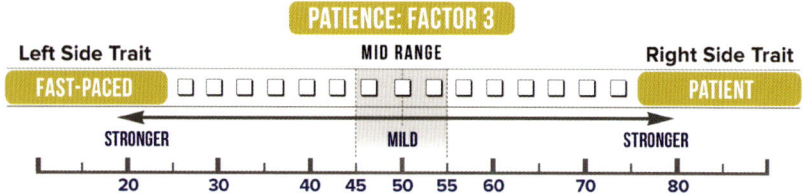

1. Looking back at the **strengths** and **struggles** for this Trait,
   a. What are some of your key **strengths** for leadership?
   b. Looking at your **struggles**, what is one area where you could adapt and become a better leader?
2. How can you apply the *Quick Coach Notes*?
3. With whom will you share this information for more insight, discussion, and accountability?

Calculate your specific Factor score by taking the *Leadership Behavior DNA* **assessment. It only takes 10 minutes to receive your personal report.**

Learn more at www.LeadershipBehaviorDNA.com/Book

ENDNOTES

1   Remember that they may not always be objective about themselves, family members, and certain others with whom they have special relationships.
2   *IKE THE SOLDIER As They Knew Him*, Merle Miller, page 26, Perigee Books (The Putnam Publishing Group), 1988, New York NY.
3   Ibid.

THE STRUCTURE FACTOR

This Factor indicates a person's need for structure, concern for details, and desire to prepare.

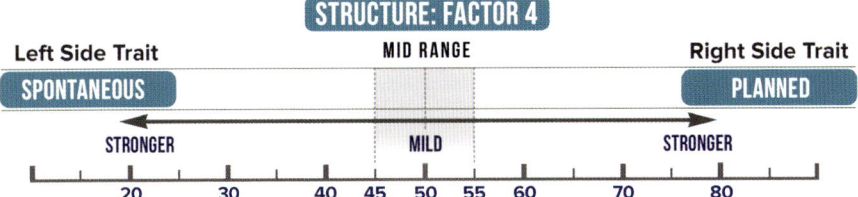

STRUCTURE: FACTOR 4

Left Side Trait	MID RANGE	Right Side Trait
SPONTANEOUS		PLANNED

STRONGER   MILD   STRONGER

20   30   40 45 50 55 60   70   80

Spontaneous Leader Qualities

[Motivated to be Free-flowing]

- Generalize, like big picture
- Spur-of-the-moment
- Flexible, respond quickly
- Verbal communication
- Instinctive approach

Planned Leader Qualities

[Motivated to be Orderly]

- Like specifics
- Structured, organized
- Task-focused, rigid
- Written guidance
- Analytical approach

— The Structure Factor —

This Factor provides insights into how a person handles details, accuracy, organization, and preparation for upcoming events. The Planned (right side) of the continuum is naturally motivated to organize, plan, schedule, and manage details to "get it right." The Spontaneous (left side) prefers to achieve "ballpark" accuracy and then move on to something else. They are naturally motivated by freedom and flexibility to "read and react" to the situation at hand and will typically resist the confining nature of Structure.

What about the Mid-Range?

Obviously, there are significant advantages for both Planned and Spontaneous personalities, depending on the role, task, or job. Mid-range folks are able to adapt in either direction as needed. As with all the DNA Behavior Factors, both the left- and right-side Traits are critical to organizational success, and both have strengths and struggles. Try to see them as of equal value and avoid value judgments on what is good or bad.

CHAPTER 12 ▶ THE PLANNED TRAIT

FACTOR 4: RIGHT-SIDE TRAIT

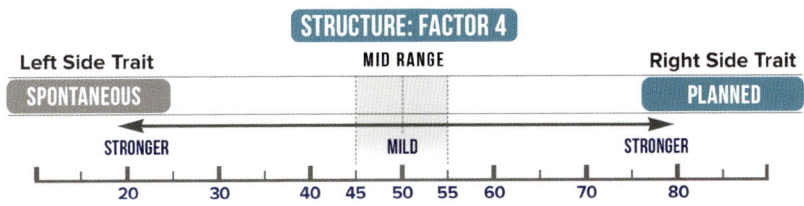

By failing to prepare, you are preparing to fail.

—Benjamin Franklin

Planned people naturally operate from a structured approach because it's their default motivation to be organized, prepared, and accurate. Most people aspire to have these attributes. But consider whether or not you are a true Planned person who is *naturally compelled* toward the **strengths** and **struggles** below. Or, due to the demands of work and culture have you overcome your spontaneous nature in order to be ordered and detailed?

Planned – Strengths and Struggles

 **Strengths in Leadership**

1. Organized, scheduled, and prepared
2. Accurate and exact with detail
3. Systematic, develop processes/procedures
4. Conduct research and analyze before deciding
5. Persistent to achieve goals, get closure

 **Struggles in Leadership**

1. Tend to be inflexible or too fixed
2. Perfectionistic to mistakes, too picky
3. May be overly reliant on procedures/rules
4. Can overprepare and sacrifice timeliness
5. Difficulty with improvising

Planned Trait examples

Well known examples from this group include: Prominent figures Mitt Romney, Meghan Kelly, Condoleezza Rice, Henry Kissinger, George Will, Stephen Spielberg; Presidents Richard Nixon, Jimmy Carter, Thomas Jefferson; military—Generals Douglas MacArthur and Omar Bradley, business—Warren Buffett, Mary Barra; sports figures—Jack Nicklaus, Greg Maddux, Nick Saban, Mike Krzyzewski.

 ## Planned – Leadership Strengths

Accurate, good with details, focused, and thorough

A key motif that runs through all the Planned *strengths* is the desire—even compulsion—to "get it right" the first time—none of this trial and error stuff for them. Precision and accuracy are paramount in their work.

The Planned group's standards of perfection do not go unnoticed, for they extend to nearly every area of their work and life. Even when they suspect something is probably true, they want to prove it before they believe it. Realistically, some that are reading this now are probably thinking: "How do these authors know this is true? I wonder if they can prove it."[1]

Since Planned people respect accuracy, they naturally check things out to understand why things are the way they are. This need to "know that they know," and asking the "why?" question is fundamental to career fields that require extensive analysis and research, including career fields like engineering, accounting, and areas of science and technology. It's easy to value this talent because so many processes rely on their precision. Think about the details required to send a payload into space orbit or design and maintain electrical distribution systems and controls that provide electricity, heating and cooling to a skyscraper. The reliability of those systems is beyond imagination. Clearly, Planned personalities shine where precision and reliability are required.

This group presses for specifics rather than generalities. This point was illustrated in an Amazing Traits Exercise Lee conducted with a group of relatively spontaneous sales managers, meeting off-site with their more structured operations/staff counterparts. The goal was to build trust between the opposite styles and improve communication to enhance cohesion.

Not surprisingly, the mostly Outgoing/Spontaneous salespeople sat on one side of the table and the mostly Reserved/Planned operations staff folks sat on the other side. In describing how they liked to be communicated with, the spokesperson for the Planned group shared their first item as "Be specific." He then leaned across the table, glared at his Spontaneous sales buddies and with much energy and animation proclaimed, "I can't work with a lot of general 'pie in the sky' stuff. I need specifics to do my job." It was the perfect message delivered in the perfect way for their audience.

A Planned person also likes discipline, along with rules and procedures to guide themselves and others. A systematic environment allows them to focus their attention on one thing at a time. They are very good at resisting distractions or attempts by others to pull them away from the task at hand. They value thoroughness tying up every loose end and accounting for every detail in a project to ensure accuracy.

Sometimes Planned people resemble the Take Charge[2] group because they can be very determined and even controlling when it comes to getting results. They have been known to walk right over someone who is blocking their way to achieving a goal involving accuracy. The difference is that afterward, they will give you back the keys to the shop. Their motivation is not to be in control; rather, they are just highly focused and insistent when it comes to getting results accurately and achieving closure on their goals.

Organized, planned, scheduled, systematic, and prepared

We recently asked participants in another Amazing Traits Exercise to think of an animal that represented their Trait. One of the highly structured and planned people said that his animal icon would be a kangaroo. Of course, the team wanted to know why, and he answered, "I like the idea of having a pouch to keep all my stuff organized." That says a lot about this group because they get uneasy with the disorder. In fact, a key **strength** of Planned people is that they promptly put things back in place, knowing they are saving time later. "Everything has a place and everything in its place" is their motto.

Planned people also like to prepare ahead of time for upcoming events or responsibilities. Waiting until the last minute may not leave enough time to "get it right." Everyone likes to be prepared, but this group takes it very seriously and will start early to make sure they are ready.

While leading a workshop at the SHRM (Society of Human Resource Managers) southeast convention on the subject of managing differences, Lee asked for a volunteer from each side of this continuum to share some insights. A young lady who said she was on the spontaneous and highly unstructured side related her experience of traveling to Europe with her best friend who was her opposite in this Factor.

She said that her idea of a good vacation was to have a very general plan but no firm schedules. She preferred the spur-of-the-moment lifestyle that offered adventure and flexibility of just going with the flow as the day developed. Her Planned friend, of course, was just the opposite and wanted definite plans for each day. They agreed to compromise and to do two days of scheduled and planned activities followed by two days of just "winging it." She said it was a great trip, and they both benefited by seeing from a new and more positive viewpoint, the benefits of the way the other side lived.

Planned people typically have an advantage in academic institutions because of their talents. Research at the Johnson-O'Conner Institute shows that people who have high graphoria (the ability to keep neat notes, homework, and records) also do better than their Trait opposites in large university classes. Their natural organizational skills and drive to prepare to give them an edge in these impersonal, self-directed environments. Spontaneous persons (typically low in graphoria) tend to achieve better results in smaller classes where there is more instructor interaction and more personal accountability for homework (typically they are Outgoing and have a strong desire to impress others.)

Planned people have a strong natural gift for creating systems. More than any other group, they are willing to invest the time and effort up front to develop plans, procedures, and processes that can be used over and over again. Since they hate to re-invent the wheel, they develop a system for something that is going to be repetitive.

Analytical, conduct research, and good with facts and data

These folks are most comfortable and productive when they can follow their own natural process (system) to research and collect facts, and then analyze them before reaching conclusions. A good mental picture is to imagine someone taking a gadget apart, examining each piece, and then carefully re-assembling it. When they get finished, they understand it, they know it's put together well, that it is accurate, solid, and well thought out. Only when they have been through these steps are, they comfortable putting their stamp of approval on the decision or finished product.

Careful, disciplined, neat, and diplomatic

The need to do things correctly carries over into every area of their lives. They are very particular with their things; they keep their desk drawers neat and they are particular with equipment. This accounts for some of their territorial nature and explains why they don't like to loan out or share their "stuff."

They typically lead disciplined lifestyles. If a picture is crooked, they notice it and straighten it immediately. They ensure that the yard is mowed perfectly and that the mower and car oil is changed on schedule. If you look in their freezer, you are likely to find that all the packages are arranged by type and all the labels are in the same direction, so they can be read easily. **For truly Planned people, there is a "right" way to do everything, and they typically provide the criteria for what constitutes "right."**

Planned – Leadership Struggles

Perfectionistic, too picky, have unrealistic standards, and self-critical

Often the *struggles* for each Trait can come from the over-extension of *strengths*, as evidenced here. With standards and expectation so high, Planned folks can become preoccupied with reaching a level of accuracy that is unreasonable. They need to distinguish between areas where 100% accuracy can mean life or death (like nuclear materials and brain surgery) versus the mundane details of everyday living.

Interestingly, these folks can be the hardest on themselves of any of the behavioral Trait groups, often undermining their self-confidence. In observing Amazing Traits Exercises, we've noticed that Planned personalities often develop their list of *struggles* before addressing their *strengths*.

Most Planned people could improve their performance, relationships, and health by realizing that personal perfection is an unattainable goal. Likewise, professional perfection is rarely required. Yes, moon shots and brain surgery require the extra work to reach a 99.999 percent accuracy rate, but most things don't.

Rigid, over-prepared but lack confidence, and overly rely on procedures

The downside of being highly organized is often a lack of flexibility. Systems and schedules are like fences; they are both helpful and problematic. They provide security, but they also can limit those who are inside if the gates are not open. Typically, highly organized and scheduled people do not like to open the gates and venture from the secure boundaries of their schedules, plans, habit patterns, rules, and procedures.

Many in this group tend to trust their fortress of plans and preparation more than themselves when it comes to execution.[3] **We all know that failing to plan means planning to fail; how-**

ever, there comes a time to step out on that preparation and act with confidence.

Paralyzed by analysis, and slow to decide

The Planned group is often described by the process of "ready, ready, ready, aim, aim, aim." Before they fire, they want every possible piece of information to make sure they fire perfectly the first time. Thus, more facts and data with detailed analysis can seem as important as actually doing something; and, for this group, it's often more comfortable and less risky. As General Colin Powell, retired Chairman of the Joint Chiefs of Staff said, "Procrastination in the name of reducing risk actually increases risk."[4]

In today's world where entrepreneurs abound, it will be those that can structure and develop a process that can actually make it as a true business organization. So Planned people have an edge in making that leap. However, we are regularly coaching these leaders that they cannot allow their Planned *strength* to become a *struggle* characterized by stubbornness and a refusal to change a strategy or key process when it is needed. Of course, the larger the business gets the harder it will be to make structural changes and see through all the impacts, which is why a planned leader will slow things down. Whereas a more spontaneous leader would, with the flick of a finger, expect everyone to jump onto the new path because he or she knows it is intuitively right. So, while Planned characteristics are needed for organizational sustainability, that leader has to also keep in touch with changing technologies and customer needs to anticipate course changes.

Unfortunately, there is another component that we all have to deal with and that is time. **A key to success is learning that a good solution timely executed is far superior to a perfect solution executed too late.** Thus, the challenge for the Planned person is to realize when enough preparation is sufficient. The perspective of an opposite-side teammate can be extremely valuable in bringing a balancing viewpoint.

Whom do you know with the Planned Trait?

1. _____

2. _____

3. _____

Quick Coach Notes

Ideal Work Environment

Highly Planned people operate at their best in situations that are neat, orderly, and systematic. They thrive where accuracy and details are important to their success and are valued accordingly.

Connecting with the Planned Trait

1. Consider and value their need for accuracy and detail.
2. Remember their need to analyze.
3. Present specifics—swayed by facts, figures, data, not emotional appeals.
4. Honor their need for structure, schedules, and rules.

Managing the Planned Trait

1. Look for ways to prepare them for change. Show them the plan—or get them involved in developing the plan.
2. Agree on expectations and give them time to work.
3. Remember their need to "get it right" the first time and help them understand that some things don't have to be perfect.
4. Correct with compassion.

Planned people should remember that perfection is not always needed and that rules and schedules are to enhance success not preclude it. Analyze but don't get paralyzed in the process. Loosen up.

DNA Behavior Style Groups with the Planned Trait

Note: See Appendix D for more information on the ten Style Groups.

- Reflective Thinker
- Strategist
- Stylish Thinker
- Relationship Builder (sometimes)

145

ENDNOTES

1 We anticipated your question. Our assessment development has always been managed by IO and Applied Psychologists who specialize in academic research and statistical validation of measurements of human behavior. See Appendix E. Additionally, the concepts shared in this book have been verified through working with thousands of individuals and hundreds of teams over more than 25 years.

2 Blends of Factors are common, so a person could be both Take Charge and Planned. As shown in the Strategist style group in Appendix D, this combination is highly result-oriented.

3 This is typically not true for Planned/structured people who also score on the Take Charge side of Factor 1. Their confidence can override these concerns.

4 *A Primer on Leadership*, Lesson 15, General Colin Powell, Retired Chairman of the Joint Chiefs of Staff.

CHAPTER 13 ▶ THE SPONTANEOUS TRAIT

FACTOR 4: LEFT-SIDE TRAIT

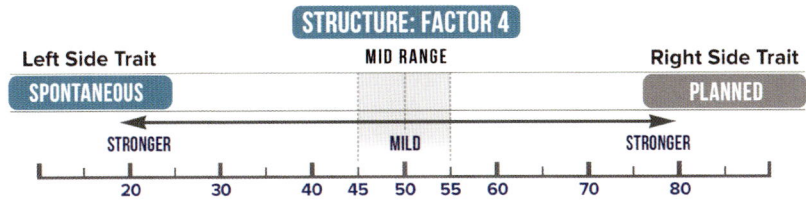

Spontaneity is everything to me, working without a net.

—Regis Philbin

Spontaneous best describes the naturally motivated behaviors of this group. These folks do their very best work when they are operating from a generalist perspective and using their "gut" instincts. When saturated in detail, their effectiveness and efficiency slow down like molasses on a cold day. With that general understanding, let's look at their **strengths** and **struggles**.

Spontaneous – Strengths and Struggles

 **Strengths in Leadership**

 **Struggles in Leadership**

1. Instinctual, improvise on the spot
2. Can operate spontaneously and without procedures
3. Give quick and reasonable assessments
4. Work with broad concepts
5. Versatile; can adapt easily

1. Prone to lack of organization
2. May overlook important details
3. May overcommit and not follow through
4. Can be underprepared and overconfident
5. Can discount rules or agenda

Spontaneous Trait examples

Famous people who exhibit the Spontaneous Trait include media personalities: Oprah Winfrey, Goldie Hawn, Billy Crystal, Bette Midler, Will Smith, Mary Tyler Moore, Ryan Seacrest, Bono, and the Ferris Bueller character. Political leaders in this group include Presidents Teddy Roosevelt, Dwight Eisenhower, and Prime Minister Tony Blair. Military leaders: Generals Norman Schwarzkopf and George Patton; sports personalities Terry Bradshaw, Bret Favre, Dion Sanders, and NASCAR's Darrell Waltrip.

Those with the Outgoing Trait are also likely to be Spontaneous so the two Traits do tend to overlap in some areas. (These two statistically have a positive correlation as do their Planned opposites with the Reserved Trait.)[1]

 ## Spontaneous – Leadership Strengths

Spontaneous, impromptu, have on-the-spot appraisals/decisions, and start quickly

All the Traits have brains that are wired uniquely, but nowhere is it more obvious than when comparing the Spontaneous Trait to its Planned opposite. The Spontaneous brain scans constantly, collecting massive data inputs from their environment through visual, audio, and other stimuli. This information is not just put away in some filing cabinet in the basement of the brain. Instead, it is somehow pictured and experienced in a way that leaves a marker on it, as it is written (randomly) to the brain's memory. This memory marker provides a hook for a quick retrieval system. The effect of this process is that spontaneous people are able to access their mental files and almost instantaneously synthesize relevant information for a quick response. Granted, their answers may not be perfect, but they are usually in the ballpark. Their off-the-cuff appraisals can be amazingly close because they have the appropriate data stored for ready access.

This Spontaneous retrieval system seems to work well for this group because, as we'll see later, they dislike and **struggle** significantly with organizing and retrieving pieces of paper, files, and such. Carrying the previous analogy further, their minds seem to work better with a random storage system in the brain than a linear physical one like a filing cabinet. How would they remember which subject it was filed under?

This ability to extract stored data and synthesize it on the fly into a plan, decision, or immediate action is a very important **strength** for those who work in highly dynamic fields like sales, customer support, or crisis management activities. The expression "on the fly" describes the way these people operate. Their conscious thinking doesn't stay very long in one place; rather, it's on the move and this enables them to cover a lot of ground in a hurry.

Another similar expression that is often used to describe this group is: "they like to wing it," and this can be the way they do some of their best work. It's as though the excitement, challenge, adventure, and danger of the moment puts them in a near crisis situation, which helps them bring their thoughts into a clearer focus.

For this reason, spontaneous people are usually at their best when there is some outside stress or pressing deadline that forces them to work quickly. More than likely those people were the ones you knew at school who did most of their work at the last minute. For them, it just would not come together until there was a crisis, but then the juices flowed, and the work got done.

Generalists, flexible, versatile, and instinctive

Spontaneous people typically see and think in general terms rather than specifics. Like a wide-angle photograph taken at high altitude, they naturally see the breadth of the landscape rather than the details. Their receptors capture the prominent features and quickly assimilate them into broad pictures and concepts. This enables them to "catch on" quickly to general ideas without knowing all the details.

We often refer to Oprah Winfrey as a prototype to explain the **strengths** of the Spontaneous Trait group. If you've watched her program, you know that her talents for spontaneity and flexibility really help make the show. She can be in the middle of a discussion but when her radar picks up someone in the audience that is a good target of opportunity she engages them in a flash.

Oprah's natural penchant to operate on instinct is prominent in her business endeavors as well. An article in *Fortune* magazine highlighted her success and pointed out that Oprah isn't bothered by the fact that she doesn't know how to read a balance sheet. She seems quite happy to delegate the details and manage her reported billion-dollar fortune from a big picture perspective. The article also reported that her idea of due diligence is to ask one question: "Can I trust you?"[2] Doesn't that sound like someone who trusts herself and her own instincts?

Unconventional, and respond candidly and openly

Watching spontaneous people like Oprah, Terry Bradshaw, and Dion Sanders, you notice that they are their own person. They say what they think, and they don't take themselves too seriously. These same characteristics often come up in our Amazing Traits Exercise during team sessions.

In one Amazing Traits exercise there were four ladies that made up the Spontaneous group. In telling about their strengths and struggles, one said, "We like to fly by the seat of the pants." This old aviation expression originally meant flying by instinct and the feel of G-forces in your seat (rather than reference precise gauges in the cockpit). They went on to say how they had attended an office costume party wearing a set of homemade wings strapped to their bottoms. Their story was a riot, and it really gave us great insights into the amazing unconventional nature of the Spontaneous Trait.

"Out of the box" thinking and expression is often the norm for spontaneous people because they rarely allow themselves to be limited. Rules, lines, procedures, and protocol are not the final word for these folks. They use them when necessary, but when their instincts are confirmed, they are likely to ignore them entirely. General Patton was a stickler for discipline, and followed orders and enforced regulations most of the time. But when the rules conflicted with his battlefield judgment, he didn't hesitate to ignore orders and rules if he was willing to take responsibility for the outcome.[3]

Spontaneous – Leadership Struggles

Disorganized, skimp on preparation and then wing it too much

Given the Spontaneous behaviors we've described above, you can imagine that trying to keep up with papers, schedules, and assignments as well as keys, glasses, cell phones, and a myriad of other "things" can be an almost debilitating experience for them.

Have you ever seemed like you were in a dust storm with issues and projects swirling, leaving commitments forgotten? This is what happens when you have a highly Spontaneous leader. We worked with a team that was chaotic because the leader was always jumping from one thing to the next and often quite disorganized. On the other side, his *strengths* were being dynamic, making in-the-moment decisions using his intuition and keeping things exciting. Never a dull moment, but it works better when there is a second-in-command who knows how to deal with the erratic swirl of the Spontaneous leader.

Generally, Spontaneous people have very good intentions of storing or situating their things in some logical order, so they can find them later. Unfortunately, they often neglect the tedious work of really organizing them, because they are in too much of a hurry to stop and "do it right the first time." Often something else attracts their attention and their mind launches into a different direction. Even when they do organize, they may not be able to remember which folder it's in or which organizational scheme they used.

Today's fast-paced environment has some good and bad news for spontaneous people. The good news is that there are a lot of good tools and training available to help with organization. The bad news is that there is a lot more to organize—more information, more meetings, more phone calls, and more e-mails—and it's coming at an increasing rate. The best advice for these folks is to get training, work at it, use good technology, and enlist highly organized teammates and associates to assist.

Detailed preparation is also a challenge for this group because it's very difficult for them to sit down and do the work. They procrastinate because it requires detailed, focused, internal processing that can be difficult—even painful for them. Their overly optimistic appraisal of how much work it's going to take also causes problems. Since they do their best work in the crisis mode, they may neglect important preparation until it's too late. The results are predictable: *They are more susceptible to incomplete assignments, missed deadlines, and often just leaving something unfinished and moving on to the next exciting thing.*

To overcome this **struggle**, here are two antidotes. First, they should step back and look at managing themselves as though they were their own boss (which of course they are). Or, if that doesn't work, then they need a coach who can hold them accountable to accomplish their preparation in a timely manner. The coach could be a good supervisor or manager. Most highly efficient executives have an assistant to help them with organization and details—and especially the Spontaneous ones.

Overlook details, impulsive, get distracted, lose focus, and don't finish

As you probably know a growing number in our population have now been diagnosed with Attention Deficit Disorder. However, an even larger number have Attention to "Detail" Disorder, and many in the Spontaneous group often fall into this category.

If you really want to see why Spontaneous people avoid details, just watch their body language when they are trying to absorb them. Their random-access memory system is not geared up to absorb and file those little pieces of data. When the minutia is streaming toward them, you can almost see a fog descend over their countenance. Very quickly, the details start deflecting off their heads.

The best thing they can do is just say, "Let's start with the big picture so I can connect the dots. Then we can fill in the details as I need them."

The **struggle** to gain focus and avoid distractions will always be a challenge for most Spontaneous people. At the same time, it offers them an area of great potential for personal and professional growth.

Developing mental discipline and learning to live by the mantra of focus, focus, focus can be a big help. Likewise, learning to prioritize tasks in order to bring projects to closure will be important.

To the highly structured Planned person, this lack of attention to detail can seem like a character flaw but, in reality, it's just the by-product of the natural talents of the Spontaneous. Recall that we have been very upfront in listing some difficult *struggles* for all the Trait groups. Rather than judge *struggles* as wrong or bad, we just need to see them as part of the package, turn the coin over and accept people for who they are, and learn to compensate for them.

Whom do you know with the Spontaneous Trait?

1. _____

2. _____

3. _____

Quick Coach Notes

Ideal Work Environment

Spontaneous people do best in environments that offer flexibility and on-the-spot responses. They need situations that allow them to work with broad concepts in impromptu settings. Most importantly, their work should involve a minimum of detailed and structured assignments.

Connecting with the Spontaneous Trait

1. Allow them plenty of freedom and flexibility.
2. Show/tell them the "big" picture/idea.
3. Minimize complexity and details.
4. Use verbal communications with examples and graphics.

Managing the Spontaneous Trait

5. Expect/encourage their out-of-the-box thinking and resist the temptation to prematurely edit their ideas.
6. Affirm their ability to respond quickly with good estimates and reasonable answers, especially to unanticipated questions.
7. Huddle with them often to discuss milestones and progress.
8. Give them a Planned teammate to help them develop systems and processes.

Spontaneous people should remember that details and structure can be powerful allies for success. Advanced planning and preparation will also help. Limit distractions and stay on task until the job is done. Tighten up.

DNA Behavior Style Groups with the Spontaneous Trait
Note: See Appendix D for more information on the ten Style Groups.

- Engager
- Influencer
- Initiator
- Community Builder
- Relationship Builder (sometimes)

Planned, Spontaneous, and Mid-Range— we need them all

In military operations, these two seemingly opposing Traits have shown that success comes from the best of both the left and right sides of the Structure Factor continuum. Staff officers comb through intelligence, weather reports, logistical data, and a hundred other sources in order to analyze all the data and plan in detail for an operation. But once the shooting starts, commanders must synthesize the dynamics of the real battlefield, make on the spot decisions, and quickly execute the best course of action. The same is true in any workplace—especially in the modern era of constant change.

This combination of structure and flexibility—tight and loose—analysis and synthesis, planning and execution, shows the critical importance of teamwork between the Planned and Spontaneous Traits.

— Self-Assessment Application —

Based on the behavioral Traits described in this chapter and the previous chapter (or based on your actual *DNA Behavior* assessment results), what is your default *DNA Behavior*? Is it more right side, left side, or clearly in the middle?

Place an "x" on the "Spontaneous to Planned" scale below that best describes you. You may also use the free Self-Assessment Worksheet to capture your strengths and struggles for this factor. Download a copy at www.LeadershipBehavior DNA.com/Book.

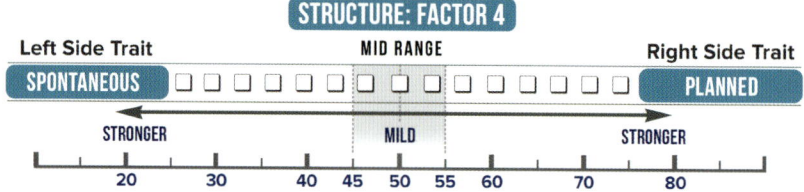

1. Looking back at the *strengths* and *struggles* for this Trait,
   a. What are some of your key *strengths* for leadership?
   b. Looking at your *struggles*, what is one area where you could adapt and become a better leader?
2. How can you apply the *Quick Coach Notes*?
3. With whom will you share this information for more insight, discussion, and accountability?

Calculate your specific Factor score by taking the Leadership Behavior DNA assessment. It only takes 10 minutes to receive your personal report.

Learn more at www.LeadershipBehaviorDNA.com/Book

ENDNOTES

1 For more on factor relationships, see Appendix F.
2 *Fortune,* April 1, 2002, page 60.
3 Taken from *General Patton's Principles for Life and Leadership* by Porter B Williamson, ISBN# 978-0918356093

THE TRUST FACTOR

This Factor indicates a person's ability to naturally trust others.

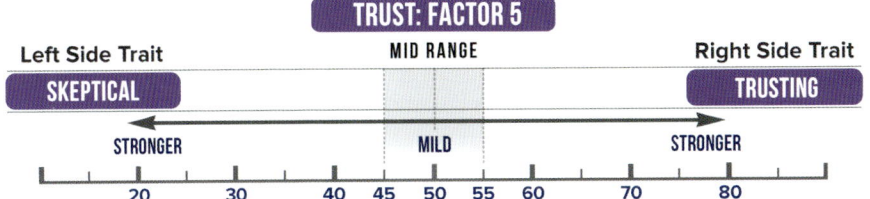

Skeptical Leader Qualities

[Motivated to Doubt]

- Suspicious
- Hesitant, dissenting
- Not easily convinced
- Calculating
- Guarded

Trusting Leader Qualities

[Motivated to Believe]

- Open-minded
- Accepting, agreeing
- Easily satisfied
- Comfortable
- Wishful

157

— The Trust Factor —

Trust is both a noun and a verb and both uses are essential to leadership and teamwork. Definitely, there are times that being skeptical and not giving trust is a very wise choice. However, in leadership and teamwork and in all situations where we are trying to work with others, trust is the essential glue for a cohesive effort. That's why leaders must be very careful and intentional in managing their skepticism and trust. It needs to be a conscious challenge because leaders need to trust as much as possible.

We want to acknowledge upfront that trust arises in many contexts. Our first thoughts are typically related to character/integrity and competence—can I trust you (integrity) and can you do the job (competence). Our ability to trust is also related to our own personal past experiences good and bad. Most of us have been burned along the way and that may have undermined our ability to trust in certain situations. These types of trust are essential, but they are not the primary focus of this chapter. Here we are going to look at another *related* and very important type of trust that affects each of us daily—the trust that comes with our natural DNA. Yes, that's right, we are born with a tendency toward being more trusting or more skeptical.

Since trust is an essential Factor for leadership and teamwork, it would seem that the right-side Trait has an advantage here. But not so fast. Remember there are **strengths** and **struggles** on both sides in every Factor. The truth is that both sides have important talents, and both will have **struggles** that require them to be intentional in situationally adapting their behaviors to respond most effectively as a leader or teammate.

CHAPTER 14 ▶ THE TRUSTING TRAIT

FACTOR 5: RIGHT-SIDE TRAIT

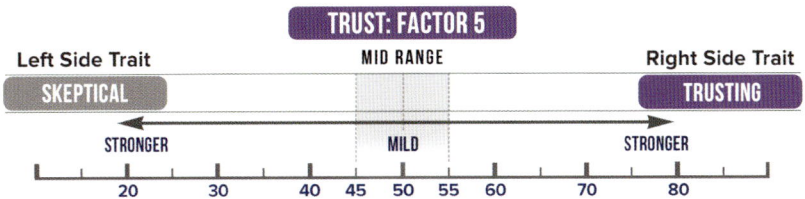

Trust is the glue of life…it's the foundational principle that holds all relationships together.

—Stephen Covey

Those scoring on the Trusting side of this continuum are naturally more open, relationship oriented, and less concerned about power and control. Consequently, they trust more easily. Their nature is to want to trust and to think that others feel the same.

The positive effect of this group is that they easily give freedom to others, allowing them to be themselves, which is essential to workplace engagement. They also are more likely to delegate and assume that others will fulfill their responsibilities without being controlled. As such, they are usually better at developing the talents of others. Let's look deeper.

Trusting – Strengths and Struggles

 **Strengths in Leadership**

1. Approachable
2. Transparent
3. Allow open dialogue
4. Trusting, let people do their jobs
5. Strong relationship-builders

 **Struggles in Leadership**

1. Easily taken advantage of
2. Take people for their word
3. Do not set boundaries
4. Get hurt easily
5. Too forgiving

Trusting Trait examples

Clearly, there are many advantages to the Trusting side of this continuum. Trust is essential for all relationships, and the fact that these folks come by it naturally gives them some real advantages at home and at work. Some well-known examples of this Trait would surely include well-known personalities Mr. Rogers, Al Roker, Oprah Winfrey, Kelly Ripa, Tyra Banks, Jennifer Garner, Halle Berry, and Kanye West, government leaders; Abraham Lincoln, Dwight Eisenhower, Bill Clinton and George H.W. Bush, and Angela Merkel; business leaders, Walt Disney, Indra Nooyi, sports personalities Dion Sanders, Terry Bradshaw, NASCAR driver Darrell Waltrip.

 ## Trusting – Leadership Strengths

Approachable, relaxed, and transparent

Those who share the Trusting Trait are comfortable to be around. They typically openly welcome you into their world, making you feel safe. Very quickly, you will feel trust toward them because they tend to be transparent; you feel they are giving trust to you.

Able to listen with an open mind

They are receptive, almost like: "The door is open, come on into my world; I'm ready to hear your ideas." These Trusting *strengths* make it easy for those with this Trait to get on board quickly to support others' ideas. They start from a perspective of "I don't see why this won't work—how can I help?" You feel the positive energy when they are involved. As our research has shown, even the most skeptical, results-oriented people, who hate "touchy-feely" stuff, admit that a leader who listened had a powerful influence on them and was crucial to their development and success.

> *"The best way to find out if you can trust somebody is to trust them." —Ernest Hemingway*

Instinct is to believe others and naturally have faith in others

These folks are very impressionable, and their first reaction is to believe that others have good intentions and the ability to do what they say they can do. They have a positive outlook about others and assume good will.

> *This attitude of believing in others is very powerful in all relationships. It meets one of the deepest needs that we all have—for someone to believe we have what it takes.*

One of the best leaders Hugh's team has worked with in the past few years is the CEO of a large tech business in the HR space. He is extremely Trusting by nature and has learned to use that talent effectively in building a large organization which grows every year. Leaders who trust will more easily be trusted by others, and they know this is the foundation of strong employee and customer relationships.

Clearly, these Trusting behaviors are crucial for relationships and for influencing others. Mastering them in some way is essential to effective leadership. But like all the other Traits, they have a downside too. Let's take a look.

Trusting – Leadership Struggles

The essence of the struggles for the Trusting Trait is that sometimes they see the world too much through "rose-colored glasses" and trust when trust is not warranted, and then things don't go well. This can hurt the larger team if expected results are not delivered. So now, we have another irony. The people who are the most trusting are likely to be those who are the least focused on results, causing skepticism as to their ability to get results, meet deadlines and keep their promises for what they or their team can do.

Fail to inspect work and too quick to assume that others will meet standards and expectations

There are many situations where the "wishful thinking" of this Trait only leads to disappointment. *To be an effective leader, teammate, or parent requires the ability to recognize when a measure of skepticism is needed; it's part of the "art" of leading.* Over time, two common expressions have carved their way into our culture: "Trust but verify" and "You can expect what you inspect." Having a degree of these as a mantra can help Trusting folks adapt their behaviors to be more effective.

Hesitant to set boundaries and get taken advantage of by others

Though we may want to believe that others have good intentions and behave with the best interests of others in mind, that's not the reality of human nature. **We all need boundaries and someone to enforce them.**

Since it's not natural for this Trait to anticipate shortcomings and see the shadow side of human nature coming, they are often let down, even blindsided. Moreover, enforcing boundaries is typically a *struggle* for trusting people. Expecting that people won't always measure up is not part of their mindset, and they typically have much discomfort in confronting people.

President Lincoln was very trusting by nature. Consequently, he experienced great frustration early in the war because there was little action and not much result on the battlefield. His top generals would not initiate the fight but delayed action in order to "recruit more soldiers," or "get more training," or "rest the horses." He patiently waited, trying to encourage them on, but it did not work. Ultimately, he had to go through three rounds of the firing of generals before he discovered that, in Grant, he had a leader who took the initiative and got results.[1]

Referring back to the very trusting CEO mentioned above, the challenge he faces is that those with a trusting nature can believe what people say too much and not hold them properly accountable. So, this was an area that we coached him in—recognizing that for Trusting leaders the results side of leadership can fall apart if they are not alert, aware, and proactive.

May "forgive and forget" too quickly

By using "forgiveness" in this context, we are really talking about ignoring, or downplaying performance and behavior problems and moving ahead as though nothing bad happened. They can easily kick the can down the road and procrastinate dealing with issues—without consequences or correction that might bring protection for the team and growth for the individual.

We often define courage as doing what is right and needs to be done even though it does not feel natural or safe

The kind of toughness needed in many situations requires this very kind of courage—the courage to lean into the pain of your natural discomfort and do the hard thing.

This Trusting Trait *struggles* with confronting others more than any other, but the reality is we all must be willing to engage with "uncomfortable" situations in dealing with others. We can't emphasize it enough: courage is the essential ingredient for personal growth and leadership development for people with all Traits and especially those on the right side of this Factor.

Whom do you know with the Trusting Trait?

1. _____

2. _____

3. _____

Quick Coach Notes

Ideal Work Environment

Trusting people operate best in a friendly workplace with a healthy group of people who are reliable and take ownership of their work.

Connecting with the Trusting Trait

1. Honor their instinct to believe in others. It's powerful in helping people develop.
2. Remember their desire to be included.
3. Keep the conversation with them friendly.
4. Remember their need for open dialogue.

Managing the Trusting Trait

1. Anticipate them being too optimistic about people and results.
2. Help them understand the value of setting and keeping boundaries.
3. Help them grow in their ability to confront others when appropriate.
4. Share stories of your mistakes and become a sounding board for them.

Trusting people need to objectively evaluate situations and people and apply skepticism where needed by courageously and kindly filtering, screening, and setting boundaries. Be discerning and respond with respectful tough love.

DNA Behavior Style Groups with the Trusting Trait

Note: As mentioned near the end of chapter 5, only the first four factors (eight Traits) are used to calculate the Style Groups, however, because of the high correlation between Trust and Relationship-related Style Groups, we have listed those here that typically come with the Trust Trait. See Appendix D for more information on the ten Style Groups.

- Engager
- Community Builder
- Adapter
- Relationship Builder
- Influencer (sometimes)
- Stylish Thinker (sometimes)
- Facilitator (sometimes)

ENDNOTES

1   *Lincoln on Leadership: Executive Strategies for Tough Times*, Donald Phillips, © Donald T. Phillips II, 1992.

CHAPTER 15 ▶ THE SKEPTICAL TRAIT

FACTOR 5: LEFT-SIDE TRAIT

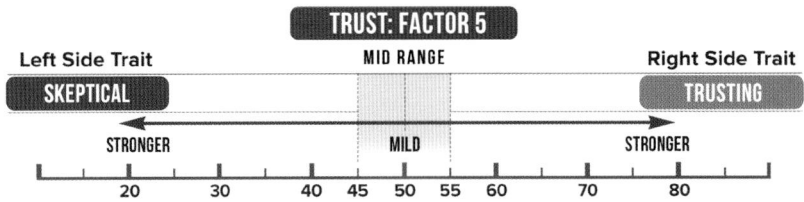

*The path of sound credence is through
the thick forest of skepticism.*

—George J. Nathan

The Trait name Skeptical is strong; it gets your attention. To some, it may seem a bit threatening or negative. But if this is your bent, you wouldn't have it any other way. You anticipate danger and take precautions, and the baser attributes of human nature prove you're right quite often. Let's look at both sides of this coin.

Skeptical – Strengths and Struggles

**Strengths in
Leadership**

1. Critical thinking, think matters through
2. Not gullible
3. Discover the truth
4. Protective of important information
5. Ask difficult questions

**Struggles in
Leadership**

1. Have difficulty letting go
2. Find it difficult to commit to others
3. Come across as negative toward others' ideas
4. Do not easily delegate
5. Make people uncomfortable

Skeptical Trait examples

Those with the Skeptical Trait naturally understand that no one is perfect and that all people have shortcomings and the potential to let you down. So, they tend to start with a Skeptical worldview and a mindset of caution about giving trust. From the time they first encounter you, it is natural for them to watch you to see if you are trustworthy or not.

Some typical examples might include entertainment and media personalities, Sean Connery, Natalie Portman, J. K. Rowling, Simon Colwell Wolf Blitzer, Rush Limbaugh, Hillary Clinton, Presidents Harry Truman, Richard Nixon, Jimmy Carter, and Barack Obama; military leaders, Generals Douglas MacArthur and James Mattis, business leaders Warren Buffett, Bill Gates, Larry Page, Steve Jobs, Larry Ellison; sports personalities like New England Patriots coach Bill Belichick, Michael Jordan, Serena Williams, Charles Barkley, and Danica Patrick.

 ## Skeptical – Leadership Strengths

Critical thinkers that dig for facts and truth

Things just don't slide by these folks without passing some tests. They have natural barriers that filter and inspect people, information, and ideas that approach their domain. They start out with the gate closed and you are only allowed in as you prove your credentials are genuine. Relating back to something said earlier, they do inspect and verify to make sure things are what they are represented to be. Their worst nightmare is to be taken advantage of. Their natural skepticism is an important tool for the way they operate.

Think matters through, ask difficult questions, and protect important information

Since people with the Skeptical Trait have a results/mission focus, they continually consider strategies to advance their agendas and get things done. They ask tough questions to get to the facts and uncover the logic underneath options or suggestions that others may offer. Their natural response is what we now call "vetting" as in vetting a candidate for a job position or political office. They themselves are cautious with handling sensitive information, and they want to know that others with whom they associate will have a similar mindset and can be trusted to protect confidentiality and privacy.

Pay attention, expect shortcomings, and confront problems

Not much gets by them; they're alert, with an eagle-eye for mistakes and shortcomings. They typically excel in areas where accuracy and quality are important. They anticipate mistakes and confront them quickly. Coach Belichick has won more Super Bowls than anyone, and he is quick to confront anyone that fails to flawlessly execute assignments—including his all-star quarterback Tom Brady.

 ## Skeptical – Leadership Struggles

Have difficulty letting go, struggle with delegation, have difficulty committing to others

Due to their lack of trust for others, they may tend to hold on to things longer than needed, or delegate and then micromanage the person doing the work. This lack of trust may also inhibit them from making commitments to others who might disappoint them. Wrapped into the package of this results-oriented Trait there is usually a good dose of independence that holds Skeptical people back from becoming too involved with others.

Make people feel uncomfortable, don't share feelings

Though their skepticism is natural for them, they may not be aware of it. They also may not be aware of how others perceive their natural distrust, which can result in negative energy coming their way in the form of relational pushback. Again, tied to their results-oriented nature, they are often not connected to their own emotions, nor those of others. Sharing feelings would tend to require great courage and a degree of trust that would not come easy. These behaviors would have to be learned over time, but the payoff would be huge.

Distrust and do not forgive easily

By nature, Skeptical people are hesitant relationally, and you may not feel "warm and fuzzy" when you meet them. On the contrary, you may feel that they are testing, evaluating, or investigating you to determine if you are worthy of being trusted. They typically come across as being more closed and secretive, not trusting that it's safe to share important information with others.

These struggles can be significant for leadership and teamwork where trust and communications are crucial for alignment, cohesion, and execution.

Ultimately, Skeptical people are not as approachable, which makes it hard for others to trust them, particularly those they are leading. And once you disappoint or let them down, you are on their bad side—and their memory is long and strong

Whom do you know with the Skeptical Trait?

1. _____

2. _____

3. _____

Quick Coach Notes

Ideal Work Environment

Skeptical people flourish where there is direct communication, clear boundaries, and high standards. They prefer talking about logic, facts, and data—things that are real and not "pie in the sky."

Connecting with the Skeptical Trait

1. Anticipate their doubts; they will ask for the facts to uncover the truth.
2. Expect that they will probe to check out your logic and see what you truly believe.
3. Be prepared to prove your case.
4. Focus on performance and results to earn their trust.

Managing the Skeptical Trait

1. Deliver on your commitments and don't let them down.
2. Keep them informed when situations change.
3. Consider how their skepticism can help you and the team be more effective.
4. Coach them on the value of trust and challenge them to be courageous in trusting others.

Skeptical people need to recognize that though their talents are vital, they can be a real "turn off" in many situations. They can benefit by showing more trust for others. Also, they can build trust by helping others reach their potential by believing in them. There will be more "wins" than "losses" by operating this way. Identify and confront your fears. Take some risks to trust others. Most will work to not let you down.

DNA Behavior Style Groups with the Skeptical Trait

Note: As mentioned near the end of chapter 5, only the first four factors (eight Traits) are used to calculate the Style Groups; however, because of the high correlation between Skeptical and Results-related Style Groups, we have listed those here that typically come with the Skeptical Trait. See Appendix D for more information on the ten Style Groups.

- Strategist
- Initiator
- Reflective Thinker
- Influencer (sometimes)
- Stylish Thinker (sometimes)

Trusting, Skeptical, and Mid-Range—we need them all

Much the same as with other talents, we find that both sides of the trust continuum have their advantages and disadvantages. That means that no matter where you are, you have something positive to offer and some room to grow. This will be important because issues of trust on teams turn out to be a bigger challenge than you might think, as we're about to see.

Baggage: The Trust Wildcard

We already have talked about the need for learned behaviors and the important role they play in growth. And, as alluded to in Chapter 4 and again at the beginning of this chapter, some of our learned behaviors from the past can have very negative outcomes, specifically those that come through pain, shame, guilt, and disappointment—such experiences can burden us with heavy baggage. These behavioral scars from extreme emotional experiences can operate as strongly as natural behavior—especially in the area of trust.

Reflect on your own feelings and behaviors related to trust. Is it possible that your ability to trust has been hijacked by pain from the past? Don't let those old experiences keep you in shackles. Forgive them, forgive yourself, and break free. Learn the positive lessons that can be found in the pain from trusting others who let you down. Let it go and then share your story with others—help them gain freedom too.

— Self-Assessment Application —

Based on the behavioral Traits described in this chapter and the previous chapter (or based on your actual *DNA Behavior* assessment results), what is your default *DNA Behavior*? Is it more right side, left side, or clearly in the middle?

Place an "x" on the "Skeptical to Trusting" scale below that best describes you. You may also use the free Self-Assessment Worksheet to capture your strengths and struggles for this factor. Download a copy at www.LeadershipBehaviorDNA.com/Book.

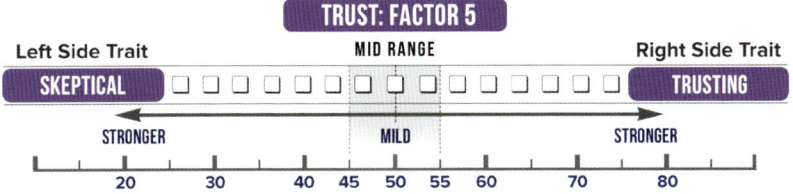

1. Looking back at the *strengths* and *struggles* for this Trait,
   a. What are some of your key *strengths* for leadership?
   b. Looking at your *struggles*, what is one area where you could adapt and become a better leader?
2. How can you apply the *Quick Coach Notes*?
3. With whom will you share this information for more insight, discussion, and accountability?

Calculate your specific Factor score by taking the *Leadership Behavior DNA* assessment. It only takes 10 minutes to receive your personal report.

Learn more at www.LeadershipBehaviorDNA.com/Book

The Pioneer Factor

This Factor indicates a person's drive to set ambitious goals and pursue them.

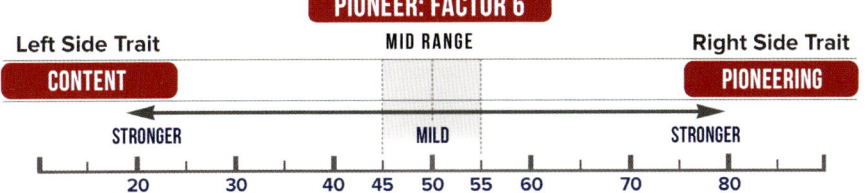

Content Leader Qualities

[Stable]

- Process focused
- Balanced
- Comfortable, not envious
- Satisfied
- Easy-going

Pioneering Leader Qualities

[Trailblazing]

- Goal focused
- Driven
- Competitive
- Ambitious
- Determined, persistent

— The Pioneer Factor —

The Pioneer Factor provides critical insight into how two different people with talents from opposite sides of the continuum can both be successful, given the proper roles and expectations. As we explore the left and right Traits you will see how people with very different motivations approach similar situations in life and relationships. People who fall on the right side (Pioneering) tend to resist the status quo, instead they look for the next hill to climb or the next challenge to overcome. They thrive on opportunities to compete and win over the challenges ahead, conquering new territories wherever possible. They become restless and frustrated without an ambitious challenge on the horizon. Those who fall on the left side (Content) are naturally motivated to operate effectively and comfortably in an established environment where the conditions and processes are known and predictable. They are more interested in life balance than conquering the next frontier.

In this chapter, we will delve into the *strengths* and *struggles* of each Trait and conclude with insights into how you can best connect with those who may be gifted radically different from you but nonetheless are crucial members of your team.

What about the Mid-Range?

As we've seen previously, mid-range scores indicate that the individual is capable of operating with the *strengths* and *struggles* associated with both Pioneering and Content Traits. Although, typically those *strengths* and *struggles* are not extreme.

Your challenge is to be a student of your own life, and understand which scenarios provide the best opportunities for you to succeed as a leader or in a particular role. Since most people intuitively discern if they prefer to be trailblazing new horizons or operating in a more stable situation (Pioneering vs. Content), they search out appropriate potential opportunities and jobs accordingly. This chapter has great value, however, in illustrating how left- and right-side Traits can collaborate to provide a healthy and productive team environment, thus the greater mission success.

CHAPTER 16 ▶ THE PIONEERING TRAIT

FACTOR 6: RIGHT-SIDE TRAIT

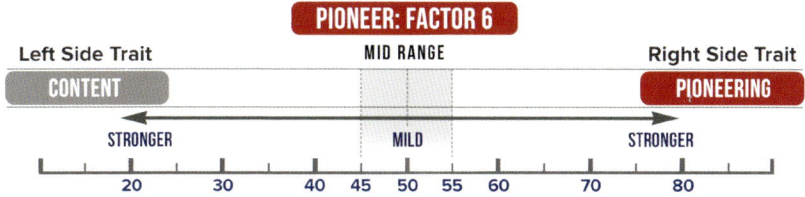

*Do not go where the path may lead. Go instead
where there is no path and leave a trail.*

—Ralph Waldo Emerson

As you might expect, Pioneering personalities are naturally motivated to overcome challenges to achieve big goals. They are hard-wired to master the unfamiliar, often at great risk and peril. They are confident visionaries who quickly become disillusioned with the status quo, day-to-day routines, and predictability of schedules. Rather, they are energized at the challenge of overcoming obstacles and charting the unknown. These pioneers won't rest until the mission is completed, the goal reached, or new conquest crushed. The more daunting the task, the better for the Pioneering people. You might think of them as "driven."

Below, is an overview of how to best understand Pioneer personalities, as well as how to position them for success as leaders.

Pioneering – Strengths and Struggles

Strengths in LeadersShip

1. Take initiative
2. Launch new programs
3. Goal-driven, restless
4. See difficult tasks through to completion
5. Competitive and confident

Struggles in Leadership

1. Too aggressive
2. May sacrifice a balanced life
3. Overly vigorous
4. May be too competitive, seem greedy
5. May tend to cut corners

Pioneering Trait examples

Examples might include entrepreneurs like Richard Branson, Jeff Bezos, Elon Musk, and Ross Perot; sales superstars Larry Ellison and Mary Kay Ash.; Presidents Teddy Roosevelt and Ronald Reagan; entertainers like Lady Gaga, Beyoncé, and Blake Lively; outdoor enthusiast, snowboarder, Jeremy Jones, mountain climbers Melissa Arnot, and Ashima Shiraishi, surfer Ian Walsh; aviators like Wilbur and Orville Wright, Charles Lindbergh, Capt. Eddie Rickenbacker, and Chuck Yeager; explorers William and Clark, Roald Amundsen, Sir Earnest Shackleton.

 ## Pioneering – Leadership Strengths

Goal-oriented, restless with the status quo, and complete tasks

Pioneers throttle up for new challenges and are motivated to define and aggressively move toward new goals. As a result, these are the people to turn to for pushing new programs that will expand market territory or increase overall efficiency in your workforce. Pioneers are wired to blaze new pathways and provide a driving force to stay on task.

Based on many years of experience, we see this Trait is almost a necessity for success in outside sales and start-up ventures and any undertaking or role that requires drive and persistence to overcome rejection and succeed in the face of a steady diet of challenge and change. Their motto would be: "It's no hill for a climber."

Lee was asked by an owner of an insurance agency to help him hire better. A quick survey showed that his top agents were strong on the Pioneering Trait. So, he began to hire more of them. But a couple of years later he called back and said he had decided that it was problematic to hire them too strongly on this Trait. Once they had learned the ropes and proven themselves, they were too ambitious; they left him and became his competitors. His plan was to dial back a bit on this Trait. He was willing to sacrifice some sales to improve retention.

Initiate, have a visionary perspective, and launch into unknown territories

Since pioneers "see" what others cannot see, they are eager to take steps, create momentum, and move rapidly toward their goals. Initiators at heart, it does not trouble Pioneers to be the first to step out in response to a challenge. Indeed, they can be easily frustrated by other personalities who hold back, wanting more details, clarity in procedures, or development of a comprehensive plan. They wholeheartedly agree with the proverbs: "He who hesitates is lost" and "Swift and resolute action lead to success; self-doubt is a prelude to disaster," and "a faint heart never filled a flush."

Competitive, vigorous, optimistic, and fearless challengers

Since they are competitive by nature, Pioneers bristle at the notion, "It can't be done." They are confident optimists, and when they accept a new challenge, Pioneers jump in with both feet, 100% committed and unwilling to take "no" for an answer. The satisfying prospects of achieving a new goal simply obscure cautions and attention to piddling, distracting details, or reasons to hesitate—confidence prevails where others might experience doubt or fear.

Pioneering – Leadership Struggles

Do too much, too fast, too aggressively, and leap before looking

Operating with a great deal of drive and initiative can have a downside. Pioneers may overlook key details, neglect to address key questions or fail to assimilate required resources to maintain their trailblazing efforts. Just as supply lines sustain army invasions, support systems, personnel, and financial resources are required for every major business thrust into the unknown. Pioneers would do well to recognize these vulnerabilities and pause long enough to listen to others who see the world through different lenses.

Excess drive can burn out others

Actions have consequences, and sometimes the impulsive launches of Pioneers land them in hot water with others. "Meep, meep!" exclaims the cartoon character Road Runner, leaving Wiley Coyote in a whirlwind of dust and confusion…an apt description of those who eat the dust of Pioneers in a hurry. Fence-Mending 101 is often required.

A few years ago, Hugh coached a strong Pioneering leader who was totally consumed with achieving ambitious goals. Further, he was so determined that there was no way he would ever change course. It was as though he was wearing blinders. He didn't seem to notice that his team was stressed to the point of near burn-out. Moreover, as soon as one goal was achieved two more were presented without pausing to celebrate or acknowledge the goals achieved.

This leader was generally not realistic in setting the goals that could be supported by the available resources and talents. Just as important, he was overzealous and ignored the fact that everyone needs a life. Ultimately, the result was that he lost good people because they never felt they could keep up or get the rewards or recognition for their efforts.

Left unsupervised, an undisciplined Pioneer may well pursue

an unsustainable pace that leads to burnout. Since their project list does not include slowing down, calculating, or pacing, Pioneers may be blinded to warning signs that would keep them in reasonable limits. Ideally, they will learn to pay attention and throttle back appropriately. If not, they will need oversight by someone with authority and a project manager to coordinate their efforts with the support systems required to reach the team goal.

Kate's Pioneering Experience

After much thought, Kate left her job with a significant financial advisory firm to open her own independent financial planning business. Kate believed that setting up an independent practice could greatly enhance her ability to deliver truly customized, client-focused support and advice. This move would also satisfy her desire to be entrepreneurial.

Kate had a strong reputation in the financial services industry and felt confident in her ability to grow her business. However, she was surprised and unprepared for the number of clients that came through the door. She was quickly overwhelmed; not just with the volume but also with the need to cover all aspects of the practice as a sole provider.

Kate had been confident she could manage the transition but now found herself dropping balls in every area of her practice. She realized she was not giving enough thought to her clients' individual needs which varied considerably. She had expected to have time to gain a deep knowledge of what the client truly wanted and then identify the most advantageous opportunities.

Kate was strong on the Pioneering Trait and full of initiative, able to accept challenges, and optimistic about the future. Hugh's team helped Kate find a level of balance. She learned to manage her strengths and also minimize her struggles. She developed processes and systems, and also hired some key staff with opposite/Content strengths to support her in the ongoing client relationship management aspects of the business. Kate was now able to focus on delivering customized service to her clients and achieve the original vision for her company.

Whom do you know with the Pioneering Trait?

1. _____

2. _____

3. _____

Quick Coach Notes

Ideal Work Environment

Pioneer personalities thrive in settings that provide freedom to discover new challenges, explore new frontiers, create new goals, and operate with a minimum of required details and tightly-defined policies and procedures. To maximize their impact, Pioneers need a support team whose *DNA Behavior strengths* provide a solid foundation for their more audacious but important excursions.

Connecting with the Pioneering Trait

1. Give them trailblazing challenges.
2. Provide them with the big picture.
3. Present them with action plans.
4. Keep them informed of progress.

Managing the Pioneering Trait

1. Keep them challenged.
2. Make sure there is clarity about goals, resources, and expectations.
3. Expect them to take territory and "fix" things.
4. Be clear about boundaries and your wiliness to use power to enforce them or they may assume all your authority too.

Pioneering people should remember that most people cannot keep up with them in terms of pace and energy— beware of burning out others. Consider the "tooth to tail" ratio. In the traditional military, for example, there may be two to five support people for each combatant. Pioneers need to consider the resources and support that is essential to sustain their initiatives.

Note: We have not included Style Group examples for Factors 6, 7, and 8. Style Groups are determined primarily by the first four Factors of one's **DNA Behavior.**

CHAPTER 17 ▶ THE CONTENT TRAIT

FACTOR 6: LEFT-SIDE TRAIT

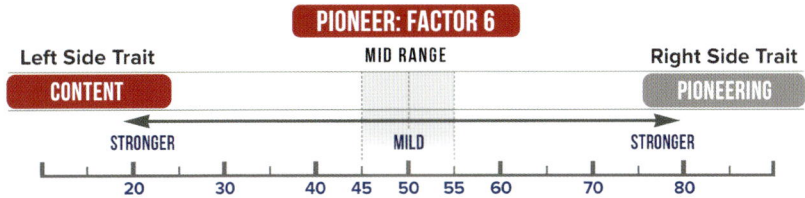

*To be content with what we possess is the
greatest and most secure of riches.*

—Marcus Tullius Cicero

Those who manifest strong Content behaviors are also very success focused, yet their approach and often their goals are quite different from their right-sided, Pioneering teammates. They measure success in terms of consistent day-to-day production achieved in a stable sustainable environment. They seek harmony and balance in their work environment and in their personal lives. Uncertainty, unpredictability, or a lack of systems can become very vexing to those with Content Traits—and their energy is expended at re-establishing normalcy all around.

Change is often perceived as a threat, and thus may be met with stubborn resistance or passive-aggressive responses. Whereas their Pioneering Trait counterparts will fall on a sword to embrace challenges on the horizon, Content personalities will do so to maintain order and familiarity around them.

Content – Strengths and Struggles

Strengths in Leadership

1. Follow the set agenda
2. Focused on realities
3. Concentrate on a balanced life
4. Satisfied, not driven to fix everything
5. Create a steady environment

Struggles in Leadership

1. Do not push forward enough
2. May be too comfortable with the status quo
3. Stay in comfort zone
4. May resist even good change
5. May respond negatively to "gung-ho" environments

Content Trait examples

Typical examples of this Trait might include entertainers: Tom Hanks, Jennifer Lawrence, Will Smith, Ed Sheeran, Daniel Radcliffe; Presidents: George H.W. Bush, Gerald Ford, military leaders' generals Omar Bradley, and Joe Dunford; business leaders Warren Buffett and Melinda Gates; and famous sports stars, Joe Torre, Derek Jeter, and Tim Duncan.

 ## Content – Leadership Strengths

Lead by example

Those sharing the Content Trait set the example for others by maintaining their focus on the here and now, and with the tasks at hand. Given a host of overwhelming tasks, they do best by setting priorities and "eating the elephant one bite at a time."

They have a unique quiet kind of competitiveness that is relentlessly reliable in performing their duty. When it comes to taking on tough duties, they are not shrinking violets—many military special operators bring this Trait into battle as do many top athletes. A good example is the Spurs power forward Tim Duncan who was an NBA All-Star fifteen times in nineteen years. Year in and year out, he consistently got the job done, and more importantly lead his team to five NBA championships. Tim was always quiet about his losses and let others claim the glory in victory.

Lead by communicating care and value to team members

Content people make key leadership contributions by building the esprit de corps in the home office. And, because people are not machines, when care and compassion are needed, Content personalities step out as thoughtful, insightful, and caring friends who soothe frazzled emotions.

Content team members grasp that we all come to work with different motivations. And they understand that without work/life balance the most are likely to burn out. By pointing out the successes and progress of others, Content persons help keep the troops motivated, appreciated, and fulfilled.

Excel at calming down, slowing down, and smoothing out surroundings

Because they are usually good listeners, Content teammates are proficient at diffusing testy or conflicted relational issues, thus becoming "go-to" people as mediators. They exude care and co-operation and project a calming influence over those ruffled emotions, as long as they are not personally involved in the conflict. As peacemakers, their leadership impact consists of restoring harmony and a steady pace back to their environments.

Promote harmony, steadiness, and loyalty

Since Content people prize harmony, they naturally flourish in environments free from interpersonal conflict. If the unresolved conflict remains, it can and will drain their time, attention, and energies away from accomplishing the real tasks at hand. And, since they invest heavily in developing caring, lasting relationships, their loyalty to both friends and their organization runs high.

Content – Leadership Struggles

Prone to a limited perspective of the big picture and next steps

While Content persons are likely captivated by the tasks of today, they may ignore or be unaware of the need for long-term plans to keep an organization viable in the decade to come. Content leaders don't deny the need for this information; rather, they yield those functions to the more Pioneering-at-heart. That's a viable option, but only as long as the team has "Pioneers" to call on. Defining the long-term goals may remain fuzzy in the mind of Content leaders simply because their radar concentrates on the practical steps required for today, not so much tomorrow.

Recently Hugh's team was engaged by the CEO of a funds management business to help the sales team get out of a rut. They found that the sales leader and many of his team members were very Content in their style. This meant that they had a very balanced approach and were quite happy going along with the status quo. This worked well for maintaining long-established customer relationships and letting the business keep going on its current easy-going path.

However, the issue was that the team did not have the competitive drive and determination to push for new sales and would not go above and beyond when necessary. This blockage left the sales results stagnant and deficient when higher energy was required to roll out new products, expand territories, and solve difficult problems.

May become overwhelmed in a fast-paced, irregular setting

"One thing at a time," says the Content person, preferring to complete a single task, start to finish, before beginning a new assignment. Leadership, however, demands flexibility and the capacity to address multiple issues in order to maintain efficiency. This can lead to a stressful environment that drains energy from the

Content persons, who by their nature strive for closure before letting go of a project.

May compromise task integrity to preserve loyal relationships

There are times when hard decisions must be made to improve efficiency and productivity by releasing or changing staff positions. Such steps prove stressful to Content leaders in at least two ways: 1) Because they are fiercely loyal and forever hopeful, and believe the best about co-workers, it becomes extremely painful for them to say, "enough is enough," and become the person who holds someone accountable or eliminates a position. 2) Even if the Content person is not responsible for terminating a person or position, it is nonetheless disruptive for the Content Trait when a teammate is terminated. Loyalty can come with an expensive emotional price tag, and Content workers may pay too great a price personally in energy and time.

Can be slow to confront and express their true feelings

In their efforts to please others and thus maintain harmony, Content leaders may be slow to verbalize their thoughts or feelings, especially if there's a chance those insights might be controversial or disruptive to the status quo. This can lead to internal turmoil, which is equally unacceptable to the Content person, leaving them in quite a bind: reluctant to express true thoughts and feelings; reluctant to be the voice that incites turmoil and needed conflict. This predicament can be resolved when someone with a "Take Charge" Trait simply asks, "What's on your mind these days?" or, "Tell me what bothers you most about your situation." Being granted permission by others in charge can be the key to unwinding a Content person who is no longer content!

Whom do you know with the Content Trait?

1. _____

2. _____

3. _____

Quick Coach Notes

Ideal Work Environment

The Content person excels best in a setting that offers a predictable pace, opportunities to relationally support others, and opportunities to complete tasks for projects from start to finish.

Connecting with the Content Trait

1. Keep the conversation comfortable and easygoing.
2. Recognize their need for stability.
3. Value their daily, consistent, reliable contributions.
4. Tone down intensity and minimize crises.

Managing the Content Trait

1. Don't expect them to take territory or initiate turn-arounds.
2. Honor their life balance needs and minimize "all-out" surges.
3. Give them clear direction to move forward.
4. Affirm them for who they are and value their contributions.

Content people should match the job setting to processes that play to their strengths of steady pace and reliability and that minimize surges in activity and are devoid of ongoing toxic conflict. They should take responsibility for honest communication with thoughts and feelings.

Pioneering, Content, and Mid-Range—we need them all

It's important to note that both Pioneering and Content people make valuable contributions to leadership roles, just in different ways. Pioneering people bring innovation, change, and the ability to compete for results—all highly sought-after values. Content people bring stability, reliability, and the capacity to faithfully operate within established systems—all critical aspects to effective organizations. Both qualities lend unique *strengths* and thus the key is to "get the right Trait to the right seat on the bus" for maximum success.

— Self-Assessment Application —

Based on the behavioral Traits described in this chapter and the previous chapter (or based on your actual *DNA Behavior* assessment results), what is your default *DNA Behavior*? Is it more right side, left side, or clearly in the middle?

Place an "x" on the "Content to Pioneering" scale below that best describes you. You may also use the free Self-Assessment Worksheet to capture your strengths and struggles for this factor. Download a copy at www.LeadershipBehaviorDNA. com/Book.

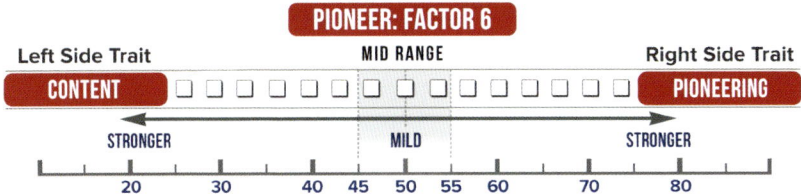

1. Looking back at the **strengths** and **struggles** for this Trait,
   a. What are some of your key **strengths** for leadership?
   b. Looking at your **struggles**, what is one area where you could adapt and become a better leader?
2. How can you apply the *Quick Coach Notes*?
3. With whom will you share this information for more insight, discussion, and accountability?

Calculate your specific Factor score by taking the *Leadership Behavior DNA* assessment. It only takes 10 minutes to receive your personal report.

Learn more at www.LeadershipBehaviorDNA.com/Book

THE RISK FACTOR

This Factor indicates a person's willingness to take risks and their ability to tolerate the consequences.

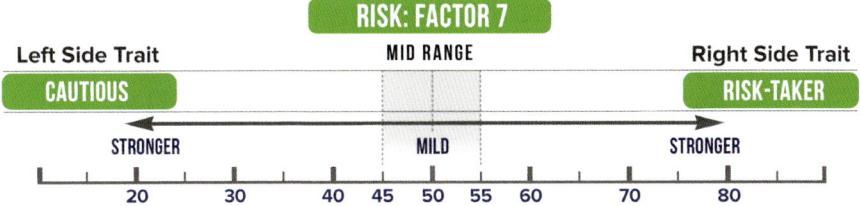

Left Side Trait	MID RANGE	Right Side Trait
CAUTIOUS		**RISK-TAKER**

RISK: FACTOR 7

STRONGER   MILD   STRONGER

20   30   40   45   50   55   60   70   80

Cautious Leader Qualities

[Safety]

- Minimize Risks
- Prefer predictability
- Like to follow proven paths
- Look for the dangers
- Seek reliability and stability

Risk-Taker Leader Qualities

[Risk]

- Take Chances
- Speculative
- Venturesome
- Daring
- Optimistic

— The Risk Factor —

Awareness of a person's comfort with risk is important in many areas and none more so than the area of financial investment. Since much of Hugh's work had centered on financial planning, this domain of human behavior has always been a keen interest for him. On a broader perspective, understanding a person's approach to risk versus reward can be important in many areas of life and work. Though it may not be a subject that most people think about regularly, perhaps it should be. After all, we all want rewards, but as in other areas, a free lunch is not the norm—risk and reward are directly related. Typically, the greater the potential reward, the greater the risk.

For entrepreneurs, understanding your risk profile is very important in making decisions to start a business, grow it, and ultimately sell it. In fact, the biggest risk often comes in deciding to sell the business. This is true in dealing with any asset.

Business leaders and boards need to understand their risk profiles in making key decisions for their companies. Too much risk-taking to aggressively expand the company without enough considered research can do significant damage. Yet, on the other side, being too cautious and not making proactive strategic decisions about growth or a new direction can leave the company in a lull or risk becoming seriously uncompetitive. This is especially true in today's world of rapid technological change.

Some people are hard-wired with temperaments that step up to risks, as reflected by the right side of the graphic above. Others gravitate toward a more cautious approach to situations and opportunities and assign their time, resources, and efforts accordingly (left side). As with other Factors, it's important to know your natural bent and keep in mind that good management includes getting the right person (yourself and others) in a corresponding position where they can best utilize their *strengths* without discounting the input of those with opposite tendencies.

Our scores on all the DNA Factors call us to reflect on our behaviors and motives with a goal of gaining clarity in one's own behavior. And, gaining the self-awareness to "connect" with oneself provides a foundation of skills for discerning and "connecting" with those of differing Traits. There is possibly no area more important to do this than for the Risk Factor. The impact of making the right or wrong decision, or in fact no decision, can have a huge impact on your life and every endeavor you are involved with, whether it be in business, career, finances, sports, or even in building a personal relationship.

Mid-range scores suggest there are particular areas where a person elects to embrace more risk, but other areas where they play conservatively and "close to the vest." For instance, some may have a penchant for high-risk investments in the stock market but be low risk in terms of physical adventure or personal self-revelation to others and vice-versa.

Human beings are incredibly complex, but the insights of **DNA Behavior** help simplify much of this complexity into usable insights for understanding self and others. And when you think about it, given the vast variety of socio-economic influences that prompt Risk-Taking behaviors, there is much to be gained by understanding our own "base of operations" that drive our internal motivations and filters and ultimately shape our behavior.

CHAPTER 18 ▶ THE RISK-TAKER TRAIT

FACTOR 6: RIGHT-SIDE TRAIT

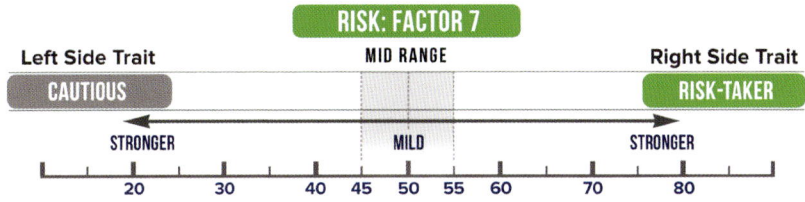

*If you are not willing to risk the unusual,
you will have to settle for the ordinary.*

—Jim Rohn

Risk-Taker leaders are comfortable with exploits into unknown territories, which could be financial, physical, practical problem solving or even intellectual. The key is that they are comfortable with higher exposures to loss or setbacks. This Trait has some overlap with the Take Charge, Fast-paced, and Pioneering Traits, yet each has a slightly different focus. All said, it's important to understand the scope of this Risk-Taker Trait for all life applications, and how the Trait relates to the overall profile of the individual.

Risk-Taker – Strengths and Struggles

 **Strengths in Leadership**

1. Willing to take chances
2. Venture into new areas
3. Face danger comfortably
4. Pursue opportunities
5. Demonstrate courage

 **Struggles in Leadership**

1. May take unnecessary risks
2. Gamble against the odds
3. Create exposures
4. May not see dangers
5. Too speculative

Risk-Taker Trait examples

Typical examples of this Trait might include famous personalities: Beyoncé, JK Rowling, Rihanna, Nicole Kidman, and Sylvester Stallone; government leaders, Presidents Teddy Roosevelt, Ronald Reagan, Donald Trump, Vladimir Putin, Emanuel Macron; business leaders Jeff Bezos, Bill Gates, Richard Branson, Elon Musk, Vera Wang, Larry Ellison Christene Barberich; sports figures Coaches Les Miles and Nick Saban.

 ## Risk-Taker – Leadership Strengths

Able to face danger calmly and take courageous action

Some people are attracted to the challenge of high-risk situations. They naturally are confident they can win or overcome the challenge. They quickly assess the pros and cons and believe they can succeed. Fear is not an issue because they believe in their own capacity—their attitude is positive. In fact, when Risk-Takers are under pressure, it is likely they will take more risk to succeed. Put another way, their solution to solve the problem will involve risk, and their analysis of risk-reward will be more aggressive.

Hugh is an extreme Risk-Taker which is masked by his very reserved personality and mid-range planful nature, but as his coach has pointed out, Risk-taking plays a big role in everything he does in business. His key is to win 80% of the time and ensure that the losses are not catastrophic. So, at times not everything looks dandy and pretty and would frighten many others, but it works for him. Also, given he is extreme on the fast-paced Trait; he can manage the chaos that comes with it. Not taking risks would be an under-achievement. From a living perspective, Hugh enjoys adventures to boost the "return on life". However, he does not take a lot of extreme physical risks because he does not think there is the upside in doing so. Though we are both on the Risk-taking side, Lee is more comfortable taking physical risks as is evidenced by the dangerous roles he's chosen and challenges he's faced in work and life situations.

In many of the risk scenarios, Risk-Takers seem to come fully alive—perhaps some would call them "adrenalin junkies" because they are attracted and feel fulfilled when they are engaged in high-risk activities. Outsiders see it as the remarkable ability some people have to look danger in the face and neither flinch nor blink! The extreme of this characteristic could range from high-risk investors, serial entrepreneurs, race car drivers, fighter pilots, and special operations military troops. Many in this group exhibit a remarkable capacity for responding to dangerous challenges with confident execution that to others looks like great courage. To them, it's just following a calling—doing what they do.

The summer of 2018 provided just such evidence. On June 23, 2018, the world became aware of the plight of 12 Thai soccer players and their coach trapped over two-and-a-half miles deep in a Thailand cave. Ten days passed before the lost group was even located, and the gravity of their confinement became clear. Floods had filled the caves; the only way out was through water.

In a race against time, each youth would have to be escorted from the darkened, murky passages on a six-hour journey to freedom and life. Complicating the rescue, not even one of the boys knew how to swim, much less use scuba gear. "It's one of the most difficult and dangerous and risky things I've ever done, not in terms of my own personal safety, but in terms of the people I was responsible for," British cave diver Jason Mallinson recounted.[1] Ultimately, one diver was lost, but all those trapped were rescued.[2]

Relentless training is helpful to overcome fear, but even when fear is lurking, the Risk-Taker, operates as though it's conquered and has retreated into the shadows. As we learned in Chapter 2, based on the normal distribution curve, one-third of the population has this Trait and is prone to this kind of Risk-taking. In many ways, they do not see themselves as extreme Risk-Takers; it's just normal behavior for them. It's much like the Outgoing person may be blind to the fear of public speaking that overwhelms most people who are not so spotlight-oriented and verbally-talented.

Readily accept exposures to potential losses for the sake of gains

We've mentioned some of the more obvious Risk-Takers from the military and Wall Street, but people with this Trait are needed and present in almost every career field. Consider surgeons, trial lawyers, real estate developers, entrepreneurs, tree climbers, and electrical linemen, all of whom have migrated in their career choice to the more risk involved roles.

Risk-taking also shows up in the way we respond to the day-to-day choices we face in life. Consider career reassignments, patients facing surgery, buying or selling a home, buying or refinancing a business, investment decisions, and retirement planning. We are all subject to an endless array of choices that carry risk and reward. Typically, Risk-Takers and Cautious people may face identical risks. Risk-Takers accept the exposures to potential losses for the sake of gains to be achieved, often without a second thought.

Able to overcome fear to function coherently

Fear has the capacity to cloud the vision and immobilize productive action, particularly the fear of failure. Risk-Takers exhibit a remarkable ability to stare fear in the eye and proceed with clear thinking and actions that lead to solutions.

FDR became the 32nd President of the United States on March 20, 1932, when our nation was gripped in the throes of the Great Depression. On the occasion of his inaugural address, he challenged the American people with this stunning reminder: "So, first of all, let me assert my firm belief that the only thing we have to fear is...fear itself—nameless, unreasoning, unjustified terror which paralyzes needed efforts to convert retreat into advance."[3]

Risk-Takers have the remarkable ability to transcend the din and clamor of the calamity at hand in order to envision the glory of what can be—as well as the practical steps A, B, and C to achieve those goals. While fear is a reality to contend with and potential losses clamor for attention, Risk-Takers are more likely to have the ability to think clearly, see potential becoming reality, and operate under the conviction that victory is within reach.

Capable of tolerating losses, and have the confidence to rebound

For Risk-Takers, coping with the potential of losses is a way of life. They are the kids who rode bikes with "no hands," the first to perform daring acrobatic feats in gymnastics, and even stepped up to the "triple-dog-dare" of touching their tongues to frozen flag poles, as Flick does in *A Christmas Story*.[4] With a well-rehearsed life history of recovering from setbacks, Risk-Takers have developed healthy attitudes of confidence to recover from losses.

 ## Risk-Taker – Leadership Struggles

Commit before considering strategic factors

Given their preoccupation with goals and the challenge at hand, Risk-Takers are prone to being oblivious to pertinent issues which, if not addressed, pose genuine threats to success. "The devil is in the details," echoes hauntingly in the path of a Risk-Taker; someone must mop up messes that result from inadequate preparations.

Coke did market surveys before releasing New Coke in 1985, but they failed to identify all the critical criteria. The results were a failed launch. In 1995, Microsoft Bob software was a bust because it was too complex for the available computing power to run it efficiently. That same year, and for similar reasons, Nintendo's Virtual Boy, an attempt to step into virtual reality was a bust as well. Of course, no one can know for sure that things will go as planned, but it looks like these big companies discounted some of the key realities of their situation.

Bright people in politics and the military have had similar issues. Militarily, the Bay of Pigs invasion of Cuba was a fiasco because it was not fully considered in light of what it would really take to win the battle. And more recently Saddam Hussein misjudged US strategic intent and committed his troops without even a credible withdrawal plan. The outcome was disastrous. His army's "Highway of death" retreat was one of history's most devasting military debacles.

"Look before you leap!" remains as time-tested counsel for Risk-Takers.

Create unnecessary exposures

While risks are a fact of life, wise management identifies and eliminates unnecessary exposures. Rather than expecting a "leopard will change its spots" or hoping a Risk-Taker will stop taking risks, prudence often dictates a collaborative approach. Working with more cautious colleagues can bring full light to unseen challenges, necessary resources and systems, and unintended consequences.

One of the entrepreneurial leaders Hugh's team works with is an extreme Risk-Taker. That is not unusual for a person who has had the courage to start up a new technology venture. The strength of this entrepreneur having a strong Risk-Taker Trait is that he was prepared to put the business and himself on the line by investing further in new technologies. The struggle was that at times he was overly vigorous and threw caution to the wind. He was blind to how much risk he was taking and not appreciating the impact on his team and shareholders. Ultimately, we coached him to hire an independent advisory board to objectively assess the risks and rewards of any major investment.

Whom do you know with the Risk-Taker Trait?

1. _____

2. _____

3. _____

Quick Coach Notes

Ideal Work Environment

Risk-Takers are most productive in settings where they have authority and resources to make things happen, but with clear responsibility and accountability for outcomes. In short, they need freedom from cumbersome restraints, so they can move both quickly and aggressively toward their "big picture" goals.

Connecting with the Risk-Taker Trait

1. Accept their comfort in taking risks that others would not consider.
2. Present them with the risks and returns.
3. Keep the discussion positive.
4. Remember that they will want to act quickly.

Managing the Risk-Taker Trait

1. Give them opportunities to take risks after evaluating whether the potential upside is truly worth the risk compared to the potential loss.
2. Help them understand that others do not have the same risk tolerance and that's okay.
3. Help them consider and evaluate how their risk-taking may be impacting others—positively and negatively.
4. Get them to walk through all the permutations and obstacles that may arise in their projects.

Risk-Takers should temper their impulses to move quickly by listening first to teammates about lurking dangers or threats they may be overlooking. Also, remember that others involved may not have the same ability to handle risk.

ENDNOTES

1   http://www.foxnews.com/science/2018/07/17/terrifying-details-thai-cave-rescue-revealed-by-divers.html

2   http://www.msn.com/en-us/news/world/%e2%80%98time-is-running-out-%e2%80%99-inside-the-treacherous-rescue-of-boys-trapped-in-a-thai-cave/ar-AAA0K6Y?ocid=ientp

3   https://en.wikipedia.org/wiki/First_inauguration_of_Franklin_D._Roosevelt#Inaugural_address

4   https://www.cinemablend.com/new/How-Christmas-Story-Actually-Filmed-Infamous-Tongue-Scene-101537.html

CHAPTER 19 ▶ THE CAUTIOUS TRAIT

FACTOR 7: LEFT-SIDE TRAIT

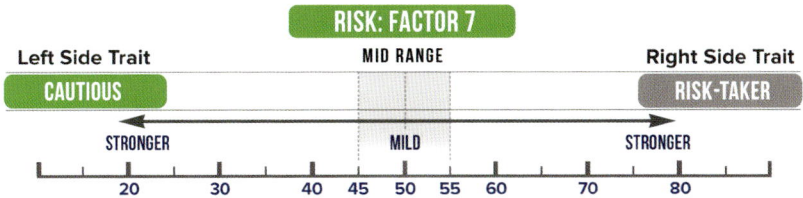

Only a fool tests the water with both feet.

—African Proverb

Cautious people view processes, goals, and life in general through lenses shaped by a concern for the safety and preservation of resources. Since they are practical in their approaches to problem-solving, they shudder at the thought of being caught off guard or unprepared, both of which could lead to errors in decision-making. Time to reflect is a valuable commodity for the Cautious person, providing an opportunity to analyze, review, and ponder possibilities, all with the intent of reducing risk, exposures, and potential inadequacies. Leery of unpredictable "variables," they prefer to concentrate on data, facts, and bodies of proven knowledge.

Cautious – Strengths and Struggles

Strengths in Leadership

1. Plan initiatives carefully
2. Preserve and protects
3. See potential dangers
4. Survey situations well
5. Follow proven paths

Struggles in Leadership

1. May miss opportunities
2. Can be overly cautious
3. May be too hesitant
4. Slow to take action
5. Often resist change

Cautious Trait examples

Typical examples of this Trait might include famous personalities: Tom Hanks, Julia Roberts, Christopher Lee, Denzel Washington, George Strait; government leaders, George Washington, Mitt Romney, and Condoleeza Rice, Angela Merkel and Queen Elizabeth II; business leaders, Warren Buffett, Peter Thiel, Ingvar Kamprad; military leaders Frederick the Great, Stonewall Jackson, Dwight Eisenhower, and Gen Colin Powell; sports figures Jack Nicklaus, Jackie Joyner-Kersee; coaches John Wooden and Mike Krzyzewski.

 ## Cautious – Leadership Strengths

Investigate to discover potential risks and exposures

Cautious people explore the lay of the land for the purpose of minimizing threats and losses. In managing finances, a Cautious person is not necessarily anti-investment; rather, they don't want to get caught off guard or make financial commitments prior to understanding pertinent details. Thus, they research, analyze, and investigate first before taking steps of action. As team members, they bring great **strength** to overall efforts by their inherent radar systems that spot potential hazards to operations and tasks.

Preserve and protect the status quo

There is a quote on investing that's often attributed to Will Rogers, the great American folk philosopher of the early 1900s, about his best friend Wiley Post, the risk-taking, aviation pioneer who always had new ideas for investment. Supposedly Rogers said, "I'm not so much concerned about the return *on* my money as I am about the return *of* my money."

Can you imagine a Cautious person's "lessons learned" from the stock market plunge in 2008-2009? From its pre-recession high in October 2007 the Dow Jones average dropped more than 50 percent in 18 months. A fund would have to grow 100% just to make it back to the point of origin. Cautious people recognize and appreciate the risk involved and typically invest conservatively. Perhaps their motto can best be expressed, "A bird in the hand is worth two in the bush," concentrating on the certainties of "what is today" over their speculations of tomorrow.

We can be glad that many professions focus on the **strengths** of the Cautious Trait. For example, engineers typically share these talents and mindset. The next time you're cruising at 36,000 feet on a transcontinental flight over vast expanses of ocean or Arctic tundra, consider the situation and you'll love and admire those Cautious people who make those engines so reliable.

Follow a steady pace and proven paths

One of Aesop's famed fables, "The Hare and the Tortoise," relates to the great race in the animal kingdom between a rabbit (hare) and a tortoise.

The hare was favored to win due to his blazing speed, quite in contrast to the plodding of the tortoise. In fact, the hare was so fast he paused to nap, thus allowing the tortoise to cross the finish line first and win the race. The story has remained popular due to the veracity of its motto:

"Don't brag about your lightning pace, for Slow and Steady won the race!"[1]

The story also illustrates the dramatic differences in current investment strategies where many adopt the appealing growth of risky stocks, preferring fast results, comparing favorably to the hare. Others adopt more of a tortoise strategy and are quite content with slow but steadier increases from reliable, trustworthy investments.

 ## Cautious – Leadership Struggles

May miss opportunities due to time-consuming analysis

Cautious people operate most comfortably when they have time to prepare and consider. The whirlwind pace and short notice decision-making required in many roles and situations can frustrate the Cautious person, who prefers time to analyze. They may miss out on golden opportunities in the meantime. In this type of dilemma, they are painfully aware of the saying, "You snooze, you lose."

Hugh's team advised a new marketing tech company on the composition of its board so that it would have a majority of independent directors to protect the interests of shareholders. The independent directors were Cautious in style, which is what the shareholders wanted given the founders were far more aggressive in their risk-taking. The **strength** was that the board played an important role in corporate governance so that the risks were carefully identified and managed. Of course, the challenge is that when the board is controlled by independent directors who are very Cautious, it can quickly block progress if the company needs to make strategic business changes to keep up with a dynamic market.

Whom do you know with the Cautious Trait?

1. _____

2. _____

3. _____

Quick Coach Notes

Ideal Work Environment

Those with the Cautious Trait naturally preserve resources and protect against loss. They thrive in stable and predictable situations. They prefer not to be put on the spot to make important decision without time for research and reflection.

Connecting with the Cautious Trait

1. Allow them time to survey the situation.
2. Provide them with the research and evidence to support your recommendations.
3. Respect their more cautious perspective and give it full consideration.
4. Help them clarify what the risks really are considering the specific situation, and also identify the safety zone.

Managing the Cautious Trait

1. Provide information that enables them to evaluate risks logically and in context.
2. Help them understand that there is also a risk in being too cautious.
3. Listen to their concerns and consider how their cautious perspective may be helpful to the team.
4. Celebrate and affirm their wise contributions.

Cautious people can mitigate the uneasiness of an environment marked by fast-paced, risky decisions by intentionally building trust relationships with leaders who are over them. Also, they should carefully consider focusing on career fields that are characterized by predictability and a steadiness of pace.

Cautious, Risk-Taker, and Mid-Range—we need them all

When laid side-by-side, the vast differences in the Cautious and Risk-Taker Traits become painfully evident. What strokes one Trait elicits stress in the other. What gives an adrenaline rush to one as risks increase, causes the other to head for cover. Those in the Mid-Range scores find there are certain conditions under which they have freedom to "let loose" and tolerate more risk and, given another set of parameters, insist on more controlled advances.

Good management creates the policy structure so each Trait clearly understands how they best contribute to the overall team success and under what conditions they will be expected to dial back their natural inclinations. With clear communications and a healthy respect for what each Trait brings to the table, people are able to capitalize on their different but complementary *DNA behaviors* to make sound decisions and talent-aligned task assignments.

— Self-Assessment Application —

Based on the behavioral Traits described in this chapter and the previous chapter (or based on your actual **DNA Behavior** assessment results), what is your default **DNA Behavior**? Is it more right side, left side, or clearly in the middle?

Place an "x" on the "Cautious to Risk-Taker" scale below that best describes you. You may also use the free Self-Assessment Worksheet to capture your strengths and struggles for this factor. Download a copy at www. LeadershipBehaviorDNA.com/Book.

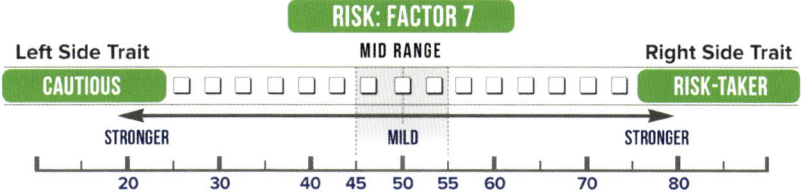

1. Looking back at the **strengths** and **struggles** for this Trait,
    a. What are some of your key **strengths** for leadership?
    b. Looking at your **struggles**, what is one area where you could adapt and become a better leader?
2. How can you apply the *Quick Coach Notes*?
3. With whom will you share this information for more insight, discussion, and accountability?

Calculate your specific Factor score by taking the *Leadership Behavior DNA* assessment. It only takes 10 minutes to receive your personal report.

Learn more at www.LeadershipBehaviorDNA.com/Book

ENDNOTES

1   http://www.storyarts.org/library/aesops/stories/tortoise.html

THE CREATIVE FACTOR

This Factor reflects a person's capacity to be original, creative, and work with new ideas.

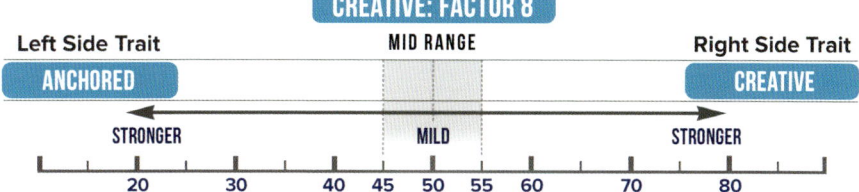

Anchored Leader Qualities

[Practical]

- Proven methods
- Solution-driven
- Needs evidence — likes facts, figures
- Tried and true
- Concrete

Creative Leader Qualities

[Ideas]

- New methods
- Ideas-driven
- Connect the "dots"
- Resourceful, explore possibilities
- Abstract

— The Creative Factor —

The Creative Factor is measured across a continuum of these two opposite Traits, Creative vs. Anchored. Scores plotting on the right side of the continuum are motivated to be Creative and are driven toward new and different ideas and concepts that reach beyond the established and into unfamiliar territories. Creative personalities are talented for original thinking and strongly pursue those ideas to innovate by creating something completely new. They are generally unimpressed with the ideas of others (and thus, the status quo) and have a zest to explore the world of possibilities. Anchored personalities (left side), in contrast, place their confidence in proven strategies, products, and processes. They can also be very innovative but typically do so with a more linear step-by-step approach.

Good management requires a keen grasp of the overall mission, coupled with an understanding of how each of these Traits— Anchored or Creative—best advances the corporate effort toward their goals. A CPA firm, for instance, would value the precision that comes from proven methods and procedures. An entrepreneurial company developing cutting-edge medical equipment, on the other hand, might place a premium on break-through theories and processes involving artificial intelligence or high-tech equipment to treat diseases in a totally new way.

Realistically, almost every organization/team needs both Anchored and Creative employees. The key to success rests in getting the right people in the right setting where they can naturally exploit their inherent *strengths*.

What about the Mid-Range

Like all the other DNA Behavior Factors many people (approximately one-third) fall in the mid-range of the Anchored vs. Creative continuum. That simply means there are areas of their lives where "Anchored" best describes their approach to living and other domains, where they tend to be more resourceful and imaginative.

As with the other seven Factors, having a grasp on your own *strengths* and *struggles* provides an insightful portal to experiencing deep satisfaction in work, as well as foreseeing the scenarios that cause stress. And especially crucial for leaders, these insights assist us in understanding, appreciating and managing people who are wired differently than we are.

CHAPTER 20 ▶ THE CREATIVE TRAIT

FACTOR 8: RIGHT-SIDE TRAIT

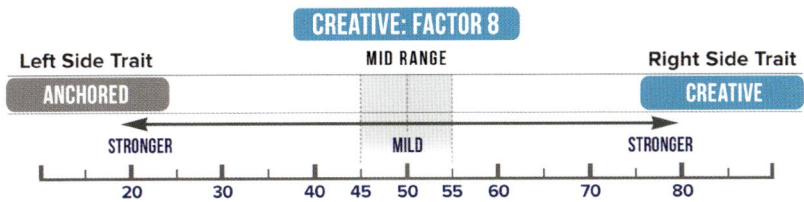

Creativity is inventing, experimenting, growing, taking risks, breaking rules, making mistakes, and having fun.

—Mary Lou Cook

Creative personalities frequently have an "itch" that is best scratched when they can think "outside the box" and allow their minds to play with disparate ideas to see if there is a way to "connect the dots." Their **strength** is to pursue the abstract in search of possibilities and solutions. Of course, this group shows up in several career fields such as design, marketing, IT, and all the arts. In the military, special operations units—those combat units that specialize in unconventional warfare—have a much higher ratio of Creatives than typical units. Given the nature of their work and the fact that these units tend to be volunteer only, this reflects their natural attraction to things that are different and more creative. It's not unusual for Creatives to share some characteristics of the Risk-Taking, Take Charge, and Pioneering Traits.

Creative – Strengths and Struggles

Strengths in LeadersShip

1. Rely on intuitive thoughts
2. Like to brainstorm
3. Develop new methods
4. Open to unusual ideas
5. Imagine new possibilities

Struggles in Leadership

1. May undervalue proven methods
2. May lack focus
3. Difficulty with following set procedures
4. Can become bored easily
5. Sometimes forget reality

Creative Trait examples

Some typical examples of this Trait are famous personalities: Beyoncé , Lady Gaga, Tyler Perry, Michael Jackson Albert Einstein, Michio Kaku, Albert Camu, C.S. Lewis, JK Rowling, government leaders, Presidents Thomas Jefferson Richard Nixon; business leaders – Walt Disney, Steve Wozniak, Larry Page, Elon Musk, Bill Gates, Mary Spio; sports icons Bernie Williams, John McEnroe.

 ## Creative – Leadership Strengths

Artistic and original

The mental images that come to mind when you think of people talented in the fields of art, music, drama, and related fields are a good place to start to understand this Trait. We can see and hear their talents and know that they are clearly different; we often say they have a gift. We all have our natural talents or "gifts", but the Creative Trait seems to be more physically, emotionally, and especially aesthetically obvious. They are often capable of touching our spirits, mystically inspiring us, and impacting us deeply.

Typically, in a group, everyone sees the correlation and knows who these people are. On one team (Lee's client), both individuals who scored high in this Trait were immediately recognized by their peers: one was a graphic artist type and the other a gifted soprano who sang in the local opera.

In another situation, a workshop participant who scored high in this area indicated that it did not seem to fit him. His comment was immediately contradicted by a teammate who said, "You are an artist at bending sheet metal." You can take a piece of metal and shape it perfectly to fit an aircraft engine nacelle." So, this creative bent is often evidenced in areas of craftsmanship.

Creativity will be displayed in many business areas, such as product and solution design, especially marketing. Of course, areas like architecture and most all of the design engineering fields will be heavily loaded with this talent.

Abstract thinkers

Creativity also extends to more abstract, conceptual thinking and includes those involved in creative writing, poetry, philosophy, math, software development, and IT areas. With a mind that operates well with symbols and imagery, they see what others do not see and connect dots in ways others don't easily conceive.

Breakthrough problem solvers

Companies, or departments within a company, frequently hit a stalemate where the solution to a nagging ordeal is elusive. Team members can sharpen their pencils, review data and trends, and evaluate team performance ad nauseam, but to no avail. Introducing, creative problem-solvers, Creative people naturally, and sometimes playfully, connect seemingly unrelated data and ideas with new possibilities that result in breakthrough solutions. They bring their abstract thinking skills to resolve an impasse.

Since they "think outside the box," what remains hidden to some may very well be obvious to Creatives.

Thomas Edison serves as a classic example of persistently pursuing a novel innovation: the light bulb! "As an inventor, Edison made 10,000 attempts to create a viable light bulb. But note the confidence in his ability to eventually breakthrough: "I have not failed 10,000 times. I have not failed once. I have succeeded in proving that those 10,000 ways will not work. When I have eliminated the ways that will not work, I will find the way that will work."[1]

After Hugh's team conducted a talent awareness program for a corporate board, they decided to replace the concrete operational based CEO with a more Creative leader. They recognized that if the business was going to change, they needed a person who could more quickly bring visionary and out-of-the-box thinking to the table.

The **strengths** of the Creative leader are that they can be very imaginative, curious and enterprising. They tend to see the pathway to the future very quickly and how to change processes and systems for delivering new services or the same service with greater efficiency. The **struggle** is that with so many new ideas hitting them they can turn the business into spaghetti very quickly and overwhelm the team. Not all innovation works unless it can be effectively resourced, planned, and executed in a workable solution within a reasonable time. We alerted the board to watch for this.

Frontier thinkers that generate lots of ideas

Creative minds are idealistic and thus they're not encumbered by the realities at hand. Rather, they are open to the enchanting lands of possibilities. Unfettered contemplations frequently prove to be a fruitful fountain overflowing with ideas and insights not considered by those who operate primarily in the practicalities of the here and now.

Lee led a training recently with a group of Air Force leaders that included a wing commander. He had the highest Creativity score on his staff. In a private conversation Lee commented, "I bet when you go on a trip you return with a note-pad filled with ideas for your team to implement—I wouldn't be surprised if they aren't dreading your list." He chuckled in agreement and replied, "Yes, that's very true, and they gave me that feedback in a recent staff meeting. I've come to realize there is no way we can implement all my ideas, so we are vetting them more."

EDS founder and business magnate, Ross Perot underscores that very point in describing the value of having creatively talented people in his organization.

"When Mort Meyerson, whose name is now a legend in the computer industry, first joined us as a young man, he bombarded us almost daily with creative ideas and changes that he thought would make the company more successful. Interestingly enough, some of the people in leadership positions got irritated. I was impressed by Mort and his creativity. One of the problems in dealing with creative people is that most of their creative ideas will not work, and you have to listen to nine bad ideas to get the idea that could make history. I always considered this to be fun and part of the process.

"In Mort's case, I learned quickly that he had a unique characteristic that most creative people do not have—he had the mental self-discipline to filter out his bad ideas. Early in Mort's career when he would come to me with a new idea, my response would be, 'Follow your nose.' Two weeks later, he would have made tremendous progress, or he would mention to me that once he had gotten into the idea, he decided it would not work and had dropped it. This made Mort unique and special."[2]

 ## Creative – Leadership Struggles

Prone to look past proven methods and disregard others' ideas

Since so much of their mental time and energy is spent on the abstract, Creative people are known to devalue previous plans and procedures as if they were inherently deficient. Their penchant is pursuing that which is "new" and inviting instead. As a result, they may *struggle* to operate within the confines of existing policy and procedures. Quite often they are rebels, and that can work to be both positive and negative.

Can become defensive or protective of their creations

While their contributions to the team effort are both innovative and needed, Creative people can be closed-minded about their work, which can come across as a self-serving, lofty attitude. And just as important and problematic, they don't take well to constructive criticism of their creations. Also, being wedded to their own originality, it's very difficult for them to value the concrete logic or the creative ideas of others. Such is often a turnoff to others making legitimate contributions to the overall successes of the group.

Prone to idea overload

Working with Creative people can be like sipping a drink from a fire hydrant: too much, too fast! Typically, it's impossible to implement their plethora of ideas, and as a result, they will have to likely let go of some of them. So, it's important to recognize that Creative leaders can wear their people out with a flurry of ideas. To his credit, the colonel mentioned earlier trusted his people, heard their feedback, and throttled back on his stream of ideas. As Ross Perot pointed out so well, rarely are all ideas doable; they must be vetted and prioritized.

Can easily lose others who don't think/communicate like them

Creative people are often gifted abstract thinkers who are quick to launch into the enticing world of their captivating ideas. Others, however, may have trouble tracking the direction of their abstract explanations that seem to ignore a concrete, here and now, linear logic flow. And, the Creative person may be oblivious to how they come across to other teammates. To help dial Creative people back into reality, ask them to 1) tell a story that illustrates their point; b) draw a picture doing the same or 3) provide an example that brings their abstract notion back down to the world of everyday life.

Whom do you know with the Creative Trait?

1. _____

2. _____

3. _____

Quick Coach Notes

Ideal Work Environment

Creative personalities operate best in a setting that offers opportunities to employ their vivid imaginations. They flourish with enthusiastic support for their new ideas as they are showcased. They like the freedom to think, create, and imagine, and ample room for originality.

Connecting with the Creative Trait

1. Expect/encourage their many ideas and out-of-the-box thinking.
2. Encourage them to brainstorm.
3. Recognize their desire to investigate ideas.
4. Resist the temptation to prematurely edit their ideas.

Managing the Creative Trait

1. Let them know you value their creative mind.
2. Help them understand that they must help in the vetting to clarify which of their many ideas can be implemented.
3. Expect them to be nonconforming and ignore rules.
4. Clarify boundaries and expectations often—and have a plan in mind.

Creative people flourish when given freedoms to brainstorm and generate innovative, cutting-edge solutions. They may struggle with boundaries and established procedures, so self-discipline and regular accountability for their results are keys to maximizing their contributions.

ENDNOTES

1 https://www.forbes.com/sites/nathanfurr/2011/06/09/how-failure-taught-edison-to-repeatedly-innovate/#5e349a6865e9
2 *Ross Perot: My Life and The Principles for Success,* 2nd edition by Ross Perot, 1996 Arlington TX, page 144.

CHAPTER 21 ▶ THE ANCHORED TRAIT

FACTOR 8: LEFT-SIDE TRAIT

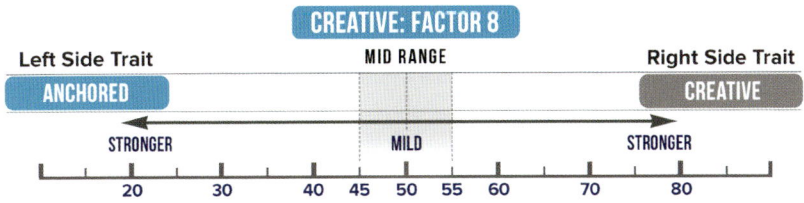

I have trouble imagining what I could do that's beyond the practicality of what I can do.

—David Byrne

Anchored personalities are also innovative, but they utilize very different tactics. Rather than dabbling in the world of possibilities and unproven plans, Anchored people are naturally going to follow an incremental, step-by-step approach to make improvements, utilizing tried and true methods as much as possible. They are especially valuable for operating proven processes that merely need ongoing tweaking to refine them to current conditions.

Anchored – Strengths and Struggles

 **Strengths in Leadership**

1. Orthodox approach
2. Focus on practical realities
3. Follow established procedures
4. Operate using evidence
5. Consistent implementation and execution

 **Struggles in Leadership**

1. May discount unconventional ideas
2. May overly rely on proven procedures
3. May procrastinate on open-ended tasks
4. Can be hesitant to act on new ideas
5. Can be overly conservative and resist change

Anchored Trait examples

Examples of the Anchored Trait include famous personalities: Andy Rooney, Barbara Walters, Chris Wallace, Morgan Freeman, Christopher Lee, Anne Hathaway, Penelope Cruz, Presidents George Washington, John Adams, Gerald Ford, and Lyndon Johnson; generals Colin Powell, Dwight Eisenhower, Omar Bradley; business—business leaders Andrew Carnegie, Sam Walton, Warren Buffett, Jim Senegal; sports coaches Bear Bryant, Nick Saban, and Joe Paterno.

 Anchored – Leadership Strengths

Use practical, logical steps to innovate

Anchored people are reluctant to expend time, energy and resources on speculative plans that their Creative friends get so pumped about. They are committed to realizing results through practical steps. Like the simplicity of step "1, 2 and then 3," Anchored personalities rely on familiar procedures that yield predictable results. Yes, they innovate, but in a different way than Creative people. Their innovations are crucial to any organization because they focus on refining or improving current products and processes that bring incremental steps of progress.

Jim Collins underscores the power of day-by-day growth in his famous story of the egg developing into a chicken. No one noticed or celebrated the process and then one day a breakout occurred. Then, of course, it was a big deal, but it didn't just happen that day. Most great organizations evolve this way—they just keep producing all the while quietly growing their capability and capacity to get better and better.

The *strength* of an Anchored person is that there is consistency and reliability in what they deliver, and decisions will be made from the framework of what they know. Thus, their contributions are like the very predictable process of going from an egg to a chicken. Slow and steady, but highly likely to produce dependable results on time.

Focus on the present and past rather than the future

When problem-solving, Anchored folks draw from past examples and current processes. Their innate sense of practicality slants them to working with processes that have some proven track record as opposed to "iffy" untested possibilities.

 ## Anchored – Leadership Struggles

Closed-minded to new possibilities

Tending to operate well on autopilot, Anchored people are naturally not attracted to new ideas, being suspicious until they see and understand the logic involved. They are practical in their approach and have little time for frivolous speculations. Hence, they are often reticent to listen openly to radical ideas and unlikely to be early adopters.

The Anchored Trait has some similarities with the Cautious Trait, since both Traits lean heavily on the practicality of what is already proven to be successful, rather than pursuing the uncertainties that come with new territories and processes.

Stubbornly hang on to what is familiar and favorite

This group actively resist giving up "tried and true" procedures in favor of experimental efforts. Victory comes from adhering faithfully to proven processes, as opposed to a "flash-in-the-pan" surge into unknown territory.

Hugh's team recently consulted with a well-established architectural business to help their leadership team unlock growth opportunities. The business was led by a CEO founder who was very Anchored. It was naturally easier for her to stay with delivering a similar hourly-based service that had worked well in the past and upon which the firm had built a solid reputation.

The problem that emerged was the younger leaders were pushing for technological and product changes because they could see that the business would slide backward in the next few years if they did not bite the bullet. Ultimately, the CEO founder appointed one of the younger leaders who was both Creative and Planned to be Chief Innovation Officer. With this combination of Traits, the CEO knew the ideas that got presented would be well conceived and researched. They set up rules of the game for reviewing and managing innovation. In the end, this was a growth path that created a "win-win" for everyone.

Slow to buy into the new team effort until they "own" it

Anchored people are slow to embrace new action plans until they see practical steps fall into place. "Seeing is believing" for Anchored people.

This was another case where Hugh's team was brought in to help coach a hard-charging pioneering and risk-taking entrepreneur who launched an existing retail restaurant chain (franchise) in a new country. The food concept this business offered was doing really well in England. However, outside England, it needed creative tweaks to fit the local culture.

The unusually anchored entrepreneur just thought if he executed on the original English food concepts, he would be milking a cash cow. So, his learning lesson was to gradually introduce menu and restaurant environment tweaks and watch the customers connect to them. Over time, he learned to get out of his own way and listen to the customer for making changes while protecting the brand and the core of the original concept.

Falter with open-ended tasks

Because Anchored people rely on predictable, step-by-step plans, they are prone to falter when the next step in the plan isn't immediately obvious—or all plans are changing quickly. Unfortunately, predictability is a diminishing value, as noted by Howard H. Stevenson and Mihnea C. Moldoveanu in their *Harvard Business Review* article:

"What is happening to predictability in an intensely competitive, rapidly changing global economy? It is being destroyed. The practices that leaders are adopting to make their organizations more competitive are ignoring the human need for predictability."

Thus, Anchored personalities *struggle* when a "new and innovative Pac-man" consumes predictability in the work setting, leaving them with a plateful of unknowns. Uncertainties about future steps often bog the Anchored person down in a quagmire of unproductivity. Situational awareness to make timely, needed changes is critical, but leaders must also be sensitive to the human challenges brought by the speed of change, especially to those with the Anchored Trait.

Whom do you know with the Anchored Trait?

1. _____

2. _____

3. _____

Quick Coach Notes

Ideal Work Environment

Anchored personalities perform best in predictable environments that offer systematic procedures that lead to goals. They excel at following through on clearly articulated plans but may struggle when next steps are not clear, or they are forced to be innovative with out-of-the-box problem solving.

Connecting with the Anchored Trait

1. Keep ideas practical.
2. Show them the logical steps.
3. Tell them past experiences.
4. Present them with concrete benefits.

Managing the Anchored Trait

1. Encourage them to innovate incrementally by taking current processes to the next step.
2. Describe abstract ideas using examples, graphics, and pictures, plus words.
3. Use dialogue and brainstorming to help them think outside the box.
4. Value their linear development process for continuous improvements in processes and system.

Anchored personalities can improve their performance by collaborating with their more daring and innovative teammates, helping them vet their ideas and bring the good ones to fruition.

Creative, Anchored, and Mid-Range —we need them all

Every organization needs both Creative and Anchored personalities. While their tendencies pull in opposite directions, a clear delineation of goals and roles can synthesize their *strengths* into a fluid, forward direction. Creatives put their best foot forward with their innovative, visionary, and cutting-edge thoughts. Anchored people bring practicality and the passion to build continuous improvements into the organization by refining well-established procedures.

— Self-Assessment Application —

Based on the behavioral Traits described in this chapter and the previous chapter (or based on your actual *DNA Behavior* assessment results), what is your default *DNA Behavior*? Is it more right side, left side, or clearly in the middle?

Place an "x" on the "Anchored to Creative" scale below that best describes you. You may also use the free Self-Assessment Worksheet to capture your strengths and struggles for this factor. Download a copy at www.LeadershipBehaviorDNA. com/Book.

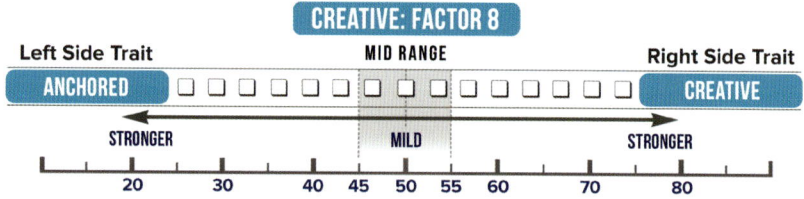

1. Looking back at the *strengths* and *struggles* for this Trait,
    a. What are some of your key *strengths* for leadership?
    b. Looking at your *struggles*, what is one area where you could adapt and become a better leader?
2. How can you apply the *Quick Coach Notes*?
3. With whom will you share this information for more insight, discussion, and accountability?

Calculate your specific Factor score by taking the *Leadership Behavior DNA* assessment. It only takes 10 minutes to receive your personal report.

Learn More at www.LeadershipBehaviorDNA.com/Book

SECTION 3

MANAGING TEAM DIFFERENCES

CHAPTER 22 ▶ MAXIMIZING DIFFERENCES TO BUILD TRUST AND TEAMWORK

Strength lies in differences, not in similarities.

—Stephen Covey

In your review of the eight Factors and sixteen Traits, we hope that you have seen that so much of what undermines teamwork is just people being themselves. That is the reality. Each person is unique and often the people we need most in our lives and work are the ones who are very different from us—often making them the ones hardest to relate to.

Struggles come with the Strengths as part of our DNA. They are just the other side of the coin and there is not much you can do about someone else's natural born struggles.

This important insight is crucial for building the trust needed to form cohesive teams—teams that can work through the stress and meet the challenges of a highly competitive and rapidly changing world.

In this chapter, we'll examine the crucial importance of celebrating differences (diversity) while at the same time building unity. You will see how understanding, accepting, and respecting people who are different rapidly builds trust. This is critical because trust is the big hurdle that teams have to cross in order to unite and execute decisions and plans to achieve mission success.

Applying the Platinum Rule in Teams

Do unto others as they would like to be done unto.

We continue to refer to the *Platinum Rule* because though it's very simple, it's often difficult to grasp and always challenging to follow. So, let's take another look. Because this short expression sounds similar to the Golden Rule, it can catch us off balance. It's also somewhat conflicting because our natural focus is often on ourselves and what others can do for us. But here we are called to focus on consideration for the other person. We're going to give them a gift. They may not have done anything special to deserve it and they may have made no effort to adapt to us, but we're bending our own style and adapting our own behaviors to meet their needs. Some would say, "That's not fair that I have to adjust my behavior for someone else—what kind of deal is that?"

In fact, we've had leaders in workshops challenge us saying, "But if I'm the boss, should they not be adapting to me?" Yes, we hope they will, but if you want to be the most effective boss you can be for that person, then you should set the example by adapting your communications and your emotions to relate in a way that works for them. Recall the story about Bob in the chapter on the Reserved Trait—Lee learned to adapt to Bob by giving him a heads-up so he could reflect on an important question before putting him on the spot in the staff meeting.

To illustrate in a more vivid way, this may help. You may have heard a version of this old saying in the workplace, "Give the dog what the dog wants to eat." If the person wants an outline versus a narrative, then give them an outline—even though you may prefer a narrative.

Another very practical way to think of the **Platinum Rule** is to consider the situation where you're a meat eater and you're having a friend over for dinner. If you know this friend is a vegetarian, wouldn't you consider serving an entree such as eggplant parmesan instead of beef stroganoff? Though this is a different context from team/work relationships, it serves as a clear example of doing unto someone else as they would like to be done unto.

Like most other rules, this one has exceptions too. There are obviously times when you don't do something for someone just because it's what they want. That's where discernment, wisdom, and courage come into play to show us how to apply our leadership balance of kindness and toughness.

The **Platinum Rule** seems to be the most difficult to apply when the other person is very different from us in their natural **DNA be-**

haviors. You know this is true if you have someone at home who is opposite from you in a specific Trait.

In the early years of his marriage, Lee knew nothing of this rule and always thought that his wife should be more like him—that would solve all their differences. Slowly, he began to realize she was a very different person. When he saw her graph showing she was on the opposite side in every Trait he thought, "Whoops!" And then one day she asked him not to talk to her until she had finished a cup of coffee. As a reserved introvert, she was overwhelmed by too many words so early in the morning. Lee wanted to honor her and began working on it. He's still coaching himself to respect her quiet time and several other **Platinum Rule** adaptations for their differences. It's difficult, but the payoff is worth the effort—45 great years of marriage and they're still growing closer.

Now, let's take the **Platinum Rule** into the workplace and examine a specific case with two very different people on the same team—Jen and Tom. They have very different roles, but they must work collaboratively to be successful. Examine the **DNA Behavior** Comparison Report graph shown below, and you'll see that their differences are stark. You will recall that that a ten-point difference in a Factor is one standard deviation, meaning there is something different in their behaviors. A spread of 20 points difference in a Factor score is a very significant difference (probably opposite) and 30 points is an extreme difference.

You can graphically see the significant differences in the natural behaviors of these two people. In Factor 2 People and 4 Structure, they are almost three standard deviations (SD) apart, and in three Factors, they are separated by roughly two SD. In Factor 3 Patience, they are on the same side but will operate somewhat differently as they diverge by 1 SD. Factor 5 Trust is the only one where they are really close.

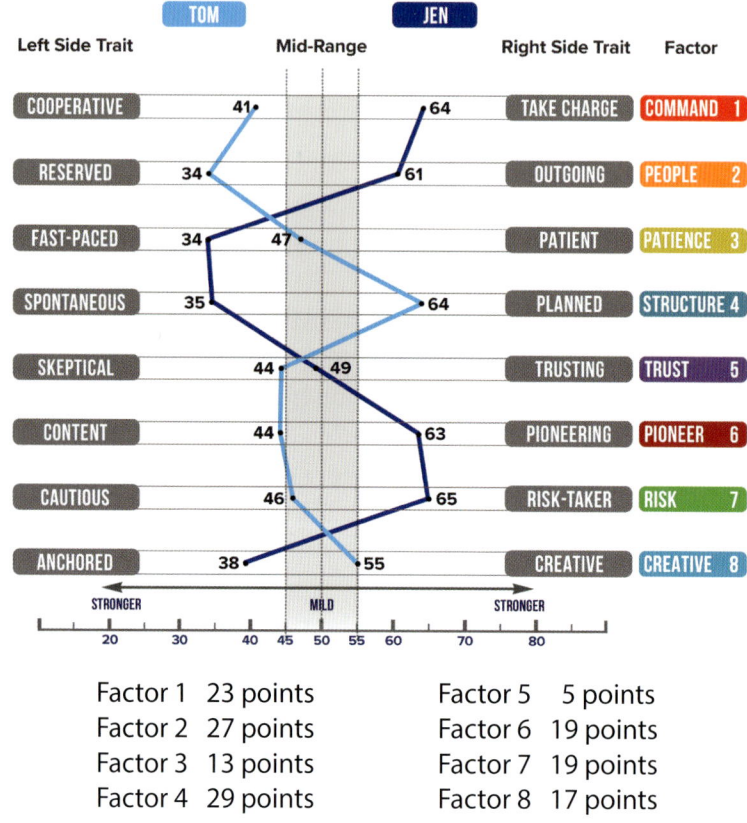

Factor	Points	Factor	Points
Factor 1	23 points	Factor 5	5 points
Factor 2	27 points	Factor 6	19 points
Factor 3	13 points	Factor 7	19 points
Factor 4	29 points	Factor 8	17 points

On the positive side, between these two people, they have *strengths* (talents) in six of the eight Traits. With the exception of Patient and Trusting, each has *strengths* that can cover for the other's *struggles*. They look like the perfect match—but because opposite-Trait *struggles* are the most irritating, it's most likely the perfect storm, unless they apply the *Platinum Rule*.

This is where scientific evidence, graphics, and numbers are a big help (like putting wheels on luggage). These two people can visually and objectively see that their *DNA Behaviors* are opposite. They can know that they can't change the other person, but they can value their *strengths* and see how they have great potential for contributing to each other's success. It won't be easy, but if each begins to apply the *Platinum Rule*, having appropriate expectations for the other, they can work together like a pitcher and catcher in baseball. Very different talents, but an amazing team.

Back to Tom and Jen above. We've actually worked with many office mates like them. If we were coaching them, we would have them share their individual *strengths* and then their *struggles*, and discuss how they are different, how that can be an advantage and how it can be an irritation. You will recall that in the previous chapters, we provided Quick Coach Notes for "Connecting with" and "Managing" each Trait. They can use those notes to point out specifics of how they would "like to be done unto." With this very transparent discussion, they can form a very trusted and respectful relationship where each values the other person's different talents and accepts their *struggles*. Typically, we would ask each to agree to work on one of their own *struggles* as a commitment to further improve their relationship; in effect, it's like giving them a gift.

Moving from Diversity to Team Unity

One of the major goals of this book is to help you better understand, accept, and respect others who are different and thus neutralize the divisive power of differences.

In team building, one of the essential challenges is to capitalize on differences and use a diversity of talents to build strong teams. However, as we have just seen, whenever you have differences, there will be a high potential for frustration or conflict.

So, we have a real dilemma: most teams need both diverse talents and unity, but differences (diverse talents) have a natural tendency to divide and prevent unity. The mutual trust that teams need can be continually undermined by their diversity, and this brings a significant and ongoing challenge to teamwork.

Diversity Has Many Forms

Diversity programs now play an important role in any work culture. They educate and remind us of the need to identify and remove any prejudice and bias that undermine fairness and respect for others in the workplace. These programs can help us change our mindsets, attitudes, and behaviors to match our professed values. Clearly, all of us can benefit from personal growth in this area.

However, challenges of diversity are much broader than race, gender, and age.

This became obvious during a team session at a plant when Lee noticed that there were worldviews from the following seven different camps:

1. **Management and unions**
2. **Racial and ethnic groups**
3. **Geographical and provincial culture (Boston MA is very different from Boston GA)**
4. **Experience: Seasoned veterans alongside "new people"**
5. **Age: Wisdom vs. boldness of youth, aka generational differences**
6. **Gender: Males and females**
7. **Natural talent/behavior differences**

During the session, he observed one team member attribute problems to no less than four of these "different-from" groups. Realistically there are many more *different* worldviews that affect teams in the workplace. For example, parents versus non-parents, single versus married, well-educated versus less educated and the many very personal differences in areas such as financial security, religion, values, family of origin, environment, and political affiliation. So, at any point, a team member has many possibilities for being different from someone else in the group.

Because some of these areas of differences are so difficult to talk about, learning about behavioral Traits provides a more acceptable and workable way to learn and value differences. And the more we can get people to see that diversity means valuing all people, regardless of their differences, the faster we will see fears and prejudices fade and the more we will see diversity with trust, respect, and unity.

Taking a broader understanding of the word diversity will help us achieve a positive perspective on diversity, i.e. capitalizing on the advantages of different talents and ideas to build highly successful teams.

Overcoming the Problems of Diverse Talents

An important goal of the earlier chapters was to help you gain a more objective viewpoint of yourself and others. If you've identified and removed some of your limiting filters and distorted (or biased) lenses, you will be able to see others from a more accurate and balanced perspective. This type of awareness will enable you to experience the powerful and positive benefits of individual differences. Now let's examine other ways that teams can overcome the divisive nature of differences and capitalize on them to build stronger teams.

Clarify areas of diversity and unity

One of the problems teams typically have is distinguishing between areas in which they need unity and areas in which they need to allow for individual differences. Consider the Diversity with Unity list below.

DIFFERENT (DIVERSITY)	SAME (UNITY)
• Talents	• Mission
• Motivations	• Commitment/loyalty
• Interests	• Organizational values
• Needs	• Opportunity
• Styles	• Policies/Discipline

Typically, teams should encourage diversity and individuality as much as possible and have a minimum of these right-side Unity items. This conceptual list will suit most organizations; however, the nature of some organizations and their missions may require more or less unity and discipline. For example, the military is going to have more on the Unity list than most civilian organizations. Regardless of the situation, it's always important for there to be clarity with a common understanding and acceptance about what needs to be the Same (Unity) and what can be Different (Diversity).

> *When there is disagreement or confusion on these two lists (diversity and unity), there is likely to be a breakdown in trust, cohesion, commitment, and teamwork. Make clarity a priority.*

Most successful companies today emphasize the importance of having a common core of values for their culture while welcoming different viewpoints and a constant influx of new ideas essential for staying viable in a fast-changing world. This tracks well with one of the common themes presented by Jim Collins and Jerry Porras in *Built to Last: Successful Habits of Visionary Companies* (the forerunner to *Good to Great*). In their classic Yin and Yang model, they point out that **visionary companies seek unwavering unity in the area of "core ideology" (core values plus purpose), but at the same time, they seek diverse ideas to stimulate progress for new methodologies and products.**[1]

> *Trusting relationships are essential to unite different talents into successful teams.*

The Team Cohesion Model below provides a conceptual view of some of the essential components in uniting diverse individuals to form a successful team. By now you have a good understanding that people are born with different behavioral talents. You have seen that opposite Traits each have their own *strengths* and *struggles* and that one Trait is not inherently better than another. Now we're looking at how to move individuals (especially those who are different) toward trust, unity, and team success.

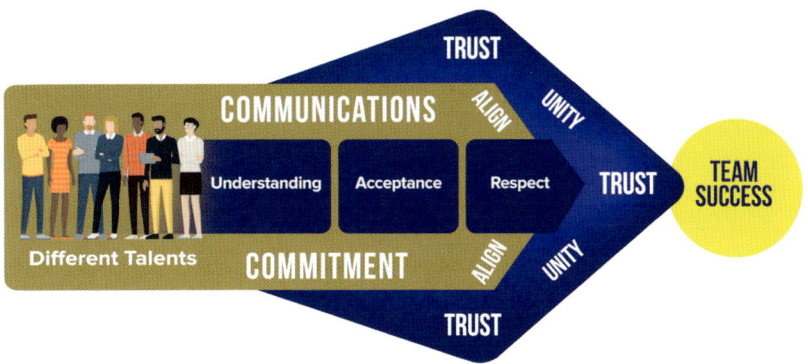

A quick analysis of the components in the above model can help us better understand teams and how an objective view of behaviors is critical for cohesion. The goal is to move from the diversity of individual talents to unity and mission success. Let's look at these components and how they can move us toward unity.

- **Communications:** Clarify—make sure everyone is on the same page.
- **Commitment:** Own your responsibilities to teammates and team goals.
- **Understanding:** Know yourself and your teammates' *DNA Behavior* and view differences as just different—not wrong.
- **Acceptance:** Value different *strengths* and accommodate different *struggles*. This is one of the major goals of this book—learning to accept those who are different. It's the only way to have a healthy relationship so you can be a good teammate (or mate/spouse).
- **Respect:** honor others and celebrate differences. The following lists provide a short summary of behaviors and actions that impact respect.

PEOPLE FEEL RESPECTED WHEN YOU	PEOPLE FEEL DISRESPECTED WHEN YOU
• believe in them • act like they're important • encourage them • show interest in them • accept them "as is" • seek their input • listen with genuine concern • honor their views/opinions • allow them to make decisions • are open and honest • recognize their turf • discover their dreams	• act like you're superior • ignore them, cut them off • focus mainly on yourself • try to change them • force your idea on them • ignore or interrupt them • minimize/discount what they've said • try to control them • are evasive, two-faced • ignore proper boundaries • criticize them

In comparing these two lists above, you can see that the behaviors that communicate respect demonstrate honor to others by giving (or giving up) something to the other person. Those that communicate disrespect, in effect, take something away (usually in order to protect or build up the person who is being disrespectful).

This giving/taking concept is very helpful in identifying whether your behaviors are communicating respect. Those who are takers will typically be focused on protecting or boosting themselves, leading to a lack of trust from others. Conversely, **those who focus on others with attitudes and behaviors that give respect are more trusted**. Relating back to the Secure versus Insecure graphics and discussion in Chapter 4, you can connect the dots and see that "givers" are more Secure and "takers" are more Insecure.

An others-oriented attitude also enables us to see that those who are different have qualities that we can admire and even want to emulate. They can be role models for our personal growth and can help us overcome some of our *struggles*. The bottom line is that **teams need givers—not takers**.

Trust

As you can see, the steps of the model are all contributing to increased trust. The more each individual shows respect for others (teammates) and commitment to the mission, the more trust accrues. Trust is crucial to teamwork because it enables teams to realize synergy and achieve more than the sum of their talents would indicate.

Align for the synergy and efficiency needed for execution

With alignment and mutual trust, individuals don't have to spend time defending themselves or apologizing for their *struggles*. Rather, they anticipate and accept each other's *struggles*. Individuals know that they can depend on their teammates to guard their blindside and look out for their interests. Their energy is freed to focus completely on the challenges of the tasks ahead. The team is positioned to achieve its goals with maximum success.

> *Our humility about ourselves, combined with our respect for our teammates, forms a powerful bond or formula for building cohesive relationships.*

Trust failures destroy teamwork

Trust is a two-edged sword. When it's broken, the effects are very destructive and can quickly break the ties that are holding a team together.

> *When trust breaks down, unity unravels, and every component of teamwork starts to collapse.*

Communication becomes more difficult; people quit trying to align, respect falls away, acceptance is replaced by criticism, and understanding breaks down. Commitment to the team quickly deteriorates and what is left is a group of talented individuals in survival mode with an every-person-for-himself (or herself) attitude.

Building trust is essential—work it

The bottom line is that Trust is such an essential and powerful ingredient in the teamwork formula that it must be continually developed and protected through conscious efforts. We've mentioned three very helpful steps.

- **Understand natural behavior and value differences.**
- **Change the way you think about others.** Rather than trying to change them, remember the two-sided coin. Instead of focusing on their *struggles*, turn the coin over and focus on their *strengths* and celebrate what they are bringing to the table and encourage their potential and dreams.
- **Practice the *Platinum Rule*.** Do unto others as they would like to be done unto.

Now let's see how you can apply these insights about working with differences to a real team.

Quick Coach Notes

Key Point

Recognize and celebrate differences. Follow the ***Platinum Rule*** to build trust and unity. Clarify issues where unity is essential and celebrate diversity in other areas. Align around core values and engage in judicious, healthy debate.

Questions

1. Are there people on your team whose "differences" are a distraction or irritation for you? What will it take for you to "turn the coin over" and focus on their ***strengths*** and ignore their ***struggles***?
2. Who do you need to respect more by applying the ***Platinum Rule*** in the way you connect and relate to them?
3. Have you been vulnerable about your own ***struggles*** by taking ownership of them and working to grow in those areas?

ENDNOTES

1   Article: "Preserve the Core/Stimulate Progress: The Yin and Yang of Visionary Companies James C. Collins and Jerry I. Porras," adapted from their book *Built to Last: Successful Habits of Visionary Companies*, Harper Business, 1994.

CHAPTER 23 ▶ BEHAVIOR PREDICTS TEAM DYNAMICS

We can't all be good at everything. This is partly the logic behind having a team in the first place, so each role can be filled with the person best suited for that role and together, every job and every strength is covered.

—Simon Sinek

No doubt, you have been wondering how all these differences impact teams. Glad you asked—it can be quite a revelation. Now let's look at a specific team to see how concepts of **DNA Behavior** apply to team dynamics. We'll analyze how group *strengths* and *struggles* impact the way a team performs internally and externally. Using the concepts of **DNA Behavior**, you'll be able to do the same but first, let's get some practice here, and then you can take on an additional team report that we'll mention on page 256. With that experience, you will be able to apply these insights to help your own team.

Team Dynamics with Real People

In our workshops, we always start out with understanding self and then others. But very quickly folks are wanting to know what the others are like: who is like me and who is different and in what way? Fortunately, there is a simple way to avail that information using the **DNA Behavior** Team Performance Report. Let's take a look.

Notice that each Factor continuum depicts all teammates and where their scores fall with placement as either left, center, or right-side Traits. Differences and similarities jump off the page. At a glance you can see why someone has been hard to understand—and know that you can't change them—they were born with different talents, both *strengths* and *struggles*. They say a picture is worth a thousand words and that's so true. Even more impressive, this picture is often worth months of exposure and experience—allowing understanding and acceptance in a single workshop.

Now let's analyze this group—Factor by Factor—and see how it reveals the dynamics of team behavior.

COMMAND: FACTOR 1

| COOPERATIVE (PRACTICAL) | MID RANGE | TAKE CHARGE (VISIONARY) |
Left Side Trait		Right Side Trait
• 29 - Isabella Martinez	• 46 - Sonja Garland	• 60 - John Doe
• 41 - DeAndre Waters	• 52 - Will DiRago	
• 43 - Karmen Light	• 54 - Jamie Jones	
• 43 - Scott Savage	• 54 - Quincy Garrison	

PEOPLE: FACTOR 2

| RESERVED (FOCUSED) | MID RANGE | OUTGOING (EXPRESSIVE) |
Left Side Trait		Right Side Trait
• 37 - Karmen Light	• 45 - Will DiRago	
• 42 - DeAndre Waters	• 46 - John Doe	
• 43 - Scott Savage	• 47 - Isabella Martinez	
	• 51 - Quincy Garrison	
	• 52 - Jamie Jones	
	• 53 - Sonja Garland	

PATIENCE: FACTOR 3

| FAST-PACED (LOGICAL) | MID RANGE | PATIENT (TOLERANT) |
Left Side Trait		Right Side Trait
• 34 - John Doe	• 45 - Jamie Jones	• 57 - Sonja Garland
• 40 - Will DiRago	• 52 - Karmen Light	• 62 - Isabella Martinez
	• 52 - Quincy Garrison	• 63 - Scott Savage
		• 66 - DeAndre Waters

STRUCTURE: FACTOR 4

| SPONTANEOUS (INSTINCTIVE) | MID RANGE | PLANNED (SYSTEMATIC) |
Left Side Trait		Right Side Trait
• 41 - Scott Savage	• 49 - Jamie Jones	• 56 - Sonja Garland
	• 51 - John Doe	• 59 - Will DiRago
	• 54 - DeAndre Waters	• 65 - Quincy Garrison
		• 68 - Karmen Light
		• 67 - Isabella Martinez

← STRONGER ——————— MILD ——————— STRONGER →

Factor 1. Mostly Cooperative or mid-range. This team is generally process-focused in order to achieve results. Only John is Take Charge. Unless John is the team leader, we can expect that decision-making is going to be slow. If John is not the leader, he may become discouraged at the slow progress of the team. This is not a start-up or turn-around team, but one that operates within an existing structure and proven processes to achieve success.

Factor 2. Group dynamics tend toward being Reserved so they will tend to be very task-focused (not multi-tasking) and seeking closure. No one is Outgoing and that means that fun and communications may be limited. Also, their ability to network is going to be limited. The good thing is that they will stay focused on work and not be chatty or distracted, looking for new opportunities.

Factor 3. More Patient than Fast Paced means they will want stability and be somewhat resistant to change. To be their best, they'll need harmony and minimum conflict. If John is the leader, he's going to have to realize that most of his people cannot keep up with his pace and desire for quick changes. Also, he'll have to soften his tone and intensity, recognizing that pressure, which works well for him, will actually slow the productivity of others. If one of the Patient folks is in charge, he or she will have to toughen up to deal in a straightforward direct way with John and Will.

Factor 4. Overall, this group is very planned and systematic. They want to get it right—the first time—and usually that takes longer. Accuracy will be a ***strength***; flexibility will be a ***struggle***.

TRUST: FACTOR 5

Left Side Trait	MID RANGE	Right Side Trait
SKEPTICAL (QUESTIONING)		**TRUSTING (BELIEVING)**
• 37 - John Doe • 41 - Will DiRago • 42 - Karmen Light • 44 - Quincy Garrison	• 47 - Jamie Jones • 53 - Sonja Garland • 55 - Isabella Martinez • 55 - DeAndre Waters	• 59 - Scott Savage

PIONEER: FACTOR 6

Left Side Trait	MID RANGE	Right Side Trait
CONTENT (BALANCED)		**PIONEERING (GOAL ORIENTED)**
• 27 - Will DiRago • 35 - Isabella Martinez • 37 - Sonja Garland • 42 - Karmen Light • 43 - DeAndre Waters • 43 - Scott Savage	• 50 - Quincy Garrison • 51 - Jamie Jones	• 63 - John Doe

RISK: FACTOR 7

Left Side Trait	MID RANGE	Right Side Trait
CAUTIOUS (CONSERVATIVE)		**RISK-TAKER (COURAGEOUS)**
• 37 - Sonja Garland • 39 - Quincy Garrison • 41 - DeAndre Waters • 42 - Scott Savage • 44 - Isabella Martinez	• 50 - Jamie Jones • 50 - Karmen Light	• 57 - Will DiRago • 60 - John Doe

CREATIVE: FACTOR 8

Left Side Trait	MID RANGE	Right Side Trait
ANCHORED (CONSISTENT)		**CREATIVE (ORIGINAL)**
• 33 - Quincy Garrison • 43 - Isabella Martinez	• 46 - Sonja Garland • 48 - John Doe • 48 - DeAndre Waters • 51 - Jamie Jones • 55- Karmen Light	• 62 - Scott Savage • 62 - Will DiRago

← STRONGER ———————— MILD ———————— STRONGER →

Factor 5. They tend to be more Skeptical, so not much is going to slip by them, and they will not be taken advantage of easily. Trusting and believing in others is not their *strength*. Becoming more flexible and situationally communicating trust will feel risky to them but will pay off with trust returned by others.

This team must grapple with the great dilemma of trust: to get trust, you must give trust. That will be a challenge for these skeptics.

Factor 6. They are heavily loaded toward being Content. Reliable production is its *strength*. Making rapid changes, taking new territory or getting new clients is not.

Factor 7. They are generally Cautious and will guard their initiatives to minimize risks. Knowing this can help the leaders above them have realistic expectations.

Factor 8. They seem to have a good balance of Creative and Anchored Traits.

Overall, this team seems to be process- and system-oriented.

Their sweet spot appears to be organizing, systemizing, inspecting, checking, and ensuring things are done properly. They seem to be well-suited for a larger, established organization (not so dynamic and entrepreneurial) and would appear to be very talented for the fields of finance, audit, internal operations, or engineering. They work best alone and will be reticent to communicate except when it's essential to get their job done. As a group it's obvious that they would not be well-suited for outside sales, which are typically almost their opposite.

With the knowledge from previous chapters, even a quick glance at this graphical team array highlights the science of how individual **DNA Behavior** differences impact team dynamics in a very real and powerful way. Teammates can visually see how they are different and use that information to have realistic expectations for each other. Each person can understand and value the different talents of everyone on the team. It's obvious to the leader that each person is unique and needs to be encouraged, managed, and communicated with differently.

In a typical workshop, after we have unpacked the eight Factors and done a couple of small-group exercises to apply the individual insights, the team is able to then look at their Team Performance

Report and analyze it much the same as we have done here with a high degree of accuracy. The discovery process and subsequent flow of learning are so logical and transparent that they facilitate a low-threat environment that frees people to be vulnerable and openly discuss their **strengths** and **struggles**.

Self-awareness and others-awareness increases objectivity which facilitates vulnerability which builds team trust.

Discussions around the Traits significantly increase understanding that opens the path for greater respect and increased trust. That's why we typically say that a workshop like this can accelerate trust in one day to a level that would normally take six months to a year of working together.

Several months ago, Hugh's team helped a staff group from a local university walk through this process. Members who in the past had very little rapport with certain "irritating" colleagues began to see how it was their natural differences **(struggles)** that were the issue. With this new understanding, they learned to value their teammates' diverse **strengths**. They began to build camaraderie and now, a year later, leadership reports that the team is working harmoniously and productively. That's a success by any measure and it's not that difficult when you follow the principles and processes described here.

As mentioned earlier, we've provided another team report graphic (very different and it includes some additional insights from the team report) in the free Fun Team Performance Report Analysis at www.LeadershipBehaviorDNA.com/Book. We encourage you to go there now and use the questions included to analyze that team. If you can grasp these basics, you will be equipped to think in terms of team dynamics in a totally new way.

Trust allows individuals to Engage and Align for Success

Before moving ahead, we have one more leadership model that has been very powerful for helping teams take advantage of their diverse talents and increased trust. We call it the Engage and Align Model™.

Engage and Align Model™

Clarify → Communicate → Collaborate

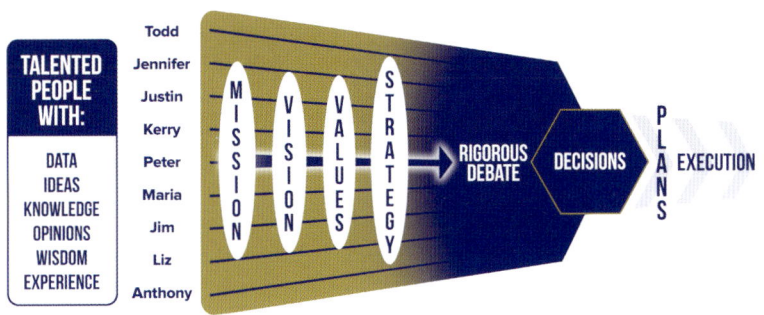

Moving from left to right on this graphic, you can see diverse, talented people coming together to discuss issues and make decisions. Each person brings his or her data, ideas, knowledge, opinions, wisdom, and experience to the discussion. Opinions and insights all must flow through the lens (or filters) of a previously determined mission, vision, values, and strategies. Anything that does not fit within those parameters is off limits. Because they have developed trust, they can have a rigorous, healthy debate on the issues and make sound decisions. Everyone has a say and the leader makes an informed decision or delegates it appropriately.

The rigorous debate (healthy, productive creative conflict) that is so essential to getting good buy-in can only occur when teams have a high level of trust—the kind of trust that comes from the humility and vulnerability typically gained from applying the principles and processes we have shared in the type of workshop described above. (This matches Steps 1 and 2 of Patrick Lencioni's *Five Dysfunctions of a Team* Model.)

From experience, we know that these concepts of **DNA Behavior** are powerful for understanding and leading yourself and others. This understanding is the foundation for trust, collaboration, and teamwork that can yield the most effective use of both individual and collective talents of the group.

But to have a healthy people culture—a culture that brings mission success, higher productivity and greater retention of top talent—requires healthy leadership. It needs leaders that are secure in themselves so that they can respect and value others.

The leader determines success more than anything else. So, as we move to the final chapter, let's focus on the responsibility of leaders to create that safe environment where all those DNA Behaviors are celebrated, developed, and exploited for the success of both mission and people.

Quick Coach Notes

Key Point

Self-awareness and others-awareness increases objectivity, which facilitates vulnerability which builds team trust. With trust, teams are more open to the rigorous debate needed to explore issues and align around the best solutions and ultimately gaining the buy in needed for smooth execution.

Questions

1. Given the description and analysis of this team above, what are the implications for your team?
2. Use the knowledge gained in this book and the questions provided along with the sample Fun Team Performance Report Analysis at www.LeadershipBehaviorDNA.com/Book to analyze this second team. You will be surprised how much of the team dynamics you will be able to quickly grasp.
3. In what ways are the two sample teams (the one in this chapter and the Fun Team Performance Report provided as an online download) similar and different from your team?
4. In what ways are you being intentional to build trust on your team so that you can have the judicious debate needed to arrive at the best decisions?

CHAPTER 24 ▶ TYING IT ALL TOGETHER & MAKING IT WORK IN YOUR LIFE & ORGANIZATION

Your life does not get better by chance,
it gets better by change.

—Jim Rohn[1]

We hope you've seen that ultimately, success at work depends on people. Of course, strategy, technology, information, resources, and capital are all essential, but they are not sufficient. People make it all happen.

A team with the right values and talents in combination with confident, engaged leadership is going to succeed. Leaders who support and develop their people, while holding them accountable for outcomes, can see them thrive and even surpass others with more resources and a better strategy. That's why organizations that understand this and emphasize a culture that values, develops and celebrates people, rises to the top and sets the pace in every sector.

It's not an accident that many on *Fortune's Most Admired Companies Top 100* list also show up on GlassDoor's *Best Places to Work*. We can draw a direct line from a keen understanding of people to a people culture to success and even dominance in an industry. Understanding the people internally allows for understanding what markets, consumers and people who are served by an organization want and need. A positive culture drives energy; positive energy drives commitment and action and action drives success.

Here's Why DNA Behavior Matters Most: It's the Tool for Building a Sustainable People Culture

Though human behavior comes naturally to each of us, working with it as leaders and teammates can be very challenging and at times frustrating. We've found that having a solid leadership philosophy aided by an objective tool can bring clarity and confidence in our attempts to relate and influence others.

Ideally, we all need to come up with our own philosophy about leadership. Obviously as all the schools teach, there has to be a focus on managing resources, solving problems, and getting results. But beyond that, a sound philosophy must answer the following questions:

- Do I believe in human potential and can I value others?
- Is my baseline mindset about others positive or negative?

We're convinced that it's crucial to have a positive perspective on people. Yet we also know that it's not always easy, especially when working in today's fast-paced, task-driven culture that rewards results and remains distant to the hearts of people.

Perhaps that's one of the greatest advantages of the ***DNA Behavior*** Discovery Process. It uses validated assessments to bring greater objective understanding through scientific measurement. The results concretely show our ***strengths*** and ***struggles*** and how we are all different. Realistically, we know we can't change others; what we can do is accept this reality in a healthy and workable way. The steps to achieving this are fairly simple:

1. First, we can set realistic expectations for people's behaviors by giving everyone space to be themselves, avoiding classifying "different" as bad or negative.

2. Second, we can set the example by adapting some of our behaviors to compensate for our ***struggles***—the ones that frustrate others and cause us to get in our own way —and use the ***Platinum Rule*** to adapt our behaviors, connecting with people in a way that makes them feel safe and more accepted.

3. Next, we can help others know their **DNA Behavior** in order to capitalize on their **strengths** and manage their **struggles**. Armed with that information, they are also equipped to learn to apply the **Platinum Rule** with others.

4. Finally, through open, objective discussion, we can share our **DNA Behaviors** and mutually agree to work on one or two of our **struggles** to compensate in the moment. Reprogramming our DNA might be impossible, but moderately adapting our behaviors in the moment is very doable and can have an enormously positive impact on our relationships and work success.

Learning to value and navigate differences has been one of the greatest benefits of our work in the human behavior area. Seeing those differences in people at home—the people we love and value the most—has helped us grow in this "people first" (people always) mindset. The objective insights from the **DNA Behavior** assessments have given us a powerful paradigm for understanding, accepting, respecting and then working with differences at work and in every environment. It's a system that is truly universal for appreciating diversity and valuing others.

Struggling to Balance Mission and People—An Every Day Challenge with a Simple Solution

Going back to our *Leadership Attributes Model* in Chapter 4, we know that good leaders have to accomplish the mission and take care of their people (Results and Relationships), leading to a balancing act that can test even the best leaders. We sometimes hear a debate about which is first or most important. After seeing the military struggle to balance the labels and priority of mission and people for generations, Lee was happy to see that the Air Force now has very creatively chosen a clever motto: "Mission First—People Always."

This foundational idea of a "people always" mindset is logical, scientifically based, and seems simple. Yet, because of the ways our brains are wired, leaders who are analytical, rational, and results-focused typically struggle when operating in this human domain. Remember, this is 40% of the population at the starting point and the higher we go in an organization, typically, the percentage of results/mission-focused leaders increases. So, for many, it's not natural for them to realize that good task management is not sufficient. They're leading people and people must be influenced—yes "results count" but you only get good results consistently from motivated and engaged people.

By simply observing a three-year-old, it's obvious that humans come well-equipped with both cognitive and emotional engines which drive our will and the choices we make. Even at that early, still formative stage of life, we can see that getting results through authority/power and fear management alone is not enough—people must be influenced in positive ways.

So, highly rational, results-oriented leaders have to deal with this thing called *human nature*, and for those who don't appreciate or don't understand it, it can be like navigating through a minefield. We hope that you now see that though human nature is diverse and complex, it can be influenced, inspired, energized and motivated toward growth for higher performance. Moreover, using the concepts of **DNA Behavior**, leaders and diverse talents can come together to form the cohesive teams so necessary for success in today's highly competitive and complex world.

Overall, we've leaned a bit more heavily on those whose natural DNA is results-oriented because typically, there are more bearing this trait at the higher levels of an organization. If you're among these people, it may seem that we've been talking more about offering "carrots" while neglecting the "sticks" that are sometimes needed to ensure consequences and accountability, but you need not worry. We agree there must be a balance. Soft love alone will not keep toddlers in line; there must be tough love too. Likewise, all successful cultures must protect organizational values and enforce high standards.

On the other hand, given the knowledge that 40% are born with a natural bent for People/Relationships, we know that many reading this book are likely to struggle with holding people accountable. Much of a good people culture comes naturally to relationship-oriented leaders, but learning to adapt their behaviors to provide the "tough" side of leadership is usually their greatest challenge. Accountability requires clear expectations, and the courage to confront poor performance and bad behavior. Procrastination is a sure sign of avoiding the issue; courage is required. Every leader must be ready to make hard decisions about people and apply negative consequences when appropriate.

Good Leaders Learn to Live in Tension—Simultaneously Pulled by both Results and Relationships

Though we often use the word "balance" in discussing results and relationships, the reality is that we will never achieve a true balance. We learn skills to move toward that state, knowing that a small change in behavior to gain a better balance can have a significant impact. Those adaptations or learned behaviors are crucial for good leadership and will quickly elevate our performance. But there is another way to look at it that is not only helpful, but likely critical for your success.

Leaders who battle to gain a balance will have to operate in a state of tension. You must feel the pull that is coming from seemingly opposite directions with seemingly opposite agendas to get results and accomplish the mission and celebrate and value your people.

In the past, we have at times called this "The Leadership Squeeze" because both mission and people are putting pressure on you—each wanting more from you. Regardless of which is the best picture for you—the tension of being stretched between the two on a rack or squeezed like a grape press—the stress is real.

The sooner you come to grips with this tension and accept it as part of your role as a leader, the better your leadership mindset will be. You will have obtained what the military calls the "high ground" for your battle to grow as a leader. You will also see the value that wisdom and community bring to your role in this struggle. This tension is the battle that great leaders recognize and accept as part of the mantle of their role. We also battle with this tension and one of our goals in this book is to help you recognize it and prepare for a victory—so you can be the great leader you want to be, and your people deserve.

The Hard Truth about Personal and Leader Development

Despite the advice and teaching from some to focus only on your *strengths*, we hope that you now understand why dealing with both your *strengths* and *struggles* is important for developing as a person and a leader. It's logical, but not easy so let's circle back for a final review of the issue of *struggles* before you begin applying natural **DNA Behavior** in your everyday life and work.

Our Struggles Can Negatively Impact Our Relationships

Grappling with Struggles

Like the elephant in the room, we find that all too often, there's never been a conversation about *struggles* and when we do get around to addressing them, we may find ourselves defensive or feeling exposed and too vulnerable. But discovering, unpacking, and integrating the insights of this book, especially with a team who knows you, has a way of revealing objective truth which benefits everyone. Think about finally seeing our own blind spots: this breakthrough tool of **DNA Behavior** provides objectivity and self-awareness that shines a light. Light brings awareness and we can see that we—like others—have a list of strengths and struggles and there is no shame in either. But using that knowledge is where the payoff comes.

Typically, when we experience others' *struggles*, we often perceive them as personal affronts or see them as problems of character or work ethic. Here, we've brought *struggles* out of the closet and given them their proper place at the table. With this perspective, this worldview, this mindset, we are able to take our focus off the negative. We can turn the coin over with our teammates and focus on their *strengths* instead of their *struggles*.

The knowledge that each of us is naturally wired with very specific *strengths* and *struggles* is liberating and facilitates clarity in understanding human nature. It's the foundation that enables the building of connections and cohesion that lead to better execution and a safer and more enjoyable workplace. Further, it means maybe not all issues can be easily resolved, as invariably some are caused by behavioral differences (people with different Traits see the same issues/events differently). But there is a big payoff when we learn to accept people as they are and learn to capitalize on the insights coming from these different viewing points.

We hope you have gained that awareness. Ideally, you've had discussions with those who know you well and trust you enough to be honest with you about what they experience. You now have the information needed to grow to a higher level as a person—to be a better teammate and a better leader. But information is not enough. You must grapple to grow.

Grappling with Growth

No one is perfect, and no one has all the right answers, but that's no reason to say "That's just the way I am." Yes, we all come equipped with **DNA Behaviors** that determine our natural bent or shape and **strengths**. But our more than 45 years of combined experience and a wealth of published research both conclude that the way we are is not an excuse for not becoming better. We must grow. We owe it to ourselves, our teammates (including families), and those we lead to grow as leaders and as people.

The word "grapple" seems so appropriate for the process of personal growth. In dealing with our **struggles**, we're not trying to reinvent ourselves. Whatever we come to the table with is good enough for greatness, if we can situationally learn to modify our behaviors (mainly to offset our **struggles**) to respond in the most effective manner.

Here, the challenge is twofold. First, it takes humility and confidence to gain self-awareness and objectively accept both the good and the bad (that sometimes is ugly). As we've said several times, accepting ourselves objectively takes both confidence and humility—key components of being genuine. With that, we must take ownership and have the courage to make the small and seemingly simple adaptations needed to grow, but they don't come naturally. Like swimming upstream, they require extra effort and progress is slow.

So, we must grapple with ourselves—with our doubts, our fears, insecurities, our shame, our old ways, and our old mindsets. We have to be intentional—with a plan and a commitment—and it's best when there is someone empowered to hold us accountable and give us feedback when we are succeeding (adapting and growing) and when we are missing opportunities.

We have encouraged you to be vulnerable in sharing not only your **strengths** but especially your **struggles**, so we thought it might be helpful for us to share three of ours. We've been aware of these for many years and though we have improved on them, we are still grappling with them. As we've pointed out, it does require intentionality and we still have to coach ourselves in the moment. When we replay the events, we celebrate successes and regret missed opportunities by recognizing them as a loss and recommitting to do better in the future.

About Hugh:

1. Hugh's greatest **strength** is his Pioneering nature which brings with it a very persistent goals focus. He can see opportunities in new fields a long way out and can be relentless in pursuit of the goal to be first. This does carry the challenge of what can be achieved in one lifetime and with that, the battle is to ensure there is ample time for family and friends. Ultimately, the key is finding good people and trusting them to come on the journey to climb the mountain with him.

2. In addition to being Pioneering, Hugh has a strong Risk-Taker Trait. He has been known to be fearless in business and this has worked 80% or more of the time. His challenge is to ensure that the losses in the 20% of failures do not take him out of the game in terms of time lost and financial cost. Further, he must grapple to not allow a loss to reduce his confidence to get back on the horse and get out there looking for the next opportunity. And as a Reserved and more guarded/private person, Hugh is adapting now to surround himself with good people who provide the sounding board necessary for risk management.

3. Another of Hugh's **strengths** is that he is extremely Fast-Paced, which comes out with strong results focus. To counter overuse, he's been committed to a "people first" mindset

for the last 18 years. Hugh grapples to temper his results drive by learning skills for managing relationships. At times in walking the tightrope of results and relationships, he's been too rigid in his mindset, and at other times too soft in holding people accountable. Nevertheless, he has greater clarity on the boundaries and is communicating them more effectively. His improved balance in leadership skills gives him the confidence to walk both sides of the street, encouraging and developing others, but clarifying expectations and applying consequences in a firm and healthy way when they are not met, or boundaries are crossed.

About Lee:

1. Lee's strongest Trait is Fast-Paced. His brain is in a constant swirl and physically, he likes to be on the go. It's easy for him to challenge things that logically don't make sense. He takes on the toughest problems with a bulldog approach, and he's comfortable confronting others, even senior leaders. But the downsides are also strong. He's constantly struggling to be more patient and less intense with others, especially those Patient people who are his opposites. He has to constantly remind himself that others have different talents that are extremely valuable. They bring stability to his life, so he is constantly coaching himself to slow down and celebrate their *strengths* and accept and accommodate their *struggles*.

2. When you put Take Charge, Fast-Paced, and Outgoing Traits together, there seems to be a blessing and a curse. Confident, with talents for both mission and people (part of the 20%) is good. But with strong opinions, candidly expressed with strong emotions, it's easy to be critical or harsh. With these three Traits, there is a lot of outward energy and it's easy to go over the top, which is definitely not a good way to positively influence others. By becoming more self-aware, he grapples to calm himself, lower his intensity, tone down, and reframe the situation to show respect and concern for others.

3. Take Charge and Outgoing Trait *strengths* are helpful for both results and people. However, when you start with strong opinions and then add an expressive Outgoing personality, it's easy to talk and difficult to listen. Such is the battle that Lee faces on a daily basis. He's grappling and making progress on this and all of these *struggles*, but they will always take intentionality and effort.

Obviously, this "grappling" is a challenge, but with a small increment of growth and change, the payoffs are huge. Most great leaders have grappled successfully. Here are some insightful words about it from Warren Buffett's website.[2]

"Warren Buffett's personality illustrates a person with some natural gifts, but also of a self-determined man who took stock of his weaknesses. He studied, practiced, and persevered to improve himself and his business acumen."

Remember, it only takes a small amount of change to yield a significant reward. And as you learn to adapt it gets easier. Most of us never fully conquer our *struggles* but adapting does become more natural.

To help you in this grappling/growing process, we've provided a one-page self-development worksheet at www.LeadershipBehaviorDNA.com/Book.

A Final Word

We have provided you, our reader, with lots of information and insights that have come from years of independent research and experience. But knowledge without action will not take you far. We've also been honest that applying this knowledge for growth is never easy. Whether you aspire to be a great football player, a concert pianist, an Olympic swimmer or a great leader or parent, you have to do the work, you have to pay the price, you have to sacrifice.

For most of us, this area of adapting human behavior is a more subtle type of sacrifice and suffering, because we're battling our

DNA, the hard-wiring in our brains. The discipline of the work seems more difficult to sustain and measure than swimming or practicing piano five hours a day. But if we want to grow and get better, we don't have a choice. We must grapple and engage in the battle.

Drawing from his POW background, Lee often shares about the power of struggle and suffering for personal growth and concludes his presentations with three lines from *The Return of the King* trailer.

> *There is no freedom without sacrifice.*
> *There is no victory without loss.*
> *There is no glory without suffering.*

Many of his POW teammates who suffered the most have lived the longest and most productive lives. Admiral James Stockdale, a seven-and-a-half-year POW, senior naval officer, and Medal of Honor recipient for his courageous performance as a POW, often quoted Aleksandr Solzhenitsyn's response to his eleven years of suffering in the Gulag Archipelago, the string of Russian prisons in Siberia: "Bless you prison."

The idea that we learn more in suffering than in the ease of life is echoed by Lee and his cellmates—all of whom were there longer than five years. When they gathered for the 40th anniversary of their return to freedom (Operation Homecoming), most agreed, "We would never volunteer to be a POW, but we would not change a thing. We came home better men."

Like surviving as a POW, personal growth takes not only discipline and commitment to keep at it, it also takes courage. To be honest, courage is the single most important issue for individual and leadership development. Grappling to grow is not for the weak or faint of heart. So, we invite you to take the courage challenge:[3]

> *Lean into the pain of your doubts and fears to do what you know is right, even when it does not feel natural or safe.*

With courage, you can do it and it's worth it. The good news is that in the end, our development will make a difference. We will become better people, better teammates, and better leaders. And in doing so we will bring freedom to the "captives," freeing others to be all they can be. That would be a great legacy for all of us.

Thank you for joining us on this journey. We wish you well.

Quick Coach Notes

Questions

1. What has been your experience with personal growth? Reflect and then list several examples of areas in which you have been intentional about growing. What can you learn from that experience?

2. From reading this book, what are the two or three struggles you are going to work on for the next six to twelve months? (We recommend that you use the free Self-Assessment Worksheet to develop your Personal Development Plan (PDP). Download a copy at www. LeadershipBehaviorDNA.com/Book.)

3. Do you have a written leadership philosophy that encompasses your beliefs about mission, people, values, standards, and growth? If not do you think it would be to your advantage to begin working on one?

ENDNOTES

1 https://www.asquotes.com/quote_of_the_day.html
2 https://www.warrenbuffett.com/traits-of-a-legend-warren-buffett-and-his-personality/
3 This is from the *Leading with Honor* Courage Challenge Card, a coaching card the size of a business card that you can carry in our pocket. You can get them in packages of ten at www.LeadershipBehaviorDNA.com/Book

▶ Acknowledgments

Writing a book is always a team effort and never more so than this one. It's time to acknowledge and thank those people who have made it possible. First, it's been a treat for us to work together on this book. We have collaborated on the subject matter for 18 years, and this effort gave us a good opportunity to express much of our research and experiences in one place. We were fortunate to have an amazing group of very talented people working alongside to keep us moving toward the finish line.

Kevin Light, managing director of FreedomStar Media, is the integrator/conductor who superbly orchestrates the many moving parts that it takes to professionally publish a high-quality book. He's had a heavy load keeping us moving on this journey, and he's managed us well.

Our two developmental editors, Mike Taylor and Sarah Weissman, did a great job helping us better express our thoughts. Then several close friends and colleagues gave us early content feedback to further improve our message. Jim Armstrong came back for an encore in this book project, producing another crisp and attractive interior layout. Our graphic artist, Sean Allen, proved talented and resilient in producing an eye-catching cover and interior graphics.

This book would have never been possible without the professional and dedicated statistical work of IO Psychologist Dr. Justin DeSimone. He provided the strong academic rigor necessary for validation of the *DNA Behavior* assessments while showing a keen understanding of our need for practical application.

We're also grateful for our clients—those we've worked with over the past two decades who have allowed us to be part of their growth experience, and in return they gave us real world stories that we share anonymously in our books and training sessions.

Book production is never over until the details are put to rest. Thanks to our copy editor Georgina Chong-You and our indexer Todd Larson for their expertise in making the finishing touches.

Our printer, Versa Press, gave it life in paper form with excellence. Our fulfillment house, PSI Distribution of Atlanta and our trade distributor, Greenleaf Book Group, continue to serve us well for over seven years.

Of course, our individual teams have been instrumental in helping us reach the finish line. Lee's assistant, Stormie Knight-Ellwanger, has been wonderful to keep him on schedule and coordinate so many aspects of the book. Working in the background at *Leading with Honor*, Liz McKenzie and Kristi Deutz have kept all the wheels turning smoothly. Lee's better-half, Mary, serves as our initial copy editor and supports his ambitious work/travel schedule, always bringing wisdom to help him stay on course.

DNA Behavior's key executives including Leon Morales, Ryan Scott, Nikki Evans and Carol Pocklington have provided a lot of encouragement and support to Hugh in keeping him out in the field practicing the leadership talents which the book addresses. Further, they have provided invaluable support in editing the book and ensuring it reflects the business culture that we are actively building. In addition, thanks to Drew Plant for his efforts in helping us position our messaging which is now gaining much stronger global traction. Hugh is lucky to have his wife Jennifer who provides a very stable home life enabling him to be out there as a pioneering leader.

Finally, we are thankful to our Heavenly Father for his mercy and grace. Our lives have been blessed beyond belief.

Appendix

▶ Appendix A

Due Diligence for Hiring

NONE OF THESE SUGGESTIONS ARE INTENDED TO SUPERSEDE LEGAL REQUIREMENTS OR YOUR COMPANY'S HUMAN RESOURCES' POLICIES AND PROCEDURES.

Common methods to gain insights into an individual's potential for success in a particular position:

- Résumé
- Assessments such as our online Leadership Behavior DNA assessment that reveal natural talents, typical struggles, results/relationship (mission/people) natural balance, and need for control, people, challenge, structure, etc.
- References
- Recommendations by people you don't know
- Recommendations by people you do know or are known to someone you know
- Past work history
- Education and training patterns and results
- Achievements of the past
- Consider the person's past work experience by type of organization.
    - Entrepreneurial people may have a hard time adjusting to the structure and restrictions in a large established corporation.
    - People who have worked in a large established corporation often have difficulty adapting to a small, more informal business without the support systems they have become accustomed to relying on.
- Interview with two or three people so they can compare notes and have a variety of questions
    - Be sure to include someone in the company of the opposite sex from the primary interviewer. (Women and men often discern very different insights in an interview.)

- Interview by the person who will be the immediate supervisor/manager
- Make sure you know what they really are passionate about and really want to do.
  - Expressed goals for the future
- Current life situation, such as willingness to relocate
- Attitude and other intangibles
- Trial with a short-term project, contract, or temporary basis

Some key factors to consider in the hiring process:

(These are not intended to be interview questions. They can serve as a general guide to help you evaluate the potential match.)

1. **Passion**
   - What does the person really want to do?
   - How strong is the desire?
   - What are the motivating factors?

2. **Natural Talents (behavioral strengths, personality, temperament)**
   - How closely do the candidates' strengths and struggles match what is most commonly found in those who succeed in this or similar positions? Use assessments to identify talents. (The Leadership Behavior DNA provides extremely accurate information, identifying natural talents to include Strengths and Struggles.) *Remember, you are not looking for average talents for the key functions of the position. For those areas, the individual should be using his or her best talents – those that have the highest potential for immediate use, as well as further development. Also, these talents should be ones that the person is highly motivated to use. For instance, corporate trainers usually love to prepare and then perform by presenting material to a group. A trainer who does not have a passion for communicat-*

ing information to a group is likely to be a boring and unmotivated speaker.

3. **Character and integrity**
   - Is this person reliable?
   - Is this person ethical?
   - Is his or her work ethic compatible with the job, mission, and organization?

4. **Experience**
   - What type of work has he or she done in the past?
   - How much of his or her experience will transfer into the position you are filling?
   - What has been the past level of achievement?
   - Are you considering the candidate more for now or growing him/her into a position later?
   - As mentioned above, how much will they have to adapt if they are moving from a large structured organization to small informal organization or vice versa?

5. **Job related**
   - Based on past performance, has the candidate demonstrated the skills that are needed in the position?

6. **Chemistry and Diversity**
   - How well will this person fit the work team?
   - Can he or she quickly become part of the group?
   - Is it likely that he or she will accept others on the team and be accepted by them?
   - Caution! Don't make the common mistake of seeing "different as wrong." Diversity is essential to a competitive workplace. Also, remember that first impressions can be biased by our past experiences.

7. **Values and Culture**
   - Will your organization's products, services, and culture be complementary to the values of the individual and vice versa?
   - Will there be conflicts? If so how significant are the potential conflicts?
   - Can everyone on the team accept the conflicts and still be good teammates?

8. **Retention and career progression**
   - Consider how long you would like to keep this person in this position.
   - Try to determine how long the candidate would want to stay in it. Evaluate in your own mind how much growth potential the person has.
   - How strongly is the candidate motivated toward career progression versus stability? Is this person looking for a stepping stone or a long-term relationship?

The Honor Code

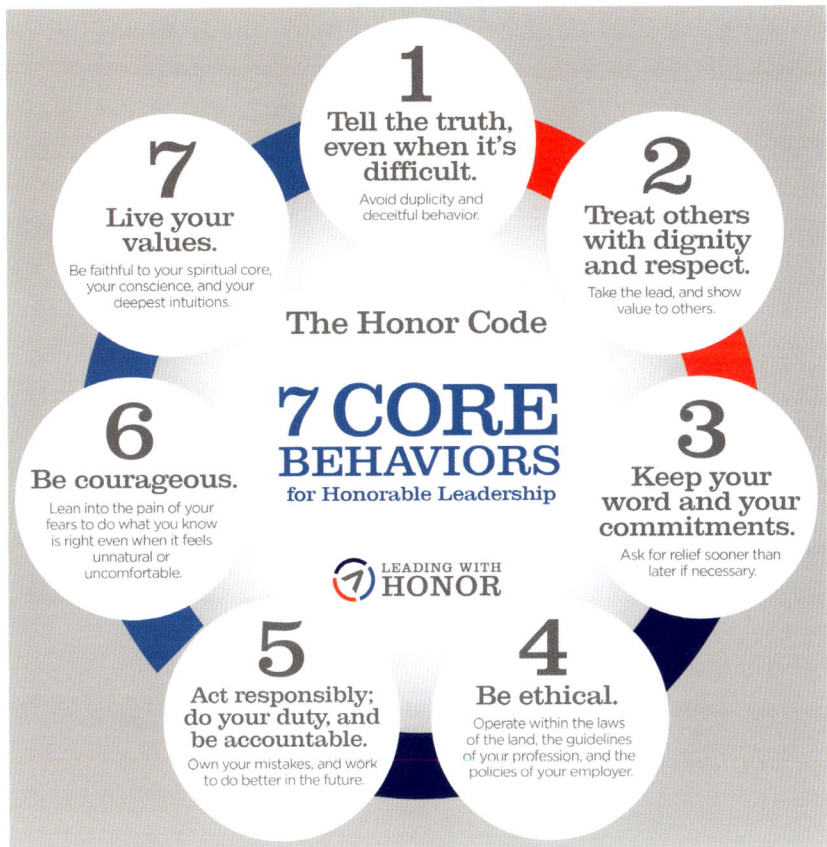

Download a copy of the Honor Code at
www.LeadershipBehaviorDNA.com/Book

▶ Appendix C

The Courageous Accountability Model™

As mentioned on page 42 of this book, the Courageous Accountability Model is a systematic process for building a positive accountability culture. The graphic below provides a visual to help you follow the critical steps that will take you through the process.

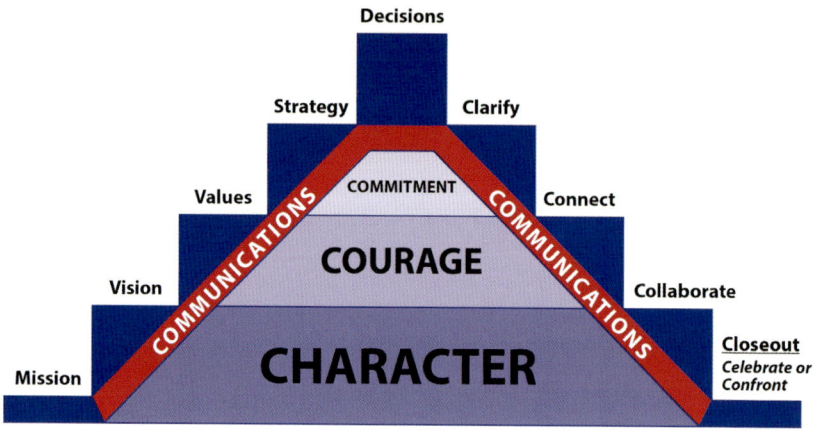

There are many ways to look at leadership. Our company uses several different leadership models, depending on the focus of the discussion. For the purpose of accountability, we believe the model presented here is simple and logical, and it provides a visual that leaders can follow in day-to-day execution.

Before walking through the model, there are two more important points to remember:

1. **Over-communicate the message**

     Notice the consistent layer of Communications throughout the entire model. Regardless of where you are in applying the model, clear, consistent communication must be the bond that holds the entire process together.

     Be intentional about over-communicating important information and decisions, and don't assume that others think like you think or hear what you are really saying.

2. **Think linear—then circular**

Models are usually shown as a linear process because there is generally a logical flow for explaining the overall course. But few things in life follow a fixed, predictable process. Reality is usually erratic and unpredictable—with things happening chaotically, which often means we have to circle back to square one before moving ahead.

So even though we will present the Courageous Accountability Model in a linear fashion, you need to remember that in real life it doesn't work that way. In the model, you may be in the Collaboration phase and realize that you must shift back to the Clarify stage in order to re-confirm something you thought was completely understood.

The Core—Character, Courage, and Commitment

The core attributes of this model are Character, Courage, and Commitment. Without these fundamentals, the day-to-day tactics of accountability are hollow and subject to collapse. More than simple words, they are critical strategies for excellence and success in your work.

- **Character** – Be aware (as a leader) of being held to a higher standard. You set the example that others will follow. Be confident yet humble.
- **Courage** – Lean into the pain of your doubts and fears to do what you know is right.
- **Commitment** – Dis-honorable behavior will corrode your will to move forward. Keep your promises and fulfill your obligations. Stay loyal to your values.

The Left Side—Mission > Vision > Values > Strategy > Decisions

On the left side of the model are the strategic steps of **Mission > Vision > Values > Strategy > and Decisions**. Anyone working in a business or organization should be well acquainted with these terms. More than buzz words used in work vernacular, they are important steps to aligning and unifying a team or organization.

These steps help define the 100,000-foot view of courageous accountability:

Mission – Defines the present state or purpose of an organization; answers the questions: Who are we, what do we do, and whom do we do it for.

Vision – The desired future state of what an organization wants to achieve over time; a picture of the future 5-10 years out.

Values – Attributes and behaviors that define what is important to the organization and its members as they interact with each other and their stakeholders.

Strategy – defining plans or actions needed to bring about a desired future, such as achievement of a goal or solution to a problem.

Decisions – A conclusion, choice, or resolution reached after consideration unusually a prerequisite for taking action or executing a plan.

The Right Side—4C's of Execution

These are the practical steps used every day to achieve healthy accountability. Let's do a quick overview of the four steps.

Clarify

It's about making sure that people understand your expectations. This requires having an alignment in your thinking. Think from the highest perspective down to the intricate details that are important for accomplishing the goal. Then clearly communicate those details.

- Make sure that mission, vision, values, policies, and guidelines are clear.
- Get alignment with your team or organization (in every level).
- Make sure people understand what outcomes are expected and what resources and ground rules are in place.
- Solicit questions and listen to make sure people have the same picture you have.

Clarify as needed until there is alignment.

Connect

In the POW camps, Lee and his comrades would risk their lives to connect with each other—overcoming every barrier thrown at us by the enemy. Connection was essential, but not just for the purpose of accomplishing the mission of resisting our captors. As human beings, they needed connection for their sanity and survival. Everyone needs connection to know they are valued and respected.

- Know you and your people's unique strengths, struggles, communication style, and results/relationships balance.
- Know how to uniquely manage each person.
- Connect with the heart by making people feel valued and important.
- Be vulnerable.

Collaborate

This may seem like an unlikely word for the accountability process, but it captures the positive, interactive experience needed for successful execution of good leadership and management.

If people are working for you, much of it should be a team effort. Even though you will be delegating authority and responsibility to achieve goals, you can never give up on your responsibility for the outcomes. An effective leader supports his or her people's efforts and facilitates their growth through collaboration.

- Develop a proactive mindset about collaboration. Welcome it; support it.
- Dialogue as needed and provide ongoing feedback to encourage and correct.
- Remember to engage in collaboration rather than withdraw or dominate.

Closeout

This step will go in one of two directions—celebrate successes or confront the issues. Also, you'll have to critique the process.

Celebrate successes. The entire process is designed to get results, to make good things happen. So there needs to be a conclusion, which is usually associated with achieving a good outcome and meeting a deadline. If you have been appropriately collaborating, you know how things are going, and you have intervened if things were not on track. So if all has gone well the closeout is about celebrating.

Confront problem issues with confidence and humility. On the other hand, if all has not gone well, then it's time for a serious confrontation as to why the expectations were not met.

Critique the process. Analyze and discuss
- What went well?
- What did not go so well?
- How could we do it better next time?
- What did we learn that can be applied elsewhere?

These four steps **Clarify** > **Connect** > **Collaborate** > and **Closeout** are like the vital organs of the body; they are crucial to effective functioning and healthy execution. Mastering them will be a lifelong process. Expect these four steps to take you out of your comfort zone, but that's usually the place of growth.

~~~~~~

The book, *Engage with Honor: Building a Culture of Courageous Accountability* (ISBN# 978-0-9838793-7-4) is designed to show you how to employ these practical steps to courageously lead your people and engage with honor.

Learn more about the Courageous Accountability Model and the book, *Engage with Honor*, at www.EngageWithHonor.com

▶ APPENDIX D

DNA Behavior Style Groups and Descriptions

Adapter

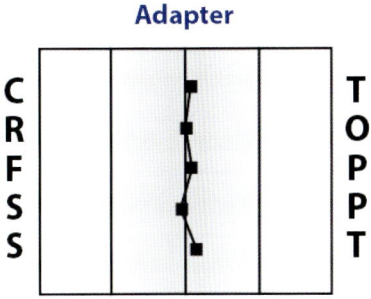

Adapters are unique in that they have the ability to adapt to the needs of their environment and display whatever behaviors are necessary for success. They are very versatile, capable of focusing on both people and tasks, and they partner and team well with others. They typically read situations and respond as needed to be effective. They can generally perform well with a variety of tasks relating to achieving their goals and managing their performance. Adapters operate most effectively when they have very clearly defined expectations and boundaries.

Community Builder

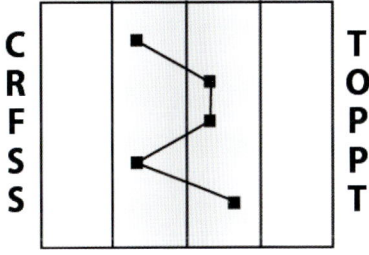

Community Builders are pleasant and energetic and excel at meeting people and promoting cooperation among groups. They influence others through friendliness, enthusiasm, empathy, and supportiveness. They bring a very positive attitude to the workplace, and in a healthy environment they will encourage others and operate diligently and collaboratively to achieve goals. They are versatile and able to engage very effectively with both people and tasks; however, they do need frequent people-interaction to capitalize on their natural relationship skills. They function best in supportive relationships that are appreciative and loyal.

Engager

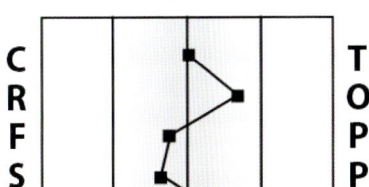

Engagers build a wide network of friends and contacts. They naturally connect with people in a broad array of situations and use their natural enthusiasm to promote ideas, products and services. They typically are high energy and they like to break the stress of work with fun and social events. They are adventurous, excited by new ideas, and motivated by variety, including meeting people from other cultures. They are passionate and expressive, leaving no doubt when they are happy or sad. They prefer new opportunities and starting (rather than finishing) projects and goals.

Facilitator

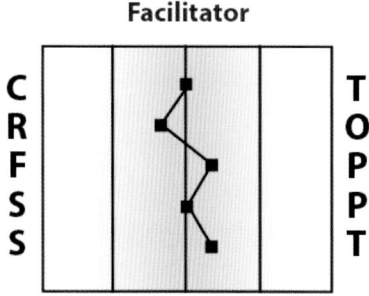

Facilitators are typically very focused on the issues at hand and will move quickly to bring closure. They are practical and usually good at finding the simplest solution. Their natural and preferred style is to lead by example. They maintain amiable relationships with a wide array of people, but they prefer privacy and productivity to social networking. As part of a team, they may hold back with their input. Being more forthright in the moment will allow them to contribute needed talents and perspectives to the group.

Influencer

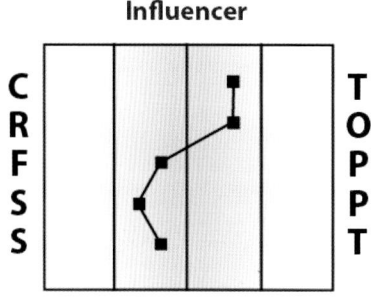

Influencers are able to engage and motivate people into action through their strong verbal talents and passion for their ideas. They need big challenges and a good team to help them achieve their goals. They prefer the limelight and want to be involved in decision-making. Influencers naturally want to help others develop. They are friendly and people-oriented until they get under pressure to deliver on their commitments, and then they become very task-focused. They are usually visionary but need and welcome help in building the structure and systems needed to achieve their goals.

Initiator

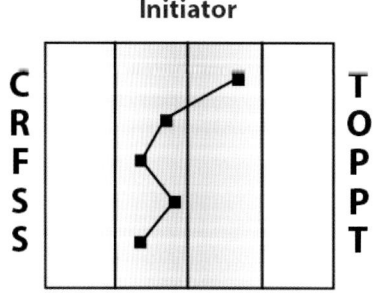

Initiators like to take bold, aggressive actions to make things happen. They like to create the rules, preferring to lead, make decisions, and set the agenda for others to follow, while monitoring the timely completion of tasks. They are results-oriented, goal-driven people who like their expectations met, while preferring not to get caught up in unnecessary details. Their decision-making will typically be fast-paced and rational. They are not afraid to take on challenging assignments and they are comfortable accepting risks to realize their ambitions. They typically are unaware of the feelings and needs of others.

Reflective Thinker

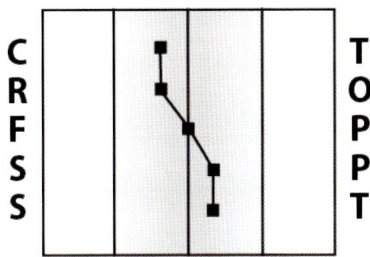

Reflective Thinkers are serious, focused and analytical in their approach to everything they do. They enjoy thinking through problems and researching information. Their accuracy and precision is valuable in any group setting, and they bring objectivity to decision-making processes. They deal in specifics and are not impressed with generalities. Typically, they will prefer to follow guidelines in completing tasks and will want to "get it right the first time." They usually dislike being put on the spot for a quick answer and will want to reflect before responding with their well thought-out ideas.

Relationship Builder

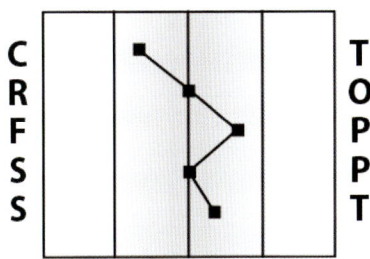

Relationship Builders thrive when given the opportunity to work with and serve others. They are friendly, kind, and empathetic, and gain fulfillment by helping others develop and achieve their potential. As leaders they are good team-builders who like to choose the right people and then help them be successful. They operate best in a stable, low-stress environment where there is an established vision, clear expectations, fairness, and consistent processes. Making rapid changes and taking risks are usually not their strengths.

Strategist

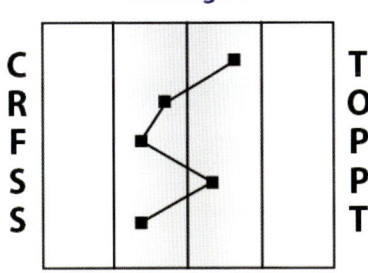

Strategists naturally blend their strong drive to reach key goals with knowledge, organized processes and high standards of quality-control. As a result, they are equipped to be strategic players in situations where achieving results is a priority. They typically envision the systems necessary to achieve ambitious goals. They follow a matter-of-fact, rational, objective approach that enhances their ability to make difficult decisions. Seeing the needs and feelings of others is not their strength, and Strategists who recognize this engage those with a "feelings" radar to help them balance their approach.

Stylish Thinker

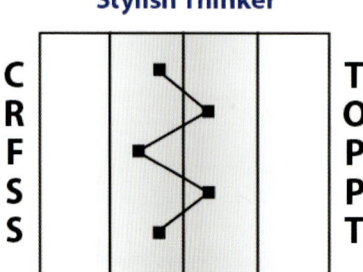

Stylish Thinkers exhibit two traits that normally do not go together: Planned (organized) and Outgoing (social). This equips them to understand systems and details and enjoy connecting with people. This unusual combination enables them to understand and analyze technical subjects and then explain or teach them to non-technical audiences. They like to test ideas in discussions with other people. They are usually strong in grasping the vision and following through on their goals. Typically they have a gift for style and like to make things look good.

▶ APPENDIX E

Summary of DNA Behavior®
Structure and Validation

The *DNA Behavior Assessment* comprises 46 sets of three non-situational items (triads of phrases) that relate to one of the eight factors using a forced choice rating (most like me, least like me) methodology.

A total of 138 items are rated. The "forced choice" rating system is used because it minimizes artificial inflation by respondents, is resistant to faking, and is less influenced by social desirability and situational biases, making it very effective for predicting behavior in the work and many other life and decision-making environments.

The 46 sets of words/phrases used in the assessment were determined by experienced subject matter experts on the DNA Behavior Research team, which included the I/O psychologists from Georgia Institute of Technology (GA Tech) who performed the independent validation work. Collectively the research and development team represented more than 100 years of relevant experience in developing and deploying behavioral assessment instruments.

- The DNA Behavior Assessment measures eight major personality factors. These measures of behavior are more specific than most other personality inventories, yielding sixteen traits and 23 subfactors.[1] The measurements capture important dimensions of behavior on how people make decisions, interact and build relationships, achieve results, handle information and complete tasks, develop trust, set and achieve goals, take and live with risks and approach innovation.

Development

- The words and phrases used in the DNA Behavior assessment were originally determined by subject matter experts (SMEs). These SMEs also created a preliminary model for predicting which items were assigned to which factors.

- Confirmatory factor analyses (CFAs) were conducted on both the major factors and subfactors in order to provide data regarding the contribution of each item to its respective factors. Mplus statistical software was used to conduct the CFAs.

- Exploratory Factor Analyses (EFAs) were conducted on both the major factors and subfactors in order to provide data regarding which items were most related to one another. EFAs were conducted using Mplus statistical software and polyserial correlations.

- The predicted model created by the SME's held up very well, with only a few adjustments required after the CFAs and EFAs were completed. The SMEs used the results of the CFAs and EFAs to inform decisions regarding which items needed to be changed as well as which items needed to be added to or taken away from each major factor and subfactor. The SMEs used this information to refine their research, ultimately reaching the final model.

Validity of Personality Factors

Convergent validity for each major factor[2] of the DNA Behavior Assessment was determined by correlating scores for that factor with an established, widely used, third-party validated personality assessment (VPA) that measures similar constructs. Each major factor of the DNA Behavior Assessment displayed high (.70 or above) correlations with the corresponding factor or subfactor from the other assessment. Specifically:

- The Command factor correlates .71 with the VPA Dominance factor.
- The People factor correlates .80 with the VPA Extroversion factor.
- The Patience factor correlates .87 with the VPA Compassion factor.
- The Structure factor correlates .84 with the VPA Conscientiousness factor.

- The Pioneer factor correlates .70 with the VPA Ambitious factor.
- The Risk-taker factor correlates .73 with the VPA Daring factor.
- The Creative factor correlates .74 with the VPA Innovation factor.

Reliability of Personality Factors

Cronbach's alpha coefficient was used to assess the internal consistency of each major factor of the DNA Behavior Assessment. For new measures, alpha coefficients above .70 are favorable and alpha coefficients above .80 are considered excellent. With the exception of the Pioneer factor, all alpha coefficients exceeded .80. Specifically:

- Command: α = .82
- People: α = .86
- Patience: α = .92
- Structure: α = .91
- Pioneer: α = .62
- Risk-Taker: α = .82
- Creative: α = .83
- Trust: α = .88

Ongoing Research

The performance of the DNA Behavior Assessment has been monitored since December 2009 on a regular basis, using new data that is received from participant usage. In December 2013, the original model was reviewed, based on a randomly selected sample of 10,000 users. A statistical re-norming exercise showed no material differences that would necessitate changes to the factor scoring model. The DNA Behavior Assessment has been used in 125 countries and translated into 11 languages. Over 1.5 million individuals worldwide benefit from DNA Behavior insights on an annual basis.

ENDNOTES

1   There are 24 subfactors shown in the report, twenty-three are validated and the additional one is a composite of several of the factors.

2   The Trust Factor was added after the original validation and therefore not included in the convergent validity exercise. Subsequent to the original validation, items for the Trust factor were selected and validated using methodologies similar to the process described above.

▶ APPENDIX F

Factor Relationship Chart

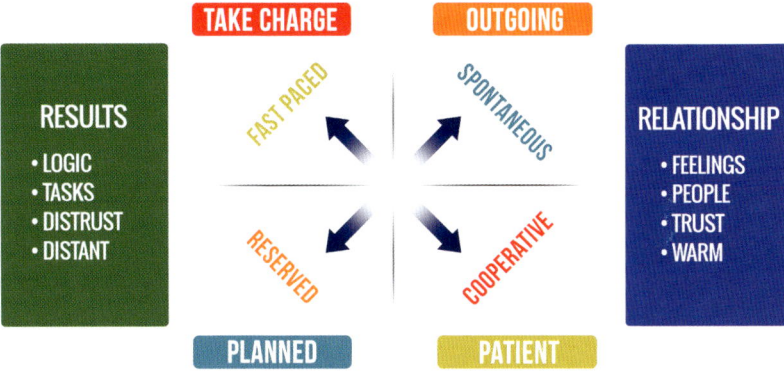

• Look Outward • Generalists
• Initiate • Move Quickly

• Look inward • Specialists
• Maintain • Move slowly

The graphic above shows the primary Traits that drive Results and Relationship. Additionally, there are positive correlations in the occurrence of the following Traits.

For example, this means that people who are Take Charge are likely to be Fast-Paced and very rarely would be Patient.

- Take Charge and Fast-Paced (also correlates with Skeptical and Pioneering Traits)
- Outgoing and Spontaneous (also correlates with Trusting)
- Patient and Cooperative (also correlates with Trusting and Content)
- Planned and Reserved (also correlates with Skeptical)

▶ APPENDIX G

Guidelines for Using DNA Behavior® Assessments

Here are some important guidelines that govern the use of DNA Behavior assessments. You will need to keep these in mind as you begin to review and apply assessment results.

1. **The assessment measures typical behaviors—normal traits.** The Factors reveal recurring patterns of behaviors common to normal people and are not designed to diagnose deviant behaviors or mental health problems.

2. **A person's scores tend to remain stable over time.** People are capable of adapting to meet the needs of new situations; however, they typically revert to their natural behaviors (happy place) when the need to adapt goes away. Knowledge, experience, and values can cause people to adapt or moderate over time from their natural behavior on a more permanent basis.

3. **There are no bad or good Trait scores.** There can be a bad job match but not a bad or good score. Every score/ point on the continuum represents important talents. All points have strengths and struggles.

4. **The assessment doesn't identify personal baggage.** No one grew up in a perfect world, and we all have acquired some baggage from painful or disappointing life experiences. Usually when you see someone acting beyond the boundaries of normally accepted behaviors, you are seeing their baggage—a reaction to pain or shame from the past.

5. **The assessment scores should not be used to put people in boxes or categories with assumed limitations.** Humans are very complex and multitalented and have an amazing ability to adapt to various situations. Behavioral profiles are guides to understand people's most obvious talents and should not be used to restrict them from opportunities to develop new talents.

6. **Decisions should never be made solely based on behavioral assessments.** They provide powerful insights for working with people and can be very helpful for decision-making. Still, they are just one piece of data and should be considered along with other sources of information and experienced-based judgment. You may want to refer to Appendix A entitled "Due Diligence for Hiring."

7. **Great leaders come with all scores and styles.** If you study leaders at all levels—Presidents, CEOs, generals, executives to front-line supervisors and volunteer club leaders—you will see that there are many ways to lead. It is the knowledge of and comfort with oneself and the desire to learn and grow that has a major impact on a person's leadership effectiveness.

▶ APPENDIX H

DNA Behavior® Scope and Use

Since 2001, **DNA Behavior International** has enabled human performance acceleration using its proprietary Financial DNA®, Business DNA® and Communication DNA® behavior tech platforms. We take an "Understanding People Before Numbers" approach to managing business and life, and power real-time management solutions through validated behavioral insights to connect, customize, and accelerate human performance.

We guide people and businesses to make smart decisions, leveraging their strengths and managing their struggles. By deploying tech and data solutions directly inside businesses, we make validated behavioral data practical in order to "Know, Engage and Grow" every employee, advisor and client. This fosters client-centered, high-performance organizations.

Our theorem: Intensified behaviors caused by unmanaged human differences, pressure, and emotions derail performance. A 2002 Harvard study shows 87% of business issues are communication-related, caused by behavioral differences. Thus, every interaction is an opportunity to adapt behavior. This necessitates understanding your natural "DNA" behavioral style and that of others.

DNA Behavior tech platforms provide real insights for real results in real time: The first comprehensive behavioral tech and data platform with *validated* personality insights, addressing financial planning, organizational development, leadership, marketing relationships and a variety of life situations.

Our technology is available to clients online; we do training and consulting, virtually and in-person. Some clients incorporate our apps into their own systems; we are the "behavioral chip" in their solutions. DNA Behavior solutions benefit1 million+ people annually in 125 countries and 11 languages, including 2.5k+ businesses leaders and 20k+ financial advisors.

Leading with Honor® is a strategic partner with DNA Behavior International and serves on the Research and Advisory Teams. Founded in 2008, we are a nationally recognized leadership and team development training and coaching company, and Lee Ellis serves as president and founder.

With more than 25 years of experience in the creation and implementation of behavioral assessment, we use this knowledge and experience and focus on organizational integrity, operational effectiveness and personal accountability for enterprise, government and not-for-profit leaders.

▶ INDEX

either/or, 43
Fast-Paced, 290
rational, 290
risky, 211
Decision(s), *see* Decision-making
Default behaviors, *see* Behavior
Default Mode Network, *see* Net-works
Delegation
of decisions, 257
of details, 150
of responsibility, 44, 66, 159, 167, 169, 287
Deoxyribonucleic acid (DNA), xix
Development
human, xiii, xiv, 315, 317
of employees, xxiii, 19-20, 37, 41, 58, 161, 122, 300, 319
of leadership, xiii, xvi-xvii, xix, 7, 10, 13, 15-16, 21, 26, 30, 34, 35, 37, 41, 51, 55, 85, 163, 232, 266, 271-272, 315
of software, 221
of talents, 8, 19-20, 159, 280, 298
of teams, 5, 6, 8-9, 18-19, 30, 37, 41, 74, 84, 301
organizational, 300
research and, 58, 146, 179, 293-294
self-development, 270, 273
Differences (individual)
acceptance of, 8, 241-242
adaptation to, 8-9
appreciation of, xiv
and conflict, xv-xvi
and DNA Behavior®, xix, 245
and empathy, xxi
and performance, xviii
and the Platinum Rule, 8
and trust, 139
assessing human differences, xiii
appreciation of, xvi, xix
in behaviors, 8-9, 12, 248
in talents, 12, 243
management of, xv-xvi, xix, xx, xxi, 6, 8, 43, 53, 237-274
manifestation of, 7
maximizing of, 237-249

respect of, 8, 241-246, 263
understanding of, xvii, xviii, xix, xx, xxii, 4, 5, 7, 17, 41, 43, 52-53, 61, 66, 119, 177, 197, 199, 216, 220, 244, 245, 248, 251, 256, 262, 263, 300
valuing of, 248
Discipline, 150, 243, 271
and commitment, 271
and the Pioneering Trait, 180-181
and the Planned Trait, 139, 141
mental, 153
self-discipline, 223, 226
Discouragement, 253
Disney, Walt, 160, 220
Distrust, *see* Trust
Diversity
and chemistry, 281
and decision-making, 257
and team unity, 241-257, 264, 281
and trust, 245, 256
appreciation of, 263
celebration of, 237, 245, 249
encouragement of, 243-244
forms of, 241-242
of cultures, 4
of DNA Behavior®, xix, 245, 264
of ideas, 244
of people, 67, 244
of personal evolution, 4
of strengths, 256
of talents, 19-20, 67, 240-257, 264, 269
respect of, 245
valuing of, 242
DNA Behavior®, 49-234, 276, 316
and adapting behavior, 28
and Community Builder, 87, 101, 122, 155, 166, 289-290
and communication, 212
and decision-making, 4, 43, 212, 293
and differences, xix, 7
and Factors and Traits, xx, 5
and inborn behavioral responses, xvi
and leadership development, xvii, xix, xxiv, 7, 14, 257

▶ ABOUT THE AUTHORS

Lee Ellis, President, Leading with Honor®and FreedomStar Media®

He is an award-winning author, leadership consultant, and expert presenter in the areas of leadership, teambuilding, human performance, and resilience. His past clients include Fortune 500 senior executives and C-Level leaders in telecommunications, healthcare, military, and other business sectors. Some of his media appearances include interviews on CNN, CBS This Morning, C-SPAN, ABC World News, and Fox News Channel. Additionally, he's made hundreds of keynote presentations in various industry sectors throughout the world.

Lee served as an Air Force fighter pilot flying fifty-three combat missions over North Vietnam. In 1967 he was shot down and held as a POW for more than five years in Hanoi and surrounding camps. For his wartime service, he was awarded two Silver Stars, the Legion of Merit, the Bronze Star with Valor device, the Purple Heart, the Air Medal with eight Oak Leaf Clusters, and POW Medal. Lee resumed his Air Force career, serving in leadership roles of increasing responsibility including command of a flying squadron and leadership development organizations before retiring as a colonel.

Lee has a BA in History and a MS in Counseling and Human Development. He is a graduate of the Armed Forces Staff College and the Air War College. He has authored or co-authored five books on leadership and career development. Lee's last book, entitled *Engage with Honor®: Building a Culture of Courageous Accountability*, has received multiple awards since its release including 2017 Award Winner Indie Excellence Book Awards, 2017 Award Winner Reader Views Reviewers Choice Award, 2017 Award Finalist International Book Awards, and 2016 Award Finalist Best Book Awards. Lee and his wife Mary reside in the Atlanta, Georgia area and have four grown children and six grandchildren.

Hugh Massie is a CEO, global human performance accelerator, behavioral insights pioneer, entrepreneur, keynote speaker, mentor, board member, devoted father, and keen golfer.

He spends his time traveling the world encouraging advisors and business leaders to discover how intensified behaviors caused by unmanaged differences, money attitudes, pressure, and emotions derail performance. He presents to advisors and leaders on how to adopt an understanding, people-before-numbers approach to managing life, finances, and business for accelerating human performance.

Hugh helps transform people and businesses worldwide by guiding them to discover *and apply* behavioral insights for making Behaviorally SMART decisions in order to better balance results and relationships. His real-world practical application of behavioral insights and the mastery of the energy of money, blended with strong financial skills, gives him the unique capability to serve as a corporate strategist, coach, mentor, trainer, board member, keynote speaker, and author.

Since 2001, as founder and CEO of DNA Behavior, and using the Financial DNA®, Business DNA®, and Communication DNA® platforms he pioneered, his solutions have impacted millions of people in over 125 countries and 11 languages, including investors with assets from $1 to over $1 billion, over 20,000 advisors, and leaders of more than 5,000 businesses.

Hugh is the author of *Financial DNA—Discovering Your Unique Financial Personality for a Quality Life* and *Leadership Behavior DNA: Discovering Your Unique Talents*, with co-author Lee Ellis, in which they share the eight factors and 16 traits that create the unique design and talents for work and relationships. Hugh also has written or contributed to many other publications and presented extensively as a keynote speaker about human performance acceleration through revealing and managing behavioral insights and money attitudes.

▶ ABOUT THE FOREWORD AUTHOR

Dr. Andrew Stricker serves LeMay Center, Air University, Maxwell AFB, as a strategist for Air Force future concepts in education.

In this role, Dr. Stricker provides strategic analysis of advances in learning and assessment sciences for innovative applications in professional military education. Prior to his arrival to Air University, Andrew served Vanderbilt University as Associate Provost for Innovation Through Technology while also holding a faculty appointment with the Vanderbilt University School of Medicine, teaching courses in biomedical informatics and human factors.

As an associate provost for the university, he was responsible for working with academic, technological, and administrative leaders to prioritize, plan, and enable innovations for improving learning, teaching, and research. Dr. Stricker also spent four years at Texas A&M University, College Station, Texas, creating and then serving as Director of the Cognition and Instructional Technologies Laboratory, and Director of the Knowledge Engineering Complex with the Texas Engineering Extension Service.

He retired from the United States Air Force with 28 years of professional experience as an Air Force officer and behavioral scientist, specializing in human development, human-factors engineering, and cognitive sciences. His graduate work was conducted at Texas A&M University, College Station, Texas and Yale University, New Haven, Connecticut. He is a member of the American Psychological Association. His current research addresses professional developmental growth with cognitive and moral reasoning in reflective practices.

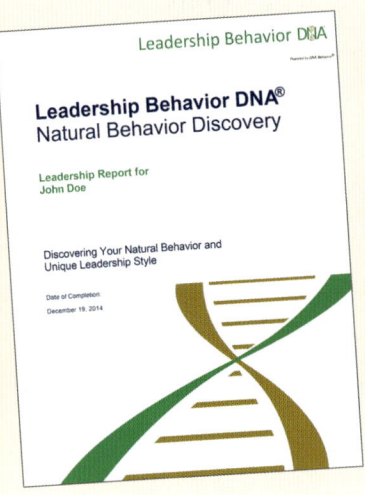
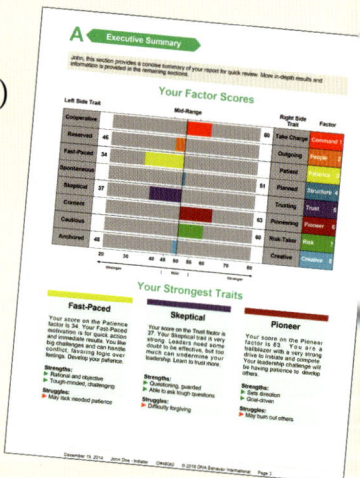

EXPERIENCE THE DNA BEHAVIOR DISCOVERY PROCESS WITH YOUR TEAM

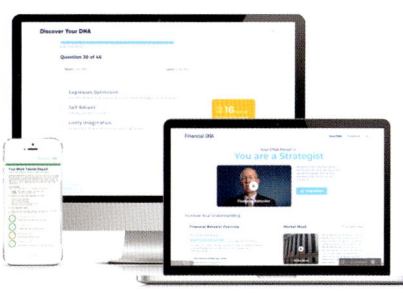

Regardless of the size of your team or organization, the DNA Behavior Discovery Process includes the assessment and a suite of available reports (including the *Leadership Behavior DNA Report*) and digital reporting options to make behavioral data practical to "Know, Engage, and Grow" every employee, advisor, and client. API delivery options are also available for enterprise use in larger organizations.

Would you like a Certified Trainer to lead your team through this Discovery Process?

Self-Paced Training, Remote Training, and Live Classroom Training options are all available depending on your specific objectives, available time, and budget requirements.

Would you like to become a Certified Advisor or Trainer?

Many of our clients like the accessibility and ease of having a Certified Advisor inside their organization that can administer and interpret reports. Also, independent consultants see the value in providing DNA Behavior as an important component of their service offering.

Get Started and Learn More at
www.LeadershipBehaviorDNA.com/Book

STAY CONNECTED TO THE LATEST NEWS, MEDIA, AND EVENTS FROM FREEDOMSTAR MEDIA!

Where is Lee or Hugh speaking?

What are the latest interviews, articles, or videos?

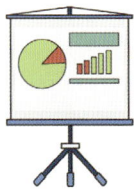

How can I get the latest research and development news on DNA Behavior?

What social media platforms can I use to follow Lee and Hugh?

Get all of the details at www.LeadershipBehaviorDNA.com/Book

Other Books Available from FreedomStar Media®

How did American military leaders in the brutal POW camps of North Vietnam inspire their followers for six, seven, and even eight years to remain committed to the mission, resist a cruel enemy, and return home with honor? What leadership principles engendered such extreme devotion, perseverance, and teamwork?

In this award-winning powerful and practical book, Lee Ellis, a former Air Force pilot, candidly talks about his five and a half years of captivity and the 14 key leadership principles behind this amazing story.

Link honor and accountability together and you have a formula for great leadership, and a healthy mindset of accountability can inspire every team and organization to achieve a higher level of excellence. The key is engaging with courage, commitment, and caring concern as opposed to motivation by fear, intimidation, and self-preservation.

In this award-winning book, Lee Ellis shares the proven model for creating a positive accountability culture that gets results.

Purchase Copies at Your Favorite Book Retailer or www.FreedomStarMedia.com

Self-study and online group training materials are also available for these resources. FreedomStar Media resources are available at special discounts for bulk purchases for sale promotions or premiums.